A TALE
OF
TWO WORLDS

BY

REVEREND RONALD KENNER

Adult Reading Material

This book is for those who see beyond the horizon or long to do so. It is for those who search beyond the limits and boundaries of the mundane existence. It is for every spiritual warrior who lifted up their sword for truth and for those who still wait for the right moment to lift theirs.

This book is about a journey and the souls that walk the journey as one in spirit. Each holds their own desires and dreams with no two alike. Yet their collective directions mesh to create a single reality that benefits the lives of all.

It is my hope that in some way the book touches the soul of the reader. I hope some have had similar experiences witnessed by the main character in his quest for discovery.

This book is the first of three books to come that carry the story to completion.

ISBN: 979-8-9852210-3-9

This book is dedicated to all my teachers in this world and the next, to those I broke bread with and those I went to war with. A dedication to my wife, Patty, who danced with me in times of joy and held me in times of sorrow and to all those who seek vision beyond the obvious who reached for a star and carry it in their heart. It's all about love, all of it.

CHAPTER 1

The sun was taking its place on the eastern horizon. A sweet silence fell over the land as the day awaited its story. Some stories would appear as they did the day before. While other stories had their scripts rewritten in the night. Nothing would be the same for them. Their desires reached beyond the things familiar. The passion for life and all that it holds was their dream to life.

Whether it be from design or from circumstance, they would be free from the chains of mortal bondage. Their measure of success would come from what they had lost rather than what they had gained.

A young man was lying in his bed awake with eyes still shut. It was a pleasant night's sleep with only a few dreams to ponder. He felt different for a very good reason. He kissed his first girl yesterday.

She was older than he which made the experience exciting. He wondered when it might happen again. He had never experienced anything like it before. At first, he was apprehensive and frightened. Her manner of embrace and the softness of her touch relaxed him until he was engaged fully in the union.

Some clothing was partially removed as hands glided across bodies in exploration. The excitement was building as the passion spilled forth. It was intoxicating for both. The sound of a slamming door startled them back to sobriety.

Her father entered the barn and gathered an arm full of fodder for the livestock. When her father left so had the thrill of their embrace. They thought it best to wait until a later time. The shock of nearly getting caught was too much for the pair.

As he lied in bed, he opened his eyes. The light of the sun met his sight as it cascaded through the window panes. He rose from his bed and dressed for the day. He could smell bread baking and knew his mother, Diane would have breakfast ready to start another day.

It was the beginning of fall when the air is cool and crisp. The leaves of oak and maple were beginning their transition. The colors of fall were always a delight to the eye. He felt alive under its canopy. He drew his inspiration from nature.

He loved to read poetry and stories of faraway places. He read every book he could get his hands on including the family Bible. It was a good way to stir the imagination for such a young man as he.

Thomas entered the warm kitchen of the house. His mother was busy as always, this time of day. She was a pleasant soul who loved her family and her place in life. Seldom was a complaint ever uttered from her lips. She always searched for the goodness in all things about people and life.

Thomas gave his mother a kiss as he did every morning. He tore off a generous portion of bread and started towards the door. "And just where are you running off to Thomas?" said Diane. "To the day," replied Thomas. "I'm off to see what this day has prepared for me mother."

The effects of yesterday's time spent with the fair maiden, awoke something inside him. He felt more alive and energetic than usual. He had always gone through life with eyes open but today was different. The memory of lips coming together for the first time weighed heavy with Thomas's.

He recalled the moment when eyes went shut and a rush overcame him. Lips locked, arms embraced, a collective energy from within merging from somewhere never experienced before. The tingling of the spine and the intoxication of the senses led to a desire to hold the moment for evermore.

The loud sound of a door closing shut broke the spell that had overcome him. The breaking of embrace, the parting of lips, delivered the eyes open as they stared intensely into the depths of each other. It was as if they had been together before. Perhaps in another time and in another place held long ago.

There was another reality going on. They felt it, sensed it, but knew not what to call it. To be aware of it was all that was needed for the tapestry of life to manifest. The essence of which gives life to living.

There was a chill in the mornings air, and he decided to embrace it. He went about his chores with a new outlook. Milking the cow was the first task of the day that awaited him. He fed the livestock in haste and returned home with milk pail in hand. He gathered the wood that would be needed to cook the evenings meal and ward off the chill of night. Now he was ready for the day and its offerings.

His special place where he often went was not far away. It was a place he had discovered as a child. To him it was a magical place, a place where his imagination and inward dreams could dance in the sun.

There was a stream that wound its way through the forest and entered this special place. It held a pool of water beside a giant oak which stood tall and majestic. Thomas felt a kinship to the tree and enjoyed many a nap beneath its canopy.

Thomas liked this time of year when leaves fell into the pool. They would float freely as gentle breezes pushed them about. He would imagine that they were mighty English war ships sailing to do battle with the French pirates.

Thomas felt the need to visit his special place to sort out the feelings from the events of yesterday's embrace.

Mary Rose is her name. She is the only daughter of Jonathan and Lydia Rose. She is the sister of Chad Rose, his best friend. The family are neighbors to Thomas and his parents, Edward and Diane Sonnet. Mary is eight years older than Thomas. She had always been like a big sister to him until yesterday. Today he wasn't sure how to feel about her. The emotions inside were looking for a different perception. One that fed a new found passion while at the same time holding a respect for friendship.

As he walked further, he could see brighter fall colors coming into view. He could hear the stream as its water cascaded over rocks and through pebbles. It gave him a sense of calm and peace. He walked to the towering oak and placed his hand on it as to say hello. He looked upwards into its branches and watched as squirrels jumped about enjoying its acorns.

Slowly he stepped to the pool to see his reflection. Pools are natures mirror. He felt different inside and wondered if he would look different outside. Thomas dropped to his knees to get closer to the reflection.

He looked at his face and studied it. Everything looked the same except for the smile he was wearing. It was then that he realized a person's outer appearance seldom reflected the inner being. Thomas realized that the eyes could deceive without intent. It's the heart that renders a better perception and the heart which can weigh intent.

His focus on the reflection began to blur. He noticed his image changing on the surface. One face would appear, and another would form in its place. The first image was that of an older man with white hair and a long white beard. His eyes were blue like sapphires. There was a wisdom about him that justified respect. He stares deeply into Thomas as if he is communicating in a way without words. Thomas was overwhelmed. Something happened. There was flash of light. Then some sort of opening, like a cover pulled back for a second or two and all things revealed. Then it was gone as fast as it appeared. The revelation was profound. He tried to jump back up to his feet but could not move.

His clarity of awareness lifted him high above the oak's stature and for a brief moment he kissed the heavens. He returned to the body still knelt at water's edge, and he was filled with elation. Still, he could not move. He was spellbound.

A strong sense of quiet peace overcame him. He could feel himself relaxing. He shifted his knees to one side so he could sit on the ground. The back of his neck was tingling as if a thousand needles were dancing about. The face on the pool was smiling back at Thomas. He nods his head at Thomas as to signal their embrace was over.

Thomas fell backwards and hit the ground with a gentle thud. His eyes wide open by what he just witnessed. He was staring blankly upwards into the sky. His gaze went beyond the clouds, beyond the blueness of the sky. In his mind's eye he saw the Absolute.

A place void of form or name. A place that sits far beyond the heavens and the furthest of stars. It created the heavens, the stars and the earth with a single thought while others sat in wait. This place where all beginnings received life. This place where all souls call home.

His eyes gently close and slowly he drifts into slumber wearing the same smile his new friend gave him only a few minutes ago. The breeze around him and within him began to stir. Nothing would ever be the same for young Thomas.

CHAPTER 2

Raindrops begin falling gently from above, cascading across yellow, orange, and red leaves on their way to the ground. The sound of which is soft at the start then ever increasing as the raindrops grow in number. The forest becomes alive with the sounds of nature. The slumbering Thomas hears the raindrops as they pelt the leaves. Some find his face beckoning him to awake from slumber. He opens his eyes and for a moment he does not recognize his surroundings.

Thomas seats himself against the oak as he struggles to make sense of it all. What once he believed real, he now questioned. Everything looked the same through the eyes, but the perception was different. Like a buried treasure once concealed, now open for discovery. Young Thomas could feel the expansion within but how to express such a feeling escaped words. As he gathered himself, he stood and looked at his surroundings. Everything around him had its place and he understood its nature. He turned towards Mary's house and wondered if she could help him understand this strange experience.

The rains had subsided, and the sun once again ruled the skies. Thomas made his way back to the road to visit Mary. In the distance he could see a wagon coming towards him. It was Mary's parents and younger brother, Chad. They waved as they passed by and seemed to be in a great hurry.

As Thomas approached the Rose's home, he saw Mary seated in the shade of an elm tree. She was busy writing in a small book. She did not raise her head on his approach or cease to write. She looked up and said, "Wait until I finish writing. Then we will talk." As he stood there, he looked around taking in the scenery, still pondering his earlier experience at the pool. Finally, Mary closed her book and looked up at Thomas.

Where was your family going in such a hurry?" asked Thomas. "Chad has been sick three days past. They are on their way to town to get help for the ailment. Mother is very worried," replied Mary.

"What were you writing in your book," asked Thomas. "Last night I had a dream about the two of us. I dreamed we were in a marriage ceremony in a small church. The minister was an elderly man with snow white hair and a long white beard. He gave me a warm smile that made me feel that everything was okay. I saw a small child standing beside us in the church. She kept tugging on my dress wanting me to lift her up," said Mary.

Thomas was surprised to hear Mary's dream. "Was the minister in her dream the same as the one he saw in the pool?" he wondered. He wanted to tell Mary about his experience but feared she would scoff at him. Mary continued with her story. "Once the ceremony was over, we embraced each other and brought our lips together. I felt complete at that moment, and I knew my destiny. It was like all the joy and all the suffering were felt in a single moment.

There was a city that stood before us, the name of which I do not know. Then I felt myself being shaken. It was mother waking me to tell me that Chad was ill, and they were taking him to town," said Mary.

Thomas stood in silence weighing Mary's dream against his vision. "Could the two be connected?" he wondered. The thought of marriage was far from Thomas's mind.

He was sweet on Rebecca, Squire Andrew Beckett's daughter. She was always flirting with him, and he enjoyed her tease. He was careful not to go too far with her because her father watched over her like a hawk. Squire was good at telegraphing his thoughts with just a look.

Thomas decided to reserve his experience for another time. Listening to Mary's dream only made things cloudier.

Mary took Thomas by the hand and invited him inside. As soon as the door was closed, Mary put her arms around Thomas and began kissing him. He did not resist her advance. Inside he was exploding as Mary pressed her lips harder against his. Their collective passion was building as their arms caressed each other and their hands performed the dance of exploration.

Mary still holding their embrace, started directing him towards her bedroom. Thomas followed her with no idea of the desired destination. Once in her bedroom she tugged on his shirt until she had removed it from his body. Her hands glided across his young muscular chest while moaning in pure delight. Thomas's hands reached up to fondle her breast. His body was trembling. Never had he felt anything so soft, so desirable. The small amount of light in the room only added to the ambiance.

The smell of lavender filled the room. It would be a fragrance that Thomas would never forget. This was his first time in such a state and such a place. It would be a time he'd always remember. It was his first time. No matter how many times he would experience similar moments in life, it would never have the magnitude of today.

The passion was burning within him. Mary's advances in the moment, was the elixir that was driving the exchange. Gently Mary directed him to the edge of her bed, then nudged him backwards until he fell. He laid there looking up at her as her eyes penetrated him. Mary reached up to her shoulders and pulled at her dress ever so slowly to reveal her bare shoulders. She continued as the dress exposed the deep cleavage of her breasts. His eyes widened as the dress moved lower.

Mary stood watching him in his excitement which in turn aroused her. It gave her a sense of power over him. Both of her breasts were exposed for his complete view. He had never seen anything so beautiful as she stood before him. Mary released the dress and it fell to the floor. His heart was pounding like a drum through his chest.

She removed her undergarment and joined him on the bed. She removed his pants then pressed her body against his. Their eyes met and their breathing began to deepen. His hands explored the curves of her body while hers danced across his. They held an embrace that put their faces so close that they were sharing the same breath.

All things love, all things beautiful in love were held in this moment between the two. A place where time and space are void. It belonged to the eternity of love, of kindness and mutual affection. Ever present, lying in wait, for a moment such as this to shed its cloak to reveal the true essence of life and the art of love.

Thomas lifted his hand to gently caress her face. He lied there seeing Mary, not like before. Rather he was seeing her through different eyes. This was not the Mary he'd known for so many years. She began to stroke the locks of his hair, while never taking her sight from him. He was afraid to blink for fear the scene would disappear. She took his hand and placed it firmly on her breast. Thomas felt his heart racing, unable to speak, he nestled his face against her.

The smell of lavender came once again into consciousness, relaxing the moment deeper. The two were surrendering themselves to the energy of creation. Thomas had never felt this way before, not knowing what to do, he lied there in pure delight.

Her eyes were a deep blue now, her breath warm, lips pursed. Emotions and feelings ruled the moment, and all other conditions had ceased to exist. Their lips meet and an energy deep within is released.

Mary reaches down to guide him into her. He stiffens at first, then relaxes to waves of pleasure. "What thing is this that gives itself without price or condition?" he thought.

He began to rock back and forth with Mary. Her breasts swelled beneath his chin. Their breathing soon turned to panting as the energy between the two was building. Thomas explodes in ecstasy and lets out a cry. Mary followed as her fingernails dug into his back. The moment held the two aloft. Then they collapsed into each other. Their bodies covered in sweat, still panting, still consuming the nectar of making love. A feeling that can only come from a special place within. As they lied there recovering from their exchange the two drift off to in peaceful slumber and nap away in embrace.

Thomas fell deeper in sleep and found himself at a place much like his special place in the forest where he loved to be. The leaves clinging to the branches were all green here, not holding the colors of fall. The only sound was that of a gentle wind that rustled the leaves. He turned and came face to face with the man he saw in the refection of the pool.

Their eyes met and without moving his lips Thomas heard him say, "My name is Nathan. I follow you in each life when you visit the material world. I help you achieve what you came here to learn and what you came here to forget." Thomas felt a kinship with him. His heart lifted in joy.

"What is my destiny? said Thomas. "To exert your will," said Nathan. "What is my will?" said Thomas. "To be yourself. Free of the opinion of others. Free to express the within in order to wipe away the things without," said Nathan. "And how shall I do that?" Thomas shouted. "Your way!" said Nathan. "It's for you to discover in each day you pull breath into your body. Use your mind to choose the way and your heart to inspire each step along life's path.

The masses wait for you to take pen in hand with eyes turned towards the heavens. You will write the psalms of the ages. They will not know their origins because they are blind in heart and scattered in mind. Just the same you will write for them. One day they will hold your work in deep regard. Far beyond your mortal life. In another time you will return to reveal the hidden treasures of your earlier work. They will not know you. You will be another face to them.

When you reach the age of twenty and six the heavens will open to you again," spoke Nathan. Thomas was numb from what he had just been revealed to him. Nathan looked at him with reassuring eyes. It gave Thomas a deep state of calm.

Thomas heard the gentle laughter of a child. He turned to see a beautiful little girl all dressed up in white clothes. She was trying desperately to catch a butterfly that was playing with her. Whenever the little girl would stand still the butterfly would land on her nose. The butterfly would tickle her chubby cheeks with its flapping wings. The little girl would let out a belly laugh. It caused Thomas to laugh with her. Nathan watched the little girl at play. He looked at Thomas and said, "The soul you see before you is your daughter to be." Quickly Thomas turned his head toward Nathan in shock. Nathan turned his head at Thomas and said, "She is beginning her transition to your world as we speak. You will wed the mother and the three of you will be joined together once again." Before Thomas could respond Nathan and the little girl were gone from sight.

"Hurry, wake up! My parents are home. Get dressed and leave through the window as fast as you can!" said Mary in a panicked voice. Thomas's feet hit the floor and he frantically got dressed. Mary opened the window for his escape. But before his exit he looked at her in her beauty one last time. Headfirst he exited the house and fell to the ground. Thomas sprang up to his feet and turned towards home.

CHAPTER 3

Thomas was putting distance between himself and the home of the Rose's. He could hear wailing and shouting coming from the house. Someone shouted, "Why did this have to happen!" It was followed by more wailing. Thomas stood still as he tried to understand what was going on. One part of him wanted to return but he thought it best not to. He could hear Mary's mother, Lydia crying in desperation. Her father was heard in mournful grieving. Whatever it was, it was serious.

A deep sadness fell on Thomas as he turned one more time to look back to the sound of weeping. He heard Mary let out a scream that sent chills down his spine. "Someone died," he thought. "Something happened to Chad."

Thomas was quiet in heart and mind as he walked home. Another storm was forming and blocked out the sun. Somewhere in the events of this day, Thomas lost his adolescence. The sound of raindrops were approaching. The thought of a rain shower soaking him seemed appealing. Gently the raindrops fell at first then escalated to a downpour. Natures cleansing felt refreshing to him as he wondered about those who cried so hard for another.

In Thomas' mind life seemed as it was meant to be. Life lays forth its path and along the way we carry our intentions and desires. He was realizing life was meant to be enjoyed in sorrow and in joy. A deep sense of relaxation offered a new outlook.

The events of life are seldom governed through mortal intent. Whether we embrace or reject the event is in our control. Life is about the choice. Choices lack the ability for error. It is the expectations of our choices which inhabit the error. The true pleasures of life can only be realized from acceptance and surrender.

Thomas felt as if he were waking from a very long dream. The type of dream you wake from when you are foggy and disoriented. Thomas felt alive for the first time in his life. He could no more stop the rain falling around him nor revive the life of his best friend, Chad.

Suddenly a bright flash of light and a deafening sound of thunder sent Thomas to the ground. Lightening had struck nearby in the forest. His left ear was ringing from the clap of the lightening. He gathered himself and continued his way home.

Smoke was rising from the chimney, and it was a welcomed sight. Thomas could warm himself from the effect of the chill from being soaking wet.

As he neared the house, he heard the ringing of a hammer striking an anvil. That would be his father repairing horseshoes to supplement the family's income.

Thomas entered the home knowing that his mother would be preparing the evening meal. Judging from the hatchet sunk into the stump, chicken and dumplings were in the pot sitting by the fireplace.

He entered his room and removed his wet clothes and sat down on the bed. He stared at the floor in disbelief of the day's events. Yesterday was his first kiss. Today was his first time lying with a woman. There had been a sad event at the Rose' home. He sat there without movement, without thought or direction.

He was sensing a drifting feeling. He felt like a feather being carried about on the wind. He felt free from all bounds and limits. A beautiful white light surrounded him and filled his soul. The light felt familiar to him, like home. His sense of self increased with each passing beath.

Suddenly his arms thrusted upwards. His head tilted back, and his shoulders followed. His eyes were shut tight, yet he was seeing wonderous things. This experience was feeding his soul and opening his spirit. He wondered if this was heaven.

A shadow was drawing near to him. As it got closer a face began to appear. It was Chad, Mary's brother. Chad was smiling and had a beautiful glow about him. Thomas could see how happy he was. He looked at Chad with inquiring eyes. "Are you dead Chad? asked Thomas. "No, I'm not dead. I've only left the world we used to share. The one that holds us with breath and body. I left that one because it was my time to leave.

All souls dwell here before and after their life on the earth. Each time our light grows until there is nothing left to learn. Only then can we shed the skin of birth, death and rebirth never to enter it again. This was my last time there in witness. I am free to join those who came before me. I will spend my energy helping others to achieve the same blessing.

Later I will share with you things about the depths of life and the expansion of love. But for now you must return my dear friend. You have a funeral and a wedding to attend to."

Slowly Thomas began to return to conscious awareness. He took a deep breath and his eyes opened. He could hear the faint sound of his mother and father talking. He dressed and went to joined his family. As Thomas entered the room, they fell silent. Both were wearing a sorrowful look. Thomas wondered what could have happen.

"Chad passed away today. He died on the way to town," said Diane. At first hearing it Thomas expected to feel sorrowful, but sorrow did not surface. Rather, he was at peace. Now he knew why everyone was so up-set at the Rose' home.

At first he wanted to run to the Rose' home and tell them that Chad was not dead. He was alive and well. Thomas realized such news would not be understood let alone welcomed. Tears needed to be shed and the regrets of life to surface for embrace.

This was how death found acceptance for those who mourned such loss. Sadness must be spilled before the alter before a higher awareness can be received.

Thomas joined his family at the dinner table in silence. Quietly they sat eating their meal. Thomas was reflecting on his day still processing the events. Everyone had finished their meal. His father stood and brought a jug of his homemade wine to the table.

Tonight, would be different. Instead of the usual two mugs he brought three. He methodically poured the mugs full. He placed one before Diane. The second he placed before Thomas. Thomas gave his father a bewildered look. His father looked at Thomas and said, "Today you showed your manhood by your reaction to the news of Chad's un-timely death. So, let the three of us raise our drink to honor him for what he gave in this world. May his soul be guarded by the angels." All lifted their mug in silence and drank as one.

Edward retired to his chair that sat before the fireplace. He prepared his pipe as always. It was the time of day for him to reflect on the day and plan the morrow.

"There is a grave to dig and a coffin to build. I will start in the morning, first thing. Jonathan and Lydia will be heartbroken having already lost their oldest son, Jeremy," said Edward. "Best we be about our sleep. Tomorrow will come and we must be up for what will come."

CHAPTER 4

The night passed swiftly. Thomas was fast asleep in his bed when he was awakened by the sound of a hammer. He rose from his bed and peered outside. He could see a light coming from his father's shed. "He's making the coffin for Chad," thought Thomas. His father was an accomplished carpenter whose talent was well known. Thomas tried to go back to sleep but the events of yesterday still haunted his mind.

He couldn't help but think how the events in life determine our direction, not so much our will. At best, one faces a number of choices brought about through the witness of events. Thomas desired to be with Rebecca, but the events steered him to Mary. Mary had gifted him, and he longed to hold her once again. Chad' passing had shifted the energy from passionate to one of empathy. He still longed to hold her but for a different reason.

The door to his room opened. His mother stood in the doorway holding a single lit candle. "It's time to get up Thomas. Your father will be needing you today," she gently spoke. She turned and walked away as quietly as she had appeared. Thomas could see the house was lit bright. He dressed himself for the day and entered the living quarters. A generous slice of cornbread and a hot mug of tea awaited him.

His father entered the home covered in saw dust. He sat down at the table beside Thomas. Not speaking a word, he began to eat in a hurried fashion. His father was in deep thought and was anxious. Thomas knew it best not to speak when his father was in this way. Edward finished the last of his meal and looked directly at Thomas. His father carried a worry look across his face.

Edward had built the coffin for Jeremy, Jonathan and Lydia' oldest son, some three years ago when he passed. Now he was building Chad's coffin for another son' burial. He was carrying a heavy sadness in his eyes was reflecting the place of his heart.

He feared one day he might be building one for his son, Thomas. The thought of losing his son would be more than he could ever bear. Love and all its benevolence can break a heart as easily as it can lift one.

Edward stood from his chair and placed his hand on Thomas' shoulder. He lowered his head, then lifted it up wearing a warm smile and said, "Let's go to the shed and sharpen the blades of our shovels. We have a grave to dig. We want our shovels to cut even lines in the soil to receive Chad's body."

Thomas swallowed hard to hold back the tears. He had never seen his father so pious. The tears kept building up behind Tomas' eyes. One escaped and went rolling down his cheek. He wanted to be strong for his family and Mary's family.

The two rose quietly and walked outside towards the shed. It wasn't so much of readying shovels as it was a time for bonding. Father and son, these two are as they set out to aid another in time of tragedy.

The sun kissed the horizon, and first light was born to this day. The air was cool but still. The dew of the ground was heavier this morning. Not a word was spoken. The silence outside reflected the silence within. Father and son, stepping before shovel and pick as if about to conduct a religious rite.

In reverence each carefully chose their tool to help bring closure to a grieving family. The sun was higher now as they walked like soldiers upon a battlefield. Their tools resting on shoulders as they walked in cadence to the beat of their hearts.

A muffled noise in the distance perked their ears. The closer they got to the Rose's home they could make out a figure standing beside a tree. It was Jonathan Rose. He had grieved all night and was weary, broken in spirit.

When Jonathan saw the two, he let out a scream and fell to his knees. Lydia his wife came running out of the house and fell to her knees to hold him. Lydia saw Thomas and Edward approaching. It was too much for her and she fainted.

Edward dropped his shovel and ran to her. He lifted her from the ground away from the heavy dew. Thomas saw Mary standing at the door appearing like a statue. She was wearing a distant stare on her face in disbelief.

Jonathan gently took Lydia from Edward and carried her inside the house. Mary broke her trance and began weeping. She sat down on the floor for she could no longer stand.

Lydia was beginning to come back in the moment. She looked up at Jonathan and in a whisper said, "Why? Why have my boys left me? Don't they know that I love them? I have always loved them. Why did my boys leave? I want to know why my babies left their mother!"

Jonathan looked up to Thomas and Edward like a lost child. He could not answer her for he wondered the same. Edward tried to speak but no words of comfort came. He too felt as a child.

Thomas was thinking back on his experience with Chad in dream state. How Chad was without tears or remorse. He was happy and in full acceptance of his position. His passing brought about heartbreak and sorrow for those who loved him so. He wondered how two contrary perspectives could arouse from the same event. It had to be a matter of perception.

Lydia raised her hand and began stroking Jonathan's face. Her eyes were tender and bleeding love towards her husband as her daughter as two friends stood in the room. Mary moved closer to her parents and wrapped her arms around them both. They rocked back and forth in embrace.

Thomas and Edward left the home and walked towards the hill that held the bodies of those souls who passed from this world to the next.

Other neighbors began to appear. Some came to help with the digging. Others came to help with the wake. They brought gifts, food, and prayers for the family. News traveled fast in the countryside. Some of the women gathered their parcels together and began making plans for the wake to come.

The one called Mildred, who lived deep in the forest, appeared from the tree line carrying parcels of her own. She was the midwife of the country people and a healer with her poultice and herb remedies.

On one occasion, The Reverend Richard and some of the town folk paid Mildred a visit one day. They went there to accuse her of witchcraft and sorcery. Their plan was to burn down her home and send her ever deeper in to the forest to be forgotten. No one really knows what happened that day. Those who went with the Reverend refused to speak of what had taken place. And Mildred went on doing what she always did, looking after those in need who dwelt in the countryside.

At the graveyard, the men searched for Jeremy's grave site. Chad would be buried beside his brother, three years past. They found his grave adorned with what flowers remained in the fields. Someone had visited the grave sometime yesterday.

The men began digging without speaking a single word. They worked in unison, each one focused on the task at hand. Thomas was in awe of the reverence the men gave. This could have been their son or father, their sister or mother. These people lived as one. They carried different names and lived in separate homes. But in heart and in soul they were one together.

The sun stood higher in the sky now. More and more neighbors and friends were gathering at the Rose' home. Jonathan and Lydia were greeting each one with the graciousness of a saint. Those who dug the grave had completed the task and were joining the others.

The clopping sound of horse's hooves was heard in the distance getting closer. The louder it became, the more people turned their eyes toward the road. A two-horse buckboard appeared with a driver and the Reverend Richard. The Reverend was not known as a man of the people. Rather he was known as a man who was quick to condemn and the last to forgive.

The buckboard was carrying the body of Chad. It was wrapped carefully in white cloth so his soul would be received in heaven.

Lydia saw the wagon and stood frozen with her hand covering her mouth. Jonathan solemnly walked to the wagon while other men followed. He stood with his head bowed before the body wrapped in white. A deep sadness overcame him. He turned and faced the other men and said, "Let us bring him home one more time, shall we?"

The men gently lifted the body from the wagon and placed it on a wide board. They carried the body towards the house. Lydia still had not moved from where she stood. Her eyes were fixed on the men carrying her son.

Other women gathered around her to give her comfort should she break from the spell that held her. Lydia looked at those that surrounded her and gave a nod as to say she was okay. She joined the pallbearers in their march to the house. Jonathan was leading the men as they walked past everyone. Some had heads bowed, others were softly giving prayers for Chad and the family. A few were in disbelief and recalling their own experiences with the loss of one so loved.

Once in the house the body was placed on the dining table. It had been covered with a white cloth. Some had brought dried flowers and placed them about the room. Candles were lit and placed at the four corners of the table that held Chad's body. Thomas was the student here as he watched the faces and the manners of all involved.

The Reverend Richard was moving amongst the crowd outside. He never passed up an opportunity to increase his flock or the church's coffers. In his mind all souls were lost and needed his brand of God to be saved.

Eventually he worked his way to the front door of the house and stepped inside. He came face to face with Mildred and was startled. The two stood silent before each other while others looked on. The Reverend nodded at Mildred, then turned his attention to the keg beside the door. He drew a full mug and downed the contents in three swallows. He composed himself and proceeded to speak to those about the room.

Whatever happened that day at Mildred's home, still burned strong in the Reverend's memory. Thomas saw what happened as the two faced each other. He could not help but wonder what could have happened on that day.

The wake was moving along in solemn fashion. Diane was deeply concerned for Lydia' state of mental health. She was lifeless and seldom spoke to anyone. It appeared that she had given up on life.

Edward summoned Thomas and the two boarded the buckboard. They drove it home and loaded the coffin he had built earlier in the day. They returned to the Roses home and passed some of those who had paid their respect and were on their way home.

The coffin was unloaded once they returned to the Rose' home. It was placed out of sight until such time as it was needed.

Thomas wondered where Mary was. He had seen her on two occasions but never once saw her mingling with others. He searched outside for her, then inside. The door to her room was shut. Thomas slowly opened the door. The light behind him crept in to reveal a dark figure seated on the bed. He stepped inside the room and closed the door behind him.

He recalled the events of yesterday he witnessed from this very room and how it made him feel. He sat down on the bed beside her. He placed his arm around her and pulled her into him. Her face nestled against his shoulder to offer comfort. She placed her arm around the small of his back and raised her head to kiss him. The kiss was what he needed to wipe away the sadness he carried for Chad. She returned the kiss with intensity. He found himself caught up in the passion of the moment as did she. His heart was pounding like a drum as the two embraced the passion to escape the holds of depression.

The two fell back on the bed as before. Thomas turned so his body was against hers. Their lips were pressed tight as their hands wildly exploring each other's body. The intensity was building without limit or regard. She wrestled to remove his pants as he was hiking her dress to the waist.

The two lied together on the bed with their lips held in embrace. She guided him into her and wrapped her legs around him. Each took a deep breath at the same moment. He began to stroke her hair while the rhythm of her movement increased. She clutched his face with one hand and pressed her lips to his neck. She began sucking on his neck without pause. He could feel her body shaking as she uttered low moans of pleasure. She held him tight never breaking their rhythm. Thomas was about to release his seed. She felt him nearing when her body stiffened as she embraced the ecstasy that came to both at the same moment. Their bodies became still, and they stopped breathing. Together they held the peak as long as it held them. Both were fighting the desire to scream from delight. Their bodies went limp, their souls meshed into one. Their panting eventually returned to breathing. Gentle kissing followed still without the first word spoken.

There were many about, inside and outside the house. It was of no matter to these two. What they had shared at such a time as this was all that mattered. It was a remorse event that brought them together. It was the remorse they held in their hearts that made the exchange of love making so intense. The memory would forever be etched in their hearts and in their souls. Not even the power of time could erase it.

Each were gathering their composure and returning themselves to the matter at hand. Thomas stood from the bed and dressed himself in the dark. He kissed her one last time before stepping towards the door. He opened the door, and the light once again came creeping back in. He turned to look at her one last time. There she sat on the bed as before. Her dark figure, the dark lady of his bottomless passion. He closed the door behind him to join the others.

He entered the room that held Chads body. He wondered if he had been missed. He looked around the room at everyone then at the body. The four white candles lit at the four corners of the table gave the body an spiritual appearance.

There, standing at the head of the table, stood Mary. Thomas froze in disbelief. He looked deep and hard at Mary, and she took notice. She smiled at him and gave a little wave. She stepped towards him. Still, he could not move.

"If it be Mary before me, then who did I embrace not a moment ago?" thought Thomas. His legs were as stiff as an oak. Mary placed both arms on his shoulders. "I've been looking for you Thomas. Where have you been and what happened to your neck?" asked Mary. Before he could respond, Lydia stepped from Mary's room and walked to the couple. Lydia's hair was in disarray as she tried to comb it in place with her fingers. Thomas realized what had just happened. He made love to Lydia not Mary. He fell faint and leaned back on the wall for support. He couldn't speak. He was numb.

"Come, let us gather together in God's love and God's passion for this soul who left his print on the lives of so many. Let us congregate as one and send him home to heaven," spoke Reverend Richard. He read some scriptures to bring a sense about life and death. He then asked everyone to bow their heads in prayer.

Lydia took Thomas's hand as she stood beside him and held it in tenderness during the prayer. It gave Thomas an ease about what had happened.

"How could this be wrong?" he thought. Both held a peace of mind and spirit. Shame or guilt failed to arrive to spoil the event. It was a new day for an ancient love had been given breath once again in the role of mortal witness. This union of two souls was designed for this moment on this occasion. It was written in the stars of the heavens and given to destiny for delivery.

No person can rearrange the position of the stars nor the destinies to be witnessed. Surrender to the day and its offerings. It is the path of the light seeker.

The Reverend finished the prayer, and Lydia released Thomas' hand. Mary placed her arms around the two and they joined the others.

The troubled look that Lydia had carried was replaced by one of peace and acceptance. Lydia was spiritually present now with the events at hand. This gave all who knew her and loved her a great sense of relief.

Reverend asked the congregation to speak out if they had a story to share about the child that gave so much joy to his parents. At first no one spoke, then from the back came a voice.

"Once he helped us harvest our apples from the orchard before a killing frost. He did it from kindness and refused to accept a wage. The apples we gifted here came from those same trees that he picked," spoke Ben Johnson. Another spoke, then another, until the room fell silent.

"Let us carry his body to its final resting place," said the Reverend. Everyone in the house exited and joined those who were waiting outside. All quietly walked to the grave site.

Some of the men remained behind. When all were out of sight the coffin was brought from its hiding place. Chads body was placed in the coffin and the lid was placed on top. It was followed by the sound of hammers driving spikes to seal the coffin. Four stout men took hold the coffin and raised it up. The procession began its journey to the gravesite for the final resting.

The graveyard was perched on a high knoll. The sun was nearing a beautiful sunset. The surrounding trees were in their brightest colors of reds, yellows, and orange. The air was cool with a gentle breeze that gave all a great sense of peace.

The pallbearers were approaching. Their steps held in cadence. They placed the coffin beside the dug grave and stood with the others.

"Our Heavenly Father, we ask that you accept his soul who loved everyone he met. He was loved by those who came today to witness," spoke Reverend. Lydia stood beside Jonathan holding onto his arm. She was still wearing a peaceful face. Unbeknownst to her, as one child was being buried, another child was held within her preparing to be born.

The pallbearers lifted the coffin and held it over the grave. Ropes were placed beneath it. Slowly they lowered it until it was at the bottom. The ropes were removed, and they stood away so that others could offer their final gifts to him.

They dropped dried flowers and handmade trinkets to rest on his coffin. It was their way to say goodbye. Thomas was reflecting on his vision with Chad. "This is the funeral I was to attend that Chad spoke of yesterday," he thought.

Thomas then turned his thoughts to Lydia. There she stood beside Jonathan. Both had their arms wrapped around each other. It would have been difficult to tell who was leaning on whom or which one was supporting the other. Perhaps both.

The procession was departing and beginning their journey home. Some were glad to see friends again and to share as a community in fellowship. It was a sad time and a good time for all.

Back at the Roses home, Mildred had restored it as it once was. It was important that the home be in a state that would allow the family to carry on and not linger in sorrow.

Thomas watched his parents embraced Lydia and Jonathan before they departed. Mary came to Thomas and wrapped her arms around him. She gave him a generous hug and kissed him on the lips. "Ouch!" she said. "What?" said Thomas. "It felt like something kicked me from inside my belly," said Mary.

"Come Thomas. Its best we be heading home," said Edward. "Mother can Thomas come with us tomorrow on our trip to town," asked Mary. "Yes, if it be his will. Of course, he can come," replied Lydia. The family had several things to do, some dealing with Chads memory. Thomas accepted the invitation. It was agreed, they would fetch young Thomas at midday.

The Sonnets left the Rose' home with torch in hand glowing yellow light to show the way. As they walked along the road, they could make out a figure ahead. It was Mildred waiting on them.

Her eyes were fixed on Thomas. She stepped towards him and took his hand. Thomas in thought realized that he could ask Mildred to explain his dreams and visions. She smiled at him and said, "That's right Thomas, you can. Just don't wait too long to ask. Otherwise, these things will fade from memory and disappear." He wondered how she knew what he was thinking. His parents were unaware of what was going on and too tired to care. They continued to the house while the two spoke. Mildred placed her hands on Thomas' shoulders and said, "Tonight you will have two visitors. One you know, one you don't. Listen to each carefully. You are a messenger and a message you shall receive." Mildred kissed him on the forehead, turned away and disappeared into the trees.

CHAPTER 5

Edward, Diane, and Thomas sat at the table held in silence as each mulled the day's events. "It's time we each go to bed. I think we've given the day and our friends the best we have to offer. Good night, Thomas," said Diane as she and Edward stood from the table. The two wrapped their arms around each other and walked to their room.

Thomas carried a lit candle to his room and undressed for the night. He blew out the candle and crawled into bed for a much needed rest. Soon he was drifting away into gentle slumber. He had already forgotten Mildred's words for it had been a very long day.

A loud thud shook his bed and stirred him from sleep. His eyes were barely opened as he scanned the darkness but saw nothing. He slowly drifted back to sleep.

His mind's eye placed him on a street made of cobblestone. He looked around and saw buildings on both sides of the street. He did not recognize his surrounding's, yet somehow it felt familiar. One of the buildings stood out from the others. It was crimson red and void of windows. The placard on the door read, "Enter Those Who Seek Knowledge."

Thomas opened the door and cautiously entered. A man was sitting at a desk. He looked up at Thomas and said, "I heard you were coming. Please sit down and let us speak." Thomas obliged his request never taking his eyes from the man.

He was older and wearing spectacles. His eyes were a deep blue, and there was an air of wisdom about him. The man smiled at Thomas and said, "My name is Isaac. I am the keeper of the gate of knowledge. Many have walked its corridors to discover the depths of knowledge.

Realize that you passed a series of trials with family, friends, and neighbors. You served well unto others and have learned from each witness. As you progress in understanding you will receive additional lessons from this world.

All things human carries a depth that escapes mortal understanding. Most find it easier to accept things on their face. They accept without question. This one thing can be attributed to the level of suffering witnessed on the planet. The lessons you witness coupled with the transcending knowledge you receive from them will forge a new awareness.

Isaac stood from his chair and walked Thomas to an inner door. "Through this door lies the knowledge of the ages. All that was, is, or will be is contained within its chambers. Know that what you learn in your journey here has not yet manifested in the world of matter.

Some that walk there, are deaf and blind to truth. There are many levels of understanding beneath the heavens. That is why the power of the story is so beneficial. To each his own understanding. Would you agree?" asked Isaac.

"Yes, I would agree with you. I need to know is this heaven?" asked Thomas. "No son. Nor is heaven behind the door. If you want to experience heaven, you will have to go within. What lives in there will show you the way," spoke Isaac as he pointed at the door.

"Now remove your shoes and know the ground you are about walk upon is holy. You will be greeted by a blessed soul of your liking. As with any lesson, it is best received when one empties their mind in order to receive clarity. Would you agree Thomas?" asked Isaac. Thomas' posture was one of reverence and awe as he looked upon Isaac. He tried to answer him but could not get the words out. All he could do was nod his head.

Isaac placed his hand on Thomas' shoulder and guided him to the door. "When you return to the world of time and space know that there is one that will act as your guide. You know her as Mildred. In this world she is called Sophia. Whenever you feel lost, she will appear. She entered into that world to help you and others like you on your chosen path," spoke Isaac.

Slowly the door began to open on its own. A cool breeze was felt by both as Thomas placed one foot inside. He turned to wave at Isaac. Just as he started to, he ran into someone. He began to apologize without even looking at who he ran into. He gathered himself and when his eyes made contact, he was looking at Mildred.

She looked much younger. Her hair was a golden rather than gray. The light of her eyes were so much brighter and filled with tenderness. She smiled at Thomas and gently kissed him on the forehead.

Her energy entered his awareness. It made him feel like he was a part of something. He felt he belonged to a fellowship that preceded time. He was becoming of his own inner being. It was intoxicating to his senses. Nothing else existed except this. A deep sense of peace overcame him, and he drifted off into the abyss.

Thomas detected the smell of fresh baked bread. The aroma always made him feel at home, safe from hunger and cold. He opened his eyes, he could see he was in his room, tucked deep beneath the covers. He laid there trying to recall the events of the evening. Seeing Mildred, the way he did, boggled the mind. "If Mildred can exist in two worlds at once, then why not everyone? Was the whole thing just some sort of dream?" he wondered.

Thomas decided he would move with the story of the day as if it were scripted, written from above. He would imagine the day as a great river. The events, be they kind or not, would be the landscape of the great river. He imagined that when he placed his foot on the floor of his room, it would be as if he were placing his foot into the water of the great river. He would surrender to the current and embrace its guidance along the journey.

The door to his room swung open and broke his thought. "It's time to get up and take care of your chores. Are you still planning on going with the Roses today?" asked Diane. "Yes mother, I am. Thank you for the care you give me daily. Thank you for your love that grows inside me each and every day," spoke Thomas. Diane turned her head to look at him. She had never heard her son speak in such a manner. "I do my best son. Your father and I hold you dear in our heart. Now get dressed and come to meal," spoke Diane.

Thomas mind turned to Lydia and their exchange at the wake. The way she kissed him, the smell of her hair, was still burning inside. He could not help but feel something deep for her. He did not understand the feeling. "Was this love, real love?" he wondered.

There was no thought given that she was married or that she was Mary' mother. These were the concerns of the material world. A world where nothing is as it seems. His feelings about the embrace was not of the energy of mortal fashion or design. Edward entered the house and the spell that held Thomas was broken.

"Thomas, once you finish your chores, I have something I want you to do for me. I'm making a grave marker for Chad. I need some of the polished stones that are held in the stream to place on his marker," said Edward. "Yes father, it would be a good thing to do for his memory," said Thomas.

The family sat eating together and using small talk to pass the time. Diane was in her best whenever the three sat to enjoy food and share the smallest of matters. This was family.

CHAPTER 6

It was the beginning of another day at the Rose' home. Another night's sleep was nearing an end. A time when the difficulties of life are void from consciousness. The only sound was the popping of embers from the evening fire.

Jonathan and Lydia were lying close to one another in peaceful slumber. The first rays of the sun's light were peeking through the bedroom window. Jonathan slowly opened his eyes and saw the light embrace Lydia's face. She appeared younger and at peace with herself. He reached for her and pulled her closer to him. He kissed her face and her eyes gently opened. She kissed him back and the two were held in love's embrace.

Their hands began to caress each other's body. Their lips exploring each other with heartfelt passion. Their arms embracing as they rolled beneath the warmth of woolen blankets. Their bodies building in heat until their breathing became as one. Jonathan gathered his bride until she was beneath him. Body against body, man and woman holding a stare that could not be broken.

Gently he entered her as she caressed his face. The two were held as one in all things shared and all things lost. Eyes met as the excitement grew. They were nearing their point ecstasy as eyes widened and bodies prepared to receive the nectar of love making. The rush entered their souls, then their bodies. Their bodies shuttered as they reached the mountain top together. Once the moment passed their bodies became limp and free of stress. Gently they kissed each other back and forth until they fell back to sleep.

Mary was lying in her bed curled tightly beneath a quilt she had fashioned. She was thinking about Chad' passing and yesterday's wake.

She thought of Thomas and their time together. She so longed to make a life for herself outside the life she was living.

She was twenty-five years old and still not married. Most of the women her age were already married with children. She felt the need to be more forthcoming in her approach with her suitors. Her mother had wed at sixteen and had her at seventeen.

Mary was not fond of country life. She wanted to live elsewhere and experience new things. She wanted to live in a town where variety and spice were commonplace.

Her thoughts turned back to Thomas. They were to meet him at midday for their trip to town. She decided to wear her finest dress. She would ask her mother for some of her rose oil to entice Thomas and his youthful desires.

Mary heard her parents moving about the home. She rose from the bed and wrapped herself in the quilt to ward off the chill in the house. She entered the room where her parents were talking. They were making plans for the journey to town. Mary noticed that her parents were calm and at ease. It was a noticeable contrast from yesterday morning.

Lydia was preparing breakfast while Jonathan prepared to begin his chores. But first he stepped behind Lydia as she stood at the fireplace. He placed his arms around her and kissed her on the neck. She stopped what she was doing and closed her eyes. Her mind traveled back to the bedroom where they had made love to each other. It gave her a deeper sense of calm. She was healing from the love she was receiving.

Lydia sat at the table that held Chad's body yesterday. She was struck with his presence about her. She could smell his hair as she sat quietly waiting for something to follow. "Chad if it's you then show me another sign," she thought. She sat there waiting, then a tug at her hair. She jumped in fright. Then another tug. This time she smiled, and her heart wept. She bowed her head and smiled in peace. Her baby was okay. Now, she would be okay.

She thought of Thomas and yesterday's interlude. Before he entered, she was sitting alone in the dark filled with grief and sorrow, ready to give up on life's hardships. Then the door opened, and he walked in without saying a word. He embraced her and she him. She didn't know why he entered or why he took her. She did not protest his advance because the thought never entered her mind. She needed to feel good about something, anything that could lift her from the darkness that consumed her. In a moments time the interlude had delivered her from the darkness she held in her heart, to a place of promise. She held no shame or regret. To condemn the act was to condemn the healing it delivered.

Her moment with Jonathan this morning gave her the insight she needed. She loved him and she loved the life they shared. She felt that she had taken her life back. The one given to her at birth. She refused to recognize herself through the servitude to others.

She had been called daughter, sister, mother, and wife. It was through these roles that she perceived herself and her self-worth. She would no longer accept the role playing to be true. Lydia was feeling free. Free of bond, free from the mindset of servitude. No longer would she see responsibility as duty beholding to another. All things from her would come as a personal choice out of care and respect born from love.

The candle held within her soul received its flame. A single trumpet on high sounded in the heavens to announce a daughter had been born to this day.

"Mother! We are ready to leave!" came a voice from outside. Lydia was startled from her trance. She rose from her chair and walked to the door. She took her shawl and joined the others at the wagon. She sat beside Jonathan as Mary took a seat in the back. Jonathan turned the wagon towards town. They would pick up Thomas on the way.

There are those who dream and those who desire. Both are busy spinning the threads that gives form to the tapestries of life. Some dream of possibilities while the fears and limitations deal with probabilities. Today these souls set out on a common journey. Each with their own intentions, each devising their own expectations. They know not what lies ahead, still they go forward. They know not the depths of their hearts yet still cling to a thing called love.

This world was created to allow all to discover the depths of the seas of life. Mountains formed so one could embrace the sky as they conquered life's peaks. All of it created so that one day, they may discover how the two are one in the same.

CHAPTER 7

The Sonnets arose this morning in melancholy. Edward was thinking about Jonathan's loss of two sons a few years apart. Diane felt sorry for Lydia and Mary. She wanted to help them get through the loss and somehow ease their pain. Thomas had lost his best friend. He and Chad grew up together as playmates. Heavy hearts filled this small valley where two families dwelt and shared.

Thomas began to prepare himself for the journey to town with the Rose'. There was much to ponder for the young man. He needed time to process the events of three days past. He decided to finish his chores first. Then he would search for the stones his father needed for Chad' headstone.

He recalled the time spent last night with Mildred and Isaac. As hard as he tried, he could not recall what happened after he met with Mildred behind the door.

There were many stories about Mildred. Some said she was a witch, others said she had magical powers. Without fail, she would always appear to deliver a mother's baby when it was time. Somehow, she always knew about the new arrivals. Not a single child was ever lost when Mildred was there to deliver.

She was revered by most and feared by a few within the community. Her gifts were welcomed when needed to aid another. Her healing abilities were well known and respected. She had more sway with the people than the church. Most believe that is why the Reverend and some of his flock paid a visit to Mildred one day. They sought to put fear in her to rid her of her place. But the fear fell to those who meant her harm.

Thomas's chores were completed. It was time to enter the forest in search of the prize stones his father requested. He approached the pool and noticed that there was more light coming to the forest floor than usual. His steps became slower as he approached with caution. A sickening feeling overcame him as he stood in disbelief. The grand oak that held his favor for so many years had been struck by lightning. It was rent in half. One half stood. The other had fallen across the stream creating a natural bridge.

Thomas remembered two days ago when a lightning bolt stuck near and shook the ground. He stepped to the tree and placed his hand on it as he always had and began to cry. He fell to his knees and continued to weep. So many changes in such a short time. So much to think about with so little understanding.

Thomas shifted to his side in a fetal position. Quiet was his mind holding a blank stare into the beyond without focus. He was in a state of transition. Like the caterpillar emerging from its cocoon. The teen and its innocence was waning as a young man was being born.

His eyes would see things differently, his mind would challenge the new perception. He turned over to sit up still wearing the blank stare.

The memories of the past were taking on a new perspective. The things once held in esteem no longer carried the value they once had. He felt as if he was starting over again. Each passing moment made him feel lighter and more at ease. He tilted his head back and allowed the sun's rays to embrace his face. His eyes were closed as he felt the winds of change within. His moment was disturbed by the sound of rustling leaves. He opened his eyes and there stood Mildred.

Mildred was wearing a gentle smile as she looked at Thomas. He was happy to see her. The sight of her made him feel safe. Thomas regained himself and stood up. She took his hand, and they began to walk. The only sound was the sound of rustling leaves beneath their feet.

Before them stood a ridge covered in tall green grass. As the suns light embraced it, and a mist could be seen rising to form a cloud. They ascended the slope together, still hand in hand. At the top they could see the glens as they wound about. Random smoke trails could be seen from chimneys of homes scattered along the countryside. Thomas stood taking in the energy. He thought of Mary, and he thought of Lydia. He thought of Chad and the moments shared with each. He was learning acceptance. The type of acceptance that comes with embracing events as they enter consciousness without judgement or reservation.

Mildred gently guided them to a sitting position. She looked deep into his eyes when a single tear appeared to the corner of her eye. The tear slowly crept down her cheek until it reached the edge of her jaw. The suns light kissed the tear and it shined like a diamond. It fell to the ground, disappearing amongst the blades of grass.

She took his hands and said, "There is so much to tell you. I will begin with the things you must know first. There are two woman you carry in your heart. Both carry your child in their womb. One you will marry out of need. The other you will love until the end of time. Both will inspire and contribute to your development in this lifetime and in others. No matter how long you travel, no matter how far you go, the two will always be with you. There will be times when you stray from their care and love. Even so, you will return to them or they to you.

They both have been with you through the ages and will continue until all things human have been realized. Your histories have witnessed other realities when you carried other names and lived in other lands.

These children, that await their arrival have also journeyed as a part of this soul family. One you shall enjoy from near. The other will know you from afar. Both will prosper from your love and the love of the mothers. It was their will to enter through you and them at this time. They are grateful to enter this world through your energies.

Thomas sat speechless. He listened to what she said about the women and children. It was a surreal moment. He was in a mild state of shock. Mildred could see it and wrapped an arm around him and said, "Come now Thomas. You will experience things far greater than what is facing you now. These days that come with change carry a promise with them. You and those you love and those you long to hold will always be cared for. They are your support, and you are theirs. See? One big soul family."

It was love that brought everyone together. It's always about love regardless of the appearance. It is out of love that the little souls decided to enter this world. Worry or denial will not shift the events that exist or the ones that will be. All is written as it was in the beginning. We are but actors on the great stage of life everlasting. Remember that Thomas. It will carry you far."

The two stood to return to the days business. Mildred reached in her pocket and handed Thomas a number of beautiful stones. "Give these to your father for Chad's grave marker. They hold healing for those who come to visit his grave," spoke Mildred. Thomas looked at her in amazement. "How did you know?" asked Thomas. "A little bird told me," replied Mildred. Thomas smiled at her response as the two descended the ridge.

They went their separate ways after they exchanged a long embrace.

CHAPTER 8

Thomas walked towards home with his head hug low. His eyes were open, but he was not seeing. His heart was beating, but he was not feeling. He was dead to his surroundings yet inside all things were swirling without pause. Where he was, held neither darkness nor light. There was no wrong and certainly no right. He was in a place where all things co-exist. They are infinite in number, yet when counted, never exceeds beyond one.

The air around him began to thicken. The back of his neck was tingling when he heard someone speak. He raised his head and there stood Nathan his spirit guide. Thomas' heart was lifted, and he was pleased.

"I see you are lost and bewildered by the revelations of the day," said Nathan. "Yes sir. I am. I feel the life I carried a few days past has dropped away. I stand here not sure who I am. I don't know if this is a dream or my time spent with Mildred was a dream," said Thomas. "It's up to you to decide which reality is the dream and which one is real. Of course there's always the possibility that both could be real, or both could be a dream. That is for you decide," replied Nathan.

"The Rose family are preparing to leave for town. Were you not going with them this day?" asked Nathan. "Yes! I forgot! I must be off. Thank you, Nathan. Will I see you again soon?" asked Thomas as he scurried off. "Yes, you will!" replied Nathan as he watched him run away.

Thomas ran all the way home. Edward was in the yard along the road. He heard Thomas coming through the woods towards him. "Here what's the hurry," said Edward. "I have the stones you asked for father. What do you think? Are they good enough?" asked Thomas as he handed them over. "Where did you find these? They vibrate as I hold them. Tell me, where did you find them?" asked Edward. "Mildred gave them to me. She said a bird told her you needed them. She said they held healing powers," replied Thomas.

Edward walked away towards his shed. All the while never taking his sight from the stones.

Thomas ran into the house to change his clothes before the Rose' arrived. He was looking forward to spending time with the family. He thought of a few stories he could tell them about Chad to hopefully cheer them up.

CHAPTER 9

Edward was finishing Chad's grave marker he made from oak wood. He sorted and arranged the stones that Mildred sent in a pattern he thought fitting. He chiseled a depression in the wood to better hold each stone. He knew the Rose' would be in town for the afternoon. That would give him the opportunity to place the marker on Chad's grave without detection.

Diane knew the Rose' would be coming home late. She decided to prepare the evening meal for the family on their return.

Thomas had the thought that Lydia could have shared what happened between them with Jonathan. His anxiety peaked as the wagon grew near. A part of him wanted to run while another wanted to hold fast. His eyes were fixated on Jonathan face. Was it friendly or displaying anger? He could not tell. Then Jonathan brought the horse to a halt.

"Come Thomas, we're running late," said Jonathan. Thomas ran to the wagon and entered from the back. Mary was waiting on him to sit beside her. She primped herself to make the strongest of impression.

Diane appeared from the house wearing a smile as she greeted the family. She wished the Rose' well on their journey and again offered her condolences. She told them that she'd have their evening meal ready for them when they returned home. They were grateful for her offering.

The wagon was once again on its way towards town. Jonathan and Lydia spoke about what needed to be done for the recording of Chad' death. They would also restock on some much needed supplies.

Mary took Thomas by the hand and said, "When we are alone, I have something I'd like to share with you. I've been thinking and I thought we might spend some personal time together today to talk about the future. Is that okay with you?" Thomas agreed with the arrangement.

Jonathan overheard her and wondered if the two were considering a relationship. Mary had a few suitors in her time, but the relationships never seemed to last. The men seemed to leave as quick as they came. He knew Mary could be a controller when she took the notion. He thought that might have been why the courtships never lasted.

They were getting close to town and saw people along the road. Some of these lived in the forest with little resources. Communities of the homeless could be found around most populated towns in those days. It was a good place for farmers and tradesmen to find seasonal labor. These people got through life by their wits and stamina. The weak, the lame and the elderly were counted among them. The children were left to fend for themselves so they too could learn the skills of survival.

There was a two-story house at the edge of town. The occupants were seldom seen. There were plenty of rumors concerning the goings on there. The children who visited the house always had food and wore better clothes than the others. Some children went in the house and never came out and were never seen again.

The parents of those lost either didn't care or were too afraid to knock on the door to ask about their child.

One less mouth to feed. One less to worry about, was their way of coping with the pain losing a child. They knew they were alone in their plight. They were looked upon as derelicts and sinners who got what they deserved.

The wagon entered town near the Stagg Inn. It was important to Lydia to record Chads death to preserve his memory in the public record. The Reverend Richard was busy preparing meat for curing in his smoke house. He saw them coming and prepared himself to receive them.

Lydia asked Thomas to accompany her to the rectory. She needed a witness to Chad's passing. He was happy to oblige her and helped her down from the wagon. Lydia enjoyed his gentleman's gesture. The two strolled toward the rectory in full conversation. There was a delightful energy building between the two.

Jonathan drove the wagon until he was in front of the trading store. He needed supplies and was looking forward to a pouch of good tobacco.

Mary planned on shopping at every store in town in search for another item for her hope chest. She loved coming to town and fantasized about living there. She was so weary of rural life and was desperate for a change.

The Reverend rushed out to greet Lydia and Thomas. They entered the rectory together and sat down beside his desk. The Reverend removed a large black book from the shelf. It held the records of the towns people and notable events.

When he opened the book, you could smell the mustiness held within its pages. The Reverend turned the pages searching for the entry of Chad's birth. "Ahh! I found it! I see your name on the same page Thomas. The two of you were born on the same month in the same year," spoke the Reverend. Thomas and Lydia watched as he completed the entry. "There it is done. Is there anything else I can do for either of you," asked the Reverend. "No, I'm sure that will do," replied Lydia.

One is born and the name and date are entered within a book of record. They pass away and the final entry is made. A name coupled with a date showing the arrival of one soul. The same name held with a different date to show its departure.

A single life be it long or be it short held within a lifeless record book. No record about what they loved or carried in life. No entry made to tell of the things they enjoyed or how many times they embraced the deepest of emotion. Nothing can be learned about someone simply by reading such an entry.

Thomas sat there recalling all the adventures he and Chad shared. They were like brothers in heart always sharing the good and hard times of life.

Lydia was recalling the day he was born to her. How he grew so fast and always wanted so much more out of life than what they could give him. He was always making fun of things to dispel worry or undue concern. He loved his parents, and he loved the life given to him.

Truly a book exist somewhere that offers the witness of every soul and every journey. A record that offers reference, guidance to become the compass to show the way to eternal bliss. A torch that dispels the sheath of darkness and ignorance.

The awareness of the moment in the rectory returns. Blessings and goodbyes are exchanged between them. Lydia gives the Reverend an offering for his church and his service. Thomas and Lydia exit the rectory together in thought of the same, called Chad.

Lydia took Thomas' hand as they walk. "I want to talk to you about yesterday's embrace," said Lydia. Thomas could feel his throat getting tighter as she continued. "I want you to know that we did nothing wrong. I want you to know that it will always be our secret. What we shared gave me hope and passion at a moment when I had no hope nor reason to live. I went from feeling dead to feeling alive again. And I still feel that way. I will forever hold that moment for as long as I live," spoke Lydia. Thomas was beside himself. He felt a great sense of relief.

Thomas was moved by her presence. She was a beautiful woman with dark hair and deep eyes. She enjoyed him as well. The two were locked in a stare. Both feeling something deep, not of mortal lust or gratification. This ran deep. Deeper than anything felt before. They were feeling a love from another time they once shared in a place called Rome.

The eternal love that gave breath, mind, and soul for the cradle of life. They would in this lifetime learn to live in the two worlds. One of man and one of God. A presence reserved for all members of creation.

CHAPTER 10

Thomas and Lydia were walking through town when they met Rebecca, the printer's daughter. Rebecca was happy to see Thomas and threw her arms around him. She gave him a warm hug and kissed him on the cheek. Any other day Thomas would embrace her with equal enthusiasm. Today was different. It felt uncomfortable with Lydia at his side.

Rebecca was known as a tease in town. She loved to flirt with the boys and even some of the men when their wives were not in plain sight.

Rebecca broke from her hug and took Thomas by the shoulders. "I have some good news for you Thomas. Father has completed binding some books you may be interested in. One is about the sun and the earth moving around each other. Isn't it crazy to think the earth is moving? Why we'd all fall down," as she laughed out loud. "There's even one of poetry. You know how much I enjoy hearing your poetry. You must come by the shop and see what else there is," said Rebecca. Thomas was excited about the publishing and his enthusiasm was mounting. "I can show you some other things while your there," spoke Rebecca in a seductive tone. The lure of new printed books was too tempting to pass up. Rebecca's father, Squire, allowed Thomas to read the books from his collection whenever he came to town. Thomas would repay the favor by doing odd jobs around the shop.

Lydia looked at Thomas and said, "Go with your friend and enjoy yourself. We will pick you up at the shop when we are ready to leave." Thomas accepted the offer and he and Rebecca set out for the print shop.

Lydia began walked towards the wagon in search of Mary and Jonathan. She brought one hand up to her mouth, the other to her stomach. She felt queasy and felt as if she would throw up. She tried to hold things back but could not. She dropped to her knees and began dry heaving. As she stared at the ground, she wondered if she was pregnant. She regained her stance and took a seat on a bench nearby.

"If I am pregnant, whose child could it be? "she wondered. "Would it matter?" she thought. "If it be Jonathan's seed, then so be it. If it be the seed of Thomas, then it must be. No matter whose seed lies within me the love for the child would be the same," she thought.

Lydia saw Mary running towards her in excitement. She was wearing a big smile as she greeted her mother. "Come see the new fabric. It comes from London, and they have it in three colors. It's beautiful mother. Come let us bargain for a yard or two of it. Lydia could see a difference in Mary. The way she was behaving. Not so much about the cloth. There was something else. "Have you seen Thomas mother? "said Mary. "Yes, he's at Andrew Becketts print shop with Rebecca," replied Lydia. The smile from Mary's face fell away. She turned and began running towards the shop.

As the print shop came into view, Mary's wrath grew. She looked about but no Thomas. Her steps quickened and her face drew tighter as one about to do battle. Mary threw opened the door to the shop and there stood Andrew busy at work. "Where is Rebecca," she asked in a loud tone. "I don't know. I have not seen her all day," replied Andrew. Mary turned and ran outside. She could hear a woman's voice coming from the back of the shop. As she rounded the corner, she could see Rebecca sitting on Thomas's lap. The two had their faces close together and ready to kiss.

"What do you think you're doing?!" yelled Mary. She ran toward the pair and shoved Rebecca. Thomas fell backwards and landed on the ground with Rebecca beside him. Mary stood over Rebecca blocking the sun. She raised her arm high and brought it down until her finger was in Rebecca's face. "If I ever catch you with your arms around him again you hussy, I'll write on the side of every building in town that you are a Jezebel! Tell me that you understand what I'm saying. Otherwise, I'm going to see how much of your hair I can pull out before the sun sets!" roared Mary as a lion about to pounce.

Rebecca looked up at the fire in Mary's eyes. She knew better than to challenge her while she laid on her back. Rebecca held her head down to show compliance. "That's better," said Mary. Mary stepped away and Rebecca gave her a look of vengeance. This battle was far from over.

Mary helped Thomas up from the ground. "I think it best that you leave with me. You could get in some serious trouble here," said Mary. Thomas was in disbelief of what had just happened. This was the first time he had witnessed Mary's wrath. The two walked towards the wagon without saying a word.

Mary took him by the hand and pulled him closer to her face. She did not want anyone to overhear what she was going to say. Do you remember the joy we shared together in my room? Do you remember how you felt when you touched my breasts and kissed my lips? How good it felt to enter me as a man? Do you remember Thomas?" she asked. "Yes, I remember," spoke Thomas.

"I would like to be with you again. Tomorrow I will meet you in the grove at the oak that sits beside the stream. There you can have me again. I will show you things about love that will please you more than you can imagine," said Mary. Thomas was curious and cautious at once.

Around the corner came Lydia and Jonathan in the wagon. It was filled with supplies and lumber. Jonathan wanted to repay Edward for the material used in making Chad' coffin. There was autumn honey and good tobacco to offer as gifts to their neighbors.

Mary and Thomas boarded the wagon and the four turned towards home. As they neared the edges of town, there stood those of the woodlands, the homeless. Their eyes reflecting the sadness that only comes from the starvation of food and love.

A strange feeling overcame Thomas. In his mind's eye he could see a figure of a body dressed in a dark hooded cloak. It had no face. The darkness that dwelled under the hood was frightening to look upon. A chill went down his back as he took a quick deep breath. Then from the darkness came a voice that said, "This world, this planet that can grow enough food to feed all the flock who gather in witness. This world that has gone astray from the family of mankind. The misguidance of human necessity has filled the land with the poverty that is heard and felt on high. When? When, I ask, will they of this planet learn to extend their arms to give love and compassion to others rather than flex arms inward, to hold more than they could ever eat, more than they could ever use? What profit does one gain from the storage of grain, when so many are hungry. Were you not sent to be your brethren's keepers? Have you not heard from the prophet it is better to give than receive? What sickness is this, that blinds one to the bounties of love?

The notion that one needs love is foolish. You are love, in truth and in manner. All things sought outside the self are fleeting, an illusion. All things sought from within are eternal and true. One renders you the slave, the other, the master. The things of heaven and of earth are not ruled from the sky. They are ruled through the heart within. The world does not define you. You define yourselves. The origin of the questions in life are from within. So too are the answers.

These souls that walk without home, without food, without hope are the reason we are here. We came to conquer ignorance and the misguidance that feeds it. We came to crush the corrupt in heart through the benevolence of others. When the day comes, when a broken heart cannot be found, nor an empty stomach can be traced, will our mission here be complete. We outnumber the stars of the sky."

Thomas shifted from the voice and became aware of the conversation between Jonathan and Lydia. The wagon was nearing home. Diane was standing in the yard collecting the last of her herbs. She saw the Rose' on approach. She turned and ran inside the house. She return holding a basket filled with generous portions of stew and enough bread for dinner and breakfast.

Jonathan stopped the wagon and stepped down. Lydia followed him and embraced Diane. Jonathan began unloading the lumber with Thomas' help. Lydia gave Diane the honey and tobacco as a gift for their kindness.

Thomas looked at Diane his mother, whom he adored and loved. Mary his soon to be girlfriend teaching him the things of manhood and the pleasures of the body. And there was Lydia who had lit the fire within him. Three women held to the love of his heart. All that separated them was the role they were playing at this time and at this place in life. All for the glory of love.

CHAPTER 11

Two weeks had passed since Chads death. Things were beginning to return to normal. It was midmorning when most chores on the farm were finished. Usually, it was a quiet time of the day. However, this morning was going to be different. Both Lydia and Mary had been complaining of not feeling well in recent days. This morning it was worse. Lydia had gone to bed because severe nausea. Mary spent time outdoors vomiting her breakfast.

Jonathan was fearful that the women may be suffering whatever it was that took Chads life. He knew he needed help but didn't know where to find it. It was then that Mildred appeared from the trees. Jonathan felt relief once he held sight of her.

"I awoke this morning and felt a need to visit you and your family. How is everyone?" asked Mildred. "Mary and Lydia are both ill. I'm afraid they have Chad's sickness," spoke Jonathan in a worried tone. "I can't lose another to death! I just can't," spoke Jonathan held in fears grip. Mildred took Jonathan by the shoulders and looked him in the eye. 'Your wife Lydia and daughter Mary are going to be alright. There is no need for alarm, please trust me. You know my truth. This illness about them will pass and when it does you will be pleased.

Jonathan, you are going to be a father and a grandfather," spoke Mildred. Jonathan stood still from what she spilled out. "What, what did you say?" asked Jonathan. He stood there looking at Mildred in a confused state. All the while Mildred still looking at him held a warm smile. She laughed as her eyes filled with light and reassurance. Jonathan was beginning to take things in. He could feel himself relaxing. "But how? How could they both be pregnant?" he thought.

Slowly he lowered himself until he was sitting on the ground. He turned to look up at Mildred. With tenderness in his face, he looked at her and said, "How?" Mildred joined him on the ground and took him by both hands. Still displaying her smile, she pulled him towards her. "You ask how it happens. I can tell you. It was a gift from above.

Jonathan, a good son to his parents, who looked after them in their time of need. Jonathan, the good husband to his loving wife, who rescued her from the grips of poverty and servitude. Jonathan, the good father to three beautiful children, who gave them all he had. Jonathan, who has need of new life and birth to soften the pains of his loss.

These are but blessings that rain down on you from above. You are blessed Jonathan. The love that lives on high has heard your prayers and seen the pain you carry in your heart. It knows the number of all the tears you shed in the loss of those you care for. These gifts that rest in the bellies of your women have come to lift you up in your time of need."

Jonathan gently lied down on his back and looked upward into the sky. It was filled with scores of white clouds. The autumn wind was rustling the leaves of the trees sending some to the ground.

Lydia came outside hearing Jonathan and Mildred talking. Mary joined them from the side of the house. "What's wrong with Jonathan? Why is he lying on the ground?" asked Lydia. He's okay. He is just overwhelmed by some news. Just let him enjoy the news and he will share it with you when he is ready," said Mildred.

Mary and Lydia joined the pair on the ground. Mary's face was still flushed, and she was still feeling nauseous. The two looked at Jonathan as he lied there looking up at the sky. He was wearing a smile on his face. He appeared to be listening to something, maybe a heralding voice or perhaps just the wind. Neither wife nor daughter had ever seen such a peaceful look on his face.

Mother and daughter turned and looked at each other, then turned their gaze upon Mildred. "He's found his inner self. Let us send him love and the warmth of our hearts. He is a good man in heart and spirit. Let's leave him so he can be alone in the moment," said Mildred.

The women rose to their feet and looked down at Jonathan. He was still wearing the same smile. A tear or two was rolling down the side of his face. There was no whimpering nor sign of repression. There was just that smile and tears of joy.

Jonathan was in a place where the things human are realized. He was in that place where all things are born and where all things return to.

The women entered the home. Lydia prepared a cup of tea for everyone. The conversations were light and cordial. Tea was served with clover honey and biscuit. Then silence. Both Lydia and Mary were feeling better. The tea and communion had a healing effect for the body and the moment. All heads were looking down at the floor held in silence.

Jonathan cried out. Mary and Lydia jumped up from the table to go to him when Mildred stopped them. "Jonathan needs this time alone with his angel. The angel is showing him what lies behind the curtain of life. To disturb the moment would deprive Jonathan of much needed knowledge of what lies ahead," said Mildred. The women hesitated at first but took their seats and returned to their tea.

The air in the house had taken on a chill. Mildred knew it was a common occurrence whenever many spirits congregated in one place. Lydia stood to fetch her shawl. She offered the same to the others, but they declined.

Jonathan was heard crying as if the world and everything in it was falling away. Lydia and Mary looked at Mildred. Mildred looked at both and said, "Go to him. He's ready for you now." The two women jumped up from the table and rushed out the door.

Jonathan was on his knees. His face was looking up to the heavens with arms outstretched. He was weeping uncontrollably as if he was waiting for an embrace from God himself. Both women fell to their knees and embraced him, knocking everyone to the ground. The three were sobbing and holding onto each other for dear life. The crying turned to laughter as they clung to each other for joy.

Mildred was still seated at the table. She finished the last of her tea. She slowly rose from the table and stood in silence. A beautiful blue orb of light entered the room and circled her three times. Mildred knew that her work here was finished. She left the house without anyone noticing.

A quiet rest and a cup of tea were all that was needed to finish the day for this special soul called Mildred.

CHAPTER 12

Evening embraced the skies, and the creatures of the day were seeking rest. Thomas was in bed curled beneath the covers. The only sound in the house was the popping and cracking coming from the evenings fire. His mind was at rest while his heart was aglow from a new love, a first love. The boyish innocence within was fading away. The times were going faster than he could process.

He was enjoying the embrace of new things and new realities. Thomas' imagination often carried the story beyond its planned destination, but he did not care. For him, fairy tales rang true, angels danced in fields of wildflowers and what lied behind the curtain was more important than all the knowledge of the world.

His eyes were getting heavier as he faded away to sleep. The place between awareness and sleep is special to all. Here the troubles and fears of the day spent are denied admittance. The gift of dreams await the weary traveler in their quest for reasons. Dreams to please, to challenge, to comfort or to bridge the gaps of uncertainty. It's all there waiting for those who seek.

A loud knock at the door startles Thomas. He rose from the bed and listened. It was quiet about the house. There was no sound of his father's footsteps across the floor to answer the knock. Thomas lied back down still listening for another knock while drifting back to sleep.

He became aware of standing on a cobblestone road facing a tall building. It was green like an emerald and held many windows. Thomas reached for the doors latch when it opened on its own. He steps inside and there stood Isaac dressed in colors of blue, gold, and white.

There was something about him that gave Thomas a deep sense of safety. "It is good to see you again Thomas. I come from a place you have forgotten in your journeys on earth. I'm here to help you along in your search. I see you have the love and care for another. What is her name?" asked Isaac. "Lydia," replied Thomas, "her name is Lydia." "And what is it that spurs such feelings for her?" asked Isaac.

"I felt a connection, like it was something that was already known. I've known her all my life but never knew such a feeling for her until now. We came together at a sad moment, and we kissed. We made as husband and wife while we held each other. I was stirred within, and the feeling has failed to leave me.

Now I can't stop thinking of her. The way she looks, the way she walks, the way she makes me feel when she touches me," said Thomas. "I only know what burns inside me. I know not it's origin. I only know that it is something I never want to let go of. Her beauty takes me to a place where love overcomes all shortcomings. A place where there are no bonds to fear or unrest to carry."

Isaac stood looking at Thomas. He could see that Thomas' eyes, though open, were not focused on the present. He was occupied with inner vision. The same vision of the prophets. A place where there is no time or space. A place between heaven and earth.

Thomas had transcended himself without realizing it. He would never look at life the same way after this. He had new eyes to which to see. It was the possibilities of what could be, that fed his yearnings.

Isaac placed his hand on Thomas' shoulder to return him to the consciousness of the world his body occupied. Thomas closed his eyes and drifted back. He could smell the wood smoke and feel the warmth of his bed.

Outside fall was beginning to yield to winter. A heavy frost covered the ground. The light of a full moon covered everything in a celestial silver light. Smoke gently raising from the chimneys of quiet homes added to the tranquility for the observer.

The night comes for the bodies to rest, while minds and hearts are elsewhere engaged in their dance. Never sleeping, always reaping the wonders of life. They journey on magic carpets at night in search of knowledge by which to grow, in search of passion by which to sow.

All share the same journey with mutual desires. This place, this journey, is for the love that lives within and nothing else. Whether we be counted as good or as bad. We are still holding each other's hand.

CHAPTER 13

It was nearly winter when days were cool, and nights are cold. It was the season for the curing of meats for winter stores. Jonathan would need help with the butchering. He decided to call on Edward and Thomas for help. He would offer a ham or backstrap as payment for their help.

Mary was thinking of her rendezvous with Thomas. She wanted to make the occasion a memorable one. She entertained thoughts of marriage with the young Thomas of seventeen years. She was worried she may never have a suitor to offer a proposal. She longed to be someone's wife, to be a caring mother and a member of society. Mary needed someone to care for.

She opened her hope chest which held her collections and the fantasies that went with each. She imagined her collection of dishes proudly displayed in her home. Her embroideries and trinkets would decorate the walls and furnishings. All she needed was a husband and a place to call home. She had pictured the scene many times over. She took a deep breath and with care closed the lid until the day came.

Lydia was busy with the morning meal. She had set the table for four even though there were only three. She wasn't ready to let Chad go just yet. Twice this morning she went to his room to wake him for the day as she always had. She saw that he was not there but dismissed the vacancy. "Maybe he rose early and already sent to do his chores," she thought.

Jonathan watched his wife move about the house in near frenzy. He knew the words to comfort her did not exist. He knew that she had to work it out her own way. He knew doing nothing would mean more to her.

At the Sonnet' home Thomas was up and dressed for the day. His thoughts turned to the meeting with Mary. He was looking forward to spending time with her. He planned to visit Andrew Beckett, the printer, afterwards. He was anxious to read the new texts Rebecca spoke of.

Thomas entered the kitchen and noticed there was something troubling his mother. Diane went about herself without a spoken word or a direct look. Edward was just waking and entered the living quarters. Thomas looked at his father and could tell he had been drinking heavy the night before. He wondered if that could be why his mother was so reserved. They often fought whenever Edward drank too much.

He was a gentle man and a loving man by nature. When he drank too much, a hidden trouble that lived within would spill out. His demon would appear for all to see and fear. Whatever was troubling him inside was held deep in secret.

The enigma of life and the enigma of love are one in the same. How someone can express love without end in one moment and turn away from love in the next is the puzzle of life. The need to be wanted, the need to be loved and cared for, can forgive, and sometimes forget such trespasses. The need for survival and the completion of one's desire will most always override reason.

There is a passage in Genesis that gave Thomas solace in such times. It was when Adam and Eve had eaten the fruit of knowledge. God said, "The man is become as one of us, to know good and evil."

To know good and evil was prophetic for Thomas. Life was about experiencing both and not one or the other. Life was not about right or wrong. It was about the mystery of right and wrong. To him, they were the same thing, only in different form.

The son and the wife loved Edward even in his worst because of his best. And so, the threads of life we make, find their place in the collective tapestries, that bears the witness in this place called Earth.

CHAPTER 14

Jonathan sat beside a tree with few leaves still clinging to its branches. The ground was littered with leaves of gold, crimson and orange. The rustling of leaves from a gentle breeze gave him a sense of peace. He closed his eyes and drifted back to those days when he held the innocence of a child.

The smell of curing leaves in the autumn air amplified the moment. His relaxing moment deepened as he thought of Mildred and the message, she gave about the pregnancies. He wondered how both women in his life could be with child. He recalled the intimacy with Lydia the morning after Chad's wake.

It was Mary being with child that baffled him. There had been no suitors calling upon the Rose' home for Mary' hand. Then he recalled Mary's conversation with Thomas when they went to town. Something about she had something to tell him when they were alone. He decided to put the matter to rest until later.

Lydia was carefully attending to her household duties. She was feeling nauseous and lightheaded lately. She was certain she was pregnant. She wondered who the father might be. Her heart, her passion was filled with thoughts of Thomas. Her devotion and reverence belonged to Jonathan. The thoughts of Thomas made her feel young and alive again. She recalled their union and had to stop with the household chores.

A delightful spell was overcoming her. The spell of young love and the embrace of possibilities. She entered Mary's room where the two held each other. She walked to the bed and slowly sat down. She closed her eyes and entered the moment in mind. A warmth was building inside her transforming time from present to past.

Her head dropping back as she took a deep breath and held it. Silence filled the room. The turbulence of passion filled her core. She could feel it coming as long as she held her breath. Her eyes were shut tight. The body held tense. She was delivered to an ecstasy moment and released a moan of pure pleasure. The same she had withheld on that day with Thomas. Her body relaxed as she fell back on the bed feeling a deep sense of relief.

Her eyes opened in a blank stare as she lied there feeling free from worry or concern. She was alive inside. She turned to one side and lifted her arm as to embrace another beside her with no one there. She lied there quietly as feelings were coming to her in waves of three and four. She was no longer aware of her body. Nor the environment in which her body lied. Lydia was elsewhere.

It was a place where all things meet. A place where all debts and misgivings are cleansed. A place that does not ask for reason or cause. This place where all the whys and how are of little or no concern. A place where peace and harmony reign above all. All present are relatives without desire or purpose. In this place there is nothing to learn and nowhere is there a single memory to be found. It's not heaven, but from here one can begin to fathom the realm of heaven.

It is from here that souls received their birth into the world of matter. They would live, prosper, fail and recover in their journey as mortals. On the day of their surrender from that world they'd return to this place once again. Lydia was content to remain here forever between heaven and earth.

She feels the touch of another, and it brings her back to the mortal reality. She feels a male vibration. Her heart surges upward. She begins to open her eyes expecting to see Thomas, yet there stood Jonathan. He's smiling down on her with warm eyes and a gentle smile. "Where were you? It was as if you were asleep in a dream. Are you okay?" he asked. She nodded her head yes as she tried to hold the magic of her moment. The energy was waning fast, and she became upset. She frowned at Jonathan as she stood. She ran out of the house without saying a word.

She entered the road and faced towards the Sonnet's home. She took a few steps in that direction and stopped. Her longing eyes filled with tears because she so longed to be held. She wanted to feel Thomas' touch.

Inside she was spinning out of control. The things that were wrong felt right. The things she once believed were right felt wrong. She dropped to her knees and placed her hands over her face. She began to weep woefully with no one else in witness.

The cool air of the day was warming as the sun grew ever higher in the sky. Lydia regained herself and rose to her feet. She brushed away the leaves that clung to her dress. She took one long look at the Sonnet's home and turned to return home.

Jonathan was seated feeding on yesterday's bread and freshly churned butter. Lydia took a seat at the table still feeling upset. "I'm going to the Sonnet home today to ask Jonathan and Thomas' help with preparing the winters store of meat," said Jonathan. Lydia lifted her head so she could hear every word. But instead, she stopped listening to him. She began planning how she could be alone with Thomas. The chore would take a couple days to complete. This would give her plenty of opportunity to devise a plan to taste the lips she so longed for.

What Lydia did not know was that Mary had similar thoughts and desires. Both women were after the same thing. One needed a lover. The other needed a husband. Both were with child by the same.

In life's entangled web, we make our beds, on which we sleep. We are the creators of life as we know it. We are the authors who write the story with pen in hand. We chose the cast and set the plots. It is us that bring joy and sadness to the stage. Life is about both ends of the rainbow.

CHAPTER 15

Mary awoke earlier this morning with only one thing in mind. It was the time she would be spending with Thomas. She wanted to please him in every way. She was determined to become the center of his attention.

She carried a dream as lovers do. She believed that happiness could only come from the love of spouse, the love of family. She realized the importance of this day and laid her plan to mind. Sadly her mind was trying to fill a need that was the business of the heart. Relationships built in such a way were like birds without wings. It would never leave the ground.

She wore the same dress on the day she made love to Thomas in her room. She pulled her hair back and tied with a green ribbon. There was just one last thing to do before she left. Get to her mother's rose water without being detected.

It was kept in her mother's bedroom. She didn't want to ask permission to use it. It would arouse Lydia' attention with a number of questions to follow. Patiently she waited for her mother to leave the house. The sound of a squeaking door hinge would be her cue.

She hears the sound she was waiting for. She dashed inside the dimly lit room and lifted the bottle of rose oil. She rubbed some on her face and her cleavage. As quick as she entered the room she exited and fled out the door of the house. She turned towards the Sonnet' house and began skipping down the road. She was happy with herself and relieved that this moment had arrived.

Thomas was already there waiting on Mary. He stood in humble awe as he stared at the oak tree. One half still standing as it littered the ground with its leaves. The other half, fallen away, lying across the stream. Thomas had never ventured across the other that side of the stream. He didn't know why. Perhaps it was because it presented something unknown which held contrast to the sanctity of his special place on earth.

He could hear the rustling of leaves coming close. He could faintly smell the fragrance of roses as it carried on the breeze. Mary appeared from the standing trees. She was looking down, being careful where to step. There were puddles about from recent rains. Thomas turned in her direction. Mary looked up and began to wave at him. She hurried her pace as she raced to embrace.

She wrapped her arms around him and held him tight. The fragrance of the rose oil was strong and gave delight to his senses. The way she held him excited him immensely. He was enjoying the attention she offered. Mary broke the embrace so she could read his face. It was as she had hoped. She pressed her lips against his and began a kiss. She glided her tongue in and out of his mouth until Thomas was filled with sexual desire. Mary broke away from their kissing and looked deep into his eyes. She too was filled with a lust for passion.

She took hold her dress at the shoulders as before and pulled it down until her breast were exposed. Thomas looked upon her breast with subtle desire. He had never seen anything more beautiful or desirable. She took his hands and placed them to her breast. He was shaking as he was held in wonderment. His hands began to caress her breasts with care. He was alive and on fire within. Mary stood before him with her eyes closed. She was allowing the moment to build the energy as his hands danced across her nipples. Both were intoxicated in the moment as the fire within each came together as one.

Mary began tugging at his shirt to remove it from his pant. She lifted the shirt over his head and dropped it to the ground. She began rubbing her breasts against his chest, while the two kissed in feverish passion without pause. She reached around to hold the small of his back while the other hand probed below his belt line. Her hand delivered him to a place of pleasure. He felt the rush as she held him, and he released his seed. His shoulders slumped to a relaxed state. He looked at Mary with grateful eyes and a smile. She returned the smile and guided him to the ground.

The two sat and continued to kiss one another. Mary was running her fingers through his hair. In a gentle soft voice she asked, "Do I please you with the fruits of my love?" "Yes," replied Thomas with dreamy eyes.

Thomas lied down and looked upward towards sky. "Is this love, or is it something else? This feeling that consumes me was it for Mary or was it because of Mary? Is love the message or is it the messenger?" he wondered.

Mary was lying beside him also held in thought. She had always been attracted to older established men who were more experienced in life. They owned property and held positions.

Thomas had none of these things. He was known for his love of books and writing nonsensical stories about people and faraway places. Mary needed someone to love and someone to love her. She was willing to release her prerequisites for a spouse and take a chance on Thomas.

She bent her face close to his and engaged her sight with his. She pressed her lips against his and they began to kiss with passion. She rolled her body on his and the kissing grew. He was calmer this time and open to whatever would come. Thomas wrapped his arms around her while she stroked his hair. Their energies were meshing. The unknown depths of souls were coming to bear. The warmth of their bodies and the passion of the moment were all that existed.

Thomas rolled over on Mary. The two removed what clothing was still clinging to their bodies. Their nude bodies embrace once more. The breathing quickened as fingers dance across each other's body. Passion building as the two danced in the world of making love.

Thomas gently enters her and softly whispers, "I love this, and I love you." Mary grabbed his buttocks to thrusts him deeper inside her. Her legs wrap around him to hold him tight. "Give me your seed Thomas! Give me your seed!" she yelled. Thomas rocked back and forth in the rhythm of their breathing. He can feel it building inside. Mary was there with him. Their eyes fixated on each other as they grow wider. Together they explode in ecstasy and the two become one. They release the sounds of pleasure that carry far into the forest. Their bodies covered with sweat mixes with rose water. They gingerly kiss one another out of love for the moment.

Thomas stood and offered his hand to help her up. She accepts the gesture and stands before him in total embrace. Something opened between the two like a flower that bears its petals. He led her to the pool of the stream. Slowly they step into the water holding hands. The chill of the water exhilarates them as they clutch each other closer for warmth. They laugh and giggle as two children at play.

They share the moment as friends and lovers. These two have walked together in other times in other roles on the stage of life. History reveals they are no strangers to each other or this world. To this place and this time of present being, they unite once again to behold the realm of mortal witness. Times of joy and times of woe await them with the embrace of each day.

A pair of eyes off in the distant witnessed the affairs of the young couple. The witness was stirred with the emotions of anger, betrayal, and jealousy. The dream of a future romance shifted to heartbreak and disappointment. Expectations withering as tears fall from the heavy eyes of witness. Anger shifts to sorrow. What once held in hope has broken the heart of one who sought the love of another. Love and its quirks were not writing a conclusion to her story. It merely was offering a different approach.

CHAPTER 16

Thomas and Mary stepped from the pool and gathered their clothes. They dressed without saying a word. Once dressed they came together and held hands. Casually they strolled together until they reached the road. They embraced one last time and set out to return to their respective homes.

Mary was taking her time returning home. She held her waist hoping that Thomas' seed had found its way to her nest. She looked upward to heaven with a great smile as she nourished the thought of being with child. "If it's a boy I will call him Chad to honor my brother. If it be a girl, I will call her Lucille, for she will be the light of my life."

She thought of her hope chest and wondered if this would be the moment, she had so long desired. She felt good about herself. A young husband, a child to love and care for with gracious parents happy for her condition. Her thoughts of marriage and motherhood gave joy to her feet. She skipped and danced on her way home.

Thomas entered his home, but no one was there. He took bread and apple butter for his meal as he prepared to leave for town. He filled his pockets with apples to eat on his return home. He ran out of the house and started for Squire Becketts print shop.

He decided to write a poem for Mary in gratitude for the way she made him feel. It would help him pass the time along the journey. "Two silver bells ringing from above, calling two souls back to love," he thought. He was pleased with the opening. He finished the poem and planned to put it to paper once he was at the print shop.

Thomas was nearing town entering the space occupied by the wood-landers. It was best to be cautious when walking here. Robbery came easy for those who hungered.

He saw children gathered along the road ahead. Their faces were dirty, their clothes were in tatters. There was no sign of hope or promise in their little eyes. They had surrendered to their position of want and poverty. Thomas' heart was heavy whenever he looked on them.

The children slowly gathered near him. They could see that his pockets were bulging with something. Thomas realized what they were looking at. He reached inside and handed each an apple. Each took hold the apple and ran off so not to be seen. They feared the older or stronger might rob them of their prize. This was their way of life, sad as it may be.

Thomas was finally in Danbury. He turned towards the print shop of Squire Beckett. The front and rear doors were opened to allow the cool breeze to enter. It helped to dry the fresh ink on paper. Thomas stepped through the door, and he was faced with Squire. "Welcome Thomas, welcome. I was wondering where you had been," spoke Squire.

"It was about matters of great importance," said Thomas. "And what might that be," inquired Squire. "To be in love, not just any love, but the love of wonder and fulfillment," spoke Thomas. Squire let out a deep laugh surprising Thomas. "Well then Thomas you must write such a story and let me print the same. This revelation of yours will be read across Europe and into the orient. Its sale will make us rich beyond belief. Song and poetry shall be born from such work," spoke Squire. Thomas didn't know if Squire was joking or being serious.

Rebecca entered the room out of breath, as if she had been in a hurry. "What brings you to town Thomas?" asked Rebecca. "I've come to see if your father has work for my hands so I may earn a wage," replied Thomas.

"I made him a business proposition daughter!" laughed Squire. "What say you Thomas, will you make me and my daughter rich with your words of love and rapture?" inquired Squire. Rebecca hearing her father's words turned to Thomas and took his hand. She placed it close to her breasts and said, "What are these words my father speaks of? Tell me Thomas, so I may too enjoy such thoughts and desires."

"It was nothing. I was thinking out loud from a dream I had last evening," spoke Thomas in embarrassment. "Oh well tell me later if you will. What work have you for Thomas?" asked Rebecca. "If none be given, I have use for him and his stories," spoke the daughter.

"God bless you daughter. I have work for him and a good wage to boot. So daughter, you will have to look elsewhere for your entertainment," spoke Squire. "Very well father but will you have need of him until days end? asked Rebecca. "Yes daughter. Now take leave so we can begin our work," said Squire.

"It's time you learn a trade young Thomas. There is no future for you on the farm. Oh, it be a labor of honor for sure. But your soul reaches for more than it can give. You are filled with the light of a dreamer. There is much within you which must come forward. But first you must develop the keen sense within you.

If you'd be inclined, I will teach you the art of print. It's a good livelihood for someone of your nature. You love to read. You'd be welcome to read my entire collection of books anytime you chose. Why you could even take over this establishment once I have passed. All you see here could be yours one day.

"When I was young as you, I stood beside what remained of the Druids. They were men and women of the stars. They came down to bring this world to a more desirable level for life and prosperity. There was a time when they defeated the Roman army of Julius Caesar. I do miss them so," spoke Squire.

"Well, what do you say Thomas. Be it in your best interest to accept my offer? Are you my apprentice or are you set on being a farmer? What shall it be dear son? Feast or famine?" inquired Squire. Thomas looked into the eyes of Squire Andrew. They were as Nathan's eyes peering up at him from the streams pool. "Yes, yes Squire. I accept your proposition," spoke Thomas in a low and broken voice. "Good choice lad. Be it so for all to hear and know," bellowed Squire.

"If you be willing, you may even be able to tame Rebecca' wild heart to be your bride one day. I would give the two of you my home and all that you see," said Squire. "You jest with me sir," replied Thomas. "No, I jest not young Thomas. I'm serious. This business, my home and daughter I would gladly give to you.

I can see in you that your path has already been written. You are too young to realize it yet. One day you will stand beside people of importance. Someday you will be known by many, yet no one will ever really know you. There is one that will. She be of dark hair and guarded words. Her shadow will follow you through life and in death. You will be the enigma as it was written from the beginning," spoke Squire from a place within.

Thomas drifted in mind to Squires words and he was absent for a moment. Something was shaking him. Then came the words, "I have something special for you!" As he was regaining his senses there stood Squire holding a book. Thomas took the book and smiled at Squire. Still, Thomas was too dazed to read the title in gold letters. He thanked Squire for the gift and carefully stepped outside. Thomas was sure to walk out of sight from Squire Andrew before sitting down to regain his composure.

He sat in wonder of what had just happened. "Was I dreaming then or am I dreaming right now?" he thought. "Is it time to return home?" Thomas stretched out on the cool grass of the village's courtyard. The sun's rays were beaming down on him restoring him back to mortal awareness.

He was a lover of nature and its effect on everyday life. To him the sun was the giver of all things. The seasons, the weather, planting, and harvest were all governed by the sun's movement in the sky. To him the sun was like God, always giving but never wanting.

"Give me grace oh heaven whose eye I have seen. Nurture me oh sun of the great sky so I may see the beauty of your creation and the source of your power. Oh, rest within me oh heaven and sun. Bring this child of God to everlasting life, to everlasting love. Take away all that stands between us. Be my guide amongst the stars and across the heavens. Take me as I am and direct my feet towards your abode so I may find my true home, my true existence and all that lies within. These things I pray to one that hears, to one who gives life. Amen," spoke the soul held to darkness.

CHAPTER 17

Mary was pleased with herself. The plans she made with Thomas went better than expected. She enjoyed their time together. Twice she had been with Thomas. It was her fertile time and with some praying she hoped to deliver a child and a husband. As she neared home, she peered upwards on the hill where Chad and Jeremy lied buried. She wondered about life and the unwanted changes it brought with no regard to objection.

Mary entered the home to see her mother sitting at the table with her head down. Right away Mary felt that something was wrong. "My, you certainly smell good Mary. Is that my rose oil you are wearing?" asked Lydia. Mary choked up and could hardly speak. "Yes, mother it is the rose oil you smell," replied Mary. "Why did you feel the need to do so daughter? "asked Lydia. "I just wanted to feel pretty today mother, that's all," replied Mary. "I see," said Lydia as she raised her head to look at Mary. "And where have you been that you felt the need to feel so pretty?" asked Lydia in a shaky voice. "I've been walking about amongst the forest enjoying the moment," replied Mary.

"What a coincidence. I too was walking amongst the forest. I followed the scent of roses that trailed behind you. And where did you think it led me daughter?" Mary could feel a weakening in her knees. Her heart began to pound inside her chest. She held the back of a chair for support. Slowly she took a seat at the table and bowed her head. "How much had her mother seen? How long was she there?" she thought.

"I was with Thomas mother. He asked me to meet him. He wanted to share some things with me. We talked for some time, that's all," replied Mary. Mary raised her head to see how much of the story Lydia believed. She could see her mother's anger building.

"I think it highly unlikely you would be so generous with rose oil just to hear the words of someone so young. What was your intent Mary?" Once again Mary bowed her head and in low sheepish voice and replied, "Thomas and I had sexual relations together. I tried to resist his advance, but his will overcame me and he had his way with me." "I see. Was this the first time daughter?" asked Lydia as she shifted her head to see Mary's face. "Yes mother, it was our first time." Again, Mary raised her face to see if her mother was ready to accept this rendition of her story.

"If you are pregnant how do expect him to care for you? He has no trade, no source of income. What do you think your father would do if he knew about this? Have you thought this out Mary? I watched you and him together. I failed to see him force himself on you. What do you think his parents would say if they knew? They are our friends. We depend on each other to survive these hard times. Your seduction will come at a very high price. I pray you will be able to pay it in full," spoke Lydia in loud tone.

Jonathan entered the house and asked, "What is going on in here? Why are you yelling mother? What has you so upset?" asked Jonathan. "Your daughter donned herself in rose oil and took to the forest to give herself to Thomas," replied Lydia. "Is this true daughter? Did you take young Thomas for your own pleasure? Did you? Look at me daughter and answer me," demanded Jonathan. "Yes father," as she quickly looked up at him, then as quick turn her eyes away. "Very well daughter. You, me, and your mother are walking up to the Sonnets home together. You are going to face his parents and tell them what you have done. I hope for your sake and Thomas' you are not pregnant," spoke Jonathan.

The news weakened Jonathan' spirit. The loss of another son and having to care for the farm alone was taking a toll on his outlook. Now he would have to face his neighbors and friends alongside Mary as she explains herself.

Jonathan washed to present himself to Edward and Diane. Lydia left the room to change her clothes. She wanted to present herself in a formal manner. Mary sat quietly in the chair with her head hung low. She worried what might happen once she told her story. She was afraid. She never once gave thought to the consequences that could arise.

"Let us ready ourselves for what is to come. Daughter you will have to stand tall and speak your story without blame or excuse. The Sonnets will honor a simple truth over a collection of half-truths. When you have finished look them in the eye and ask for their forgiveness and understanding. They are good people," spoke Jonathan.

He loved his daughter and carried no anger in his heart for her actions. He was however disappointed in her. He understood the sexual desire of young people and the need to explore and discover. It was the aftermath of such endeavors that sometimes changed the path for all involved.

The three walked side by side along the road to the Sonnets. The air was cool, and a breeze was about. Leaves were seen sweeping the land as the wind carried them off to some final destination far from their place of origin.

The winds of change were about at every turn of life and living. What is true for nature is also true for mortal, for all mortals bow to nature and its ways.

As they neared the Sonnet home, Jonathan took out his pipe. He packed it with the last of his golden leaf. He enjoyed the pipe when there were important things to contemplate. Jonathan was a good man and a wise man of good heart and character. He decided he would accept whatever Edward and Diane felt was best.

Edward saw the three approaching and called out for Diane. Diane came outside and stood beside Edward. They stood in silence knowing it wasn't a social call. They took each other's hand to brace for whatever news was coming.

Jonathan stepped up to Edward and shook his hand. "Thank you, neighbor, for Chads headstone. It truly honors his life and his time with us. We appreciate your kindness and charity. I know he looks down from heaven with favor to you and yours," spoke Jonathan.

"The reason we are here is because Mary has something to tell you both. May I ask where Thomas is?" inquired Jonathan. "Most likely he is at Squire's looking for a wage," replied Diane.

Mary took one step towards the Sonnets with her head hung. She raised her head looking at each and said, "I've come to tell you that Thomas and I were in the woods this day. We had adult relations with each other." Diane gasped and placed her hand over her mouth. She took hold of Edward and held on to his arm. She stared at Mary in disbelief. Edward became stiff in posture. His face was like stone.

He was reflecting on his and Diane's past. How they came together and why they had to get married. The two were originally from Sussex and moved to Danbury.

Mary continued with her revelation. "Thomas and I have been friends for such a long time. Our families break bread together and live as true protestant Christians. Today Thomas and I went further in our relationship. Today Thomas gave me his seed and I pray it grows in fertile soil," said Mary. "That's enough! Don't encourage more worry for them! I apologize for my daughter's behavior. A green switch will find the small of her back and bum," said Lydia.

Mary began to cry hearing the words from her mother. Diane moved towards Mary and put her arms around her, holding her tight. Diane was recalling the pain she went through when she learned that she was pregnant with Thomas.

Jonathan reached for his pipe. He asked Edward if there was a fire in the house that could render a hot coal to light his pipe. "Come Jonathan, let us smoke and speak of the news that found us today," said Edward. The two men went inside while the women took their own measure of the situation.

Thomas was on approach to his home, unaware of what was going on. He was preoccupied in mind. Besides everything that happened in a few short weeks, now he had to think about Squire' offer and how he would tell his parents.

Lydia was the first to see him. Her anger shifted to pleasure at the sight of him. Lydia's heels rose from the ground to escalate her height so she would be noticed by Thomas. He looked up and saw her standing there. Thomas hurried his walk in excitement. Lydia opened her arms to receive him. His mother and Mary were obstructed from view from the corner of the house. Diane watched as Lydia shifted from whatever she was observing. Just then Thomas appeared. He threw himself at Lydia and she embraced him and kissed him on the cheek. Diane saw the exchange and did not understand it. Lydia came to her senses seeing the look on Diane' face. She quickly released Thomas and returned to the event at hand.

"What's this? Mary why have you been crying?" asked Thomas. "I told them about us Thomas. I told them about what we did today. About our meeting in the woods," replied Mary. The smile on Thomas's face dropped away. He looked at his mother then Lydia, then Mary. He was trying to get a sense of where all this had gone. "It's okay. We don't expect two young people to refrain from their natural desires, do we Lydia?" said Diane in a curt tone. "No, no we don't," replied Lydia. Thomas heard his mother's acceptance, but they were in the company of others. Diane always saved her true thoughts and feelings for times in private.

Thomas and the women stepped inside the Sonnet home to see the men seated at the table. Pipe smoke had filled the air as Diane placed another sick of wood in the fireplace. She opened the window to release the smoke from the room. "Please stay for supper so we can share the friendship deserving of neighbors and friends," said Diane. "Very well. I will return home to fetch bread and jam along with some greens from the garden. Mary, you stay here and help Diane prepare. Thomas and I will get what is needed for the meal," said Lydia. Thomas grabbed a basket from the floor and followed Lydia out the door.

Thomas was swinging the basket back and forth as he strolled beside Lydia. "I hope you don't mind helping me Thomas," spoke Lydia. "Oh, no. I'm happy to be spending time with you," said Thomas." "I must say that I think of you often. I saw you and Mary together today in the woods. I have to say that I was aroused and angry at the same time. I want you to take me like that, the way you took Mary. I want you to take me as soon as we get inside the house. I want you to take me on Mary's bed as you did before," said Lydia. Thomas was dumbstruck by Lydia's words but aroused like never before.

The two entered the home and went straight to Mary's bedroom. Lydia was completely undressed before Thomas could shed his shirt. She shoved him down to the bed and reached for his pants. In one swift move she stripped them and slung them across the room.

She leapt on him and pressed her lips against his. She started kissing his face, then his chest and then his waist. Thomas lied there receiving the fruits of pleasure from one such as her. Her lips and tongue worked their way across his body until she came back to his face.

Lydia looked at him and said, "Surely Mary did not give you the attention as I just delivered. She is a girl. I am a woman. A woman that wants you inside her." Thomas surrendered himself to her seduction. He had never felt like this before. He was on fire, and she was the source of its fuel. Lydia took hold of him and the two copulated. His eyes rolled back into his head as she rocked back and forth making the sounds of pleasure. Her breasts were swinging side to side as she delivered the desire, they both sought. When she felt him nearing his orgasm, she would pause, then start again. She would prolong the moment for as long as she could.

Thomas watched as her breast swayed in their dance of seduction. He lifted his head to take one to his mouth. All the while Lydia rocking back and forth without pause. Bodies hot and covered in sweat continued the dance as both continued to uttered sounds of pleasure.

Their breathing coupled and they became one to each other and the moment. Lydia and Thomas reached their orgasm together. Her back flexed lifting her face away from his. Her eyes were shut tight as the orgasm delivered its rapture. Her body went limp, and she fell against him there still feeling the rush and passion from their moment sexual exchange.

They lied there together against each other, still breathing as one. They continued kissing each other as if it would be their last time together. Arms embraced bodies. Eyes held in deep possession refusing to surrender the moment to a mundane existence.

Thomas held deep feelings for Lydia. She was like an ocean who's depth and greatness could never be held in conception. His feelings for her and the desire for her touch would motivate him beyond any preconceived limitations.

Lydia wanted Thomas for a lover and a giver to satisfy the unquenchable thirst she held. It was more than sex, more than lust. It was about heart and soul not held in time but in eternity.

The two rose from the bed and quietly dressed. They continued to kiss and embrace when they came near to each other. They gathered the parcels and set out to join the others.

As they walked Lydia took his hand. She looked at Thomas and said, "To you I send my blessings, to you I send my love. To me send your blessings, to me send your love. We shall be of one heart and one of love. Do this for me as I shall do it for you. May our passion of the flesh never grow old or be forgotten. May the love we share never take leave from our hearts. May our souls find refuge amongst the sorrows of life. Take me when you will it to be. These things I profess to you forever." Lydia's words clung to his heart. Her poetic manner of speech and her tone brought a tear to his eye.

They would have to wait for another day and another time to share in love as they stepped inside to join the others.

CHAPTER 18

The days waxed on for these souls along their journey. Lydia stood at the window to see Mary in the yard. She was on her knees with her face inches from the ground. She was gaging uncontrollably. Lydia knew her daughter was pregnant, and she knew the father's name.

Lydia's emotions were a mix of frustration and empathy for Mary. Preparations for a wedding would be the next order of business. Lydia placed both hands on her tummy and gently began to rub it back and forth. She too was pregnant, but she was not certain the fathers name.

Lydia turned away and returned to preparing the mornings meal. The gestures of her body were present in the room, but the heart and mind were elsewhere searching.

Mary's sickness had subsided. She turned sideways and stretched out on the cool earth. It refreshed her and gave relief to her body. As she laid there on the ground a smile came over her face. She realized her condition. She imagined a wedding with a new life to follow. She would finally have someone by her side in slumber and the day's journey. She was feeling better and stood. She looked towards the Sonnet's home, took a deep breath, and made a wish for love and prosperity.

Jonathan was returning from caring for the livestock. He saw his beautiful daughter standing there. He stepped beside her and placed his arm around her shoulder. He gave her a hug and kissed her on the head. "No matter the outcome of this day or the days that follow I will always love you. Nothing in this world can come between a father and the love for his daughter," said Jonathan. Mary placed both arms around her father and buried her face in his chest. Lydia looked out the window and saw the two held in embrace. Her hand came to her face to hold back the emotions.

Lydia was surrendering to a destiny that was out of her control. She so wanted to express the love within her, but love stood in her way. The love and devotion for Jonathan and the love of a daughter silenced the love she held for another. Joy and sadness resting together like a single coin owning two faces.

Thomas was awake still lying in bed. He had accepted Squire's offer of apprenticeship in the art of publishing. It was time to tell his parents. Surely, they would be pleased with his choice. He could earn a modest wage while learning a valuable trade. It would also afford him the opportunity to read Squire's personal library.

Diane opened Thomas's door. "Get up young man and come to meal. Your father and I need to speak to you about some choices you need to make. Thomas sprung from his bed. He was anxious to hear what his parents had to say. As he entered the warmth of the room, he could see the table set for a lavish breakfast. Fresh baked bread, eggs and sausages, butter and clover honey adorned the table like a holiday meal. Thomas joined his parents at the table and Diane gave the blessing.

"We will be helping Jonathan on this day in the slaughter of hogs for their winter stores," spoke Edward to Thomas. This pleased Thomas. He enjoyed being with his father and Jonathan. It gave him the feeling of being more like a man than a boy. He always applied himself to every detail so that he would be accepted as an equal.

Just as Thomas had finished his first sausage, he told his parents about Squire Andrew's proposal, short of marrying Rebecca. Diane did not care for Rebecca because of her flirty behavior and her reputation with the towns people. Edward and Diane listen to his words but made no comment which surprised Thomas. The family went on with their meal quietly enjoying every bite. After each had their fill Diane began to clear the table.

Edward took his pipe from his pocket and lit it from the tables candle. Thomas knew that whenever his father lit his pipe this early there was something important to discuss. Edward took two long draws on his pipe then looked Thomas in the eye.

"You are no longer a boy. You son are a man. What you and Mary shared was your entrance to manhood. With that comes a far-reaching responsibility. You took a woman's body and when you did you took the woman. It was a few short moments that the two of you shared. Those fleeting moments can very well turn into a life time. Whatever the outcome you both will be responsible for the results of those few moments. So, let me be a little clearer to you.

If Mary is pregnant with your child, then responsibility for her and the child's wellbeing falls to you. Your future will be assigned to you through circumstance and provision. By becoming a father, you will become a husband. You will know what is like to toil day after day to provide for their wellbeing. The dreams and desires of life you once carried will have to wait for another time. Do you understand these things I say to you Thomas?" asked Edward.

He sat stunned by his father's words. Diane stepped towards Thomas so she could see his reaction. He sat there motionless feeling the gravity of his father's words. He turned his head towards his father and said, "Yes father I hear your words." Thomas stood from the table and went to his room. He dropped on to the bed and pulled the covers over his head.

Diane entered his room and sat down on the edge of his bed. She placed her hand on the covers he hid under. "I want you to know that your father and I support you no matter the outcome. Your father and I had a similar path in our youth. You were the gift we received from the passion we felt for each other on that warm summer's night. We made a life together with you in the middle. There were times when we were scared and in need. But we prevailed out of love for each other and our love for you. I carry no complaint or regret.

There were the sharp tongues of the gossipers that lashed out against us, but we paid them no mind. The towns pastor and some of the congregation shunned us at services. The very same pastor that fondled me when I was a little girl.

You will never find more hypocrisy in this world than what you will find in the clergy and their flock. Sinners all are they that lift a finger and raise it to one of lesser sin. Now come out from those covers and face what waits to embrace you on this day. Your father is waiting for you," said Diane.

Slowly the covers receded to expose a timid face. He opened his arms to embrace the messenger and her message. Thomas rose from his bed and followed his mother to join his father. "Best be going on our way Thomas. The nights frost is almost gone," spoke Edward.

Edward and Thomas entered the Rose's property. Lydia came out of the house and told them that Jonathan had already left to prepare things. Edward thanked her and the two began their climb up the hill to the barn. Thomas lagged a little behind so he could look at Lydia a little longer. She took notice and gave Thomas a warm smile and a wink. Thomas swelled with joy.

Mary watched as the scene played out between Lydia and Thomas. She gave the scene a half-hearted excuse and forgot it. Mary decided to join the Sonnets and her father. "I'll make my presence with them and share in the day. If all goes well my new love interest will be my husband and his father will be my father also," thought Mary.

Lydia stepped into the house to see Mary standing at the window. "What did Mary see?" she wondered. "Mother, I have decided to join the men at the barn with the chore of the day. I will come down near noon day and help with the meal," said Mary. Lydia thought it strange that Mary would offer to help her. She had never offered before. "Thomas, she wants to impress Thomas!" thought Lydia. "Yes daughter, come and help me. We will prepare a meal they won't soon forget."

Mary ran from the house and climbed the hill before her. Once at the top you could see the Sonnet' home. She stood there looking when something came over her. It was a strange feeling, nothing like anything she had felt before. Her eyes had ceased to focus on any one thing.

In her mind's eye she was seeing three babies. They were playing and laughing together as they descended towards her. Mary was still as she watched the children play. Her heart soared with joy and happiness. She wanted to laugh then she wanted to cry as the babies got closer. She reached for them but only one came close to her. The other two babies descended into the house where Lydia was. Mary felt the child enter her. A deep sense of warmth overcame her, and she felt faint. As she regained her composure, she heard her mother cry out from the house then silence.

Mary wondered what she had witnessed. "Angels! I believe they were angels that came from heaven to bless us one and all," she thought. She took a deep breath and felt alive within. Rather than join the men she decided to rejoin her mother in the home. She felt a strong need to be with her mother.

Mary entered the home to see her mother busy cleaning while she sang Celtic tunes. Lydia was dressed in one of her finest dresses and her hair was down around her shoulders. A faint smell of rose oil filled the home as Lydia moved about cleaning and singing, oblivious to Mary's presence. "Mother, did I hear you let out a scream as I left the house?" asked Mary. "I felt a sharp pain in my womb daughter. It passed as quick as it came. Why are you not with the men as you said?" asked Lydia. "I felt it best to be by your side mother," said Mary.

The hours of the morning passed away one by one. The smell of roast and potatoes fills the air about the house. The fireplace had warmed the home in preparation to receive three worn and hungry men. The women sat quietly at the table ever listening for the sound of voices on approach.

The laughter of Jonathan was heard first. They jumped to their feet and took their position. Mary stood by one of the chairs to present herself. Lydia moved to the fireplace to set the table with food. One by one the men entered the warm home and sat down at the table.

Mary took tea and served each one starting with her father then Edward and lastly to Thomas. She pressed her body against Thomas as she poured. Loaves of bread were placed on the table along with a grand bowl of meat and vegetables. The men were pleased as they looked on the feast. "When you men finish having your fill, know that there is apple cobbler to please a sweet tooth," said Lydia.

The men ate and shared in conversation from an array of topics. Mary and Lydia tended to the men keeping their mugs filled with strong tea and adding to the bowl anytime one could see the bottom. After a generous slice of cobbler, the men looked more like they were ready for a nap rather than a return to work. Jonathan and Edward lit their pipes to finish the occasion. Lydia cleared the table as the conversations fell off into silence.

The country life and its simplicity can turn the smallest of comforts into blessings for the soul. These folks who gather together on this day at this place, do so for survival, for love and for friendship. Their reward is in knowing that no matter the circumstance no matter the trouble, together they stand together as one in heart.

Jonathan and Edward stood and went outside to finish their pipes. "Mary, we need water from the well to clean these dishes. Fetch a pail or two of water please," said Lydia. Mary was two steps out the door when Lydia grabbed Thomas.

She guided her lips to his and held him tight to her breasts. Thomas was smitten by this beautiful woman and her forwardness. He began rubbing her back while in embrace. His hands dropped to her buttocks, and he lifted her off the floor. He forced his tongue into her mouth, and she returned the gesture. Lydia gave a deep groan and began kissing him feverishly. Edwards voice was heard at the door and the two began to break their embrace.

"Here what is this with you two?" said Jonathan. "Thomas was just thanking me for the meal and our hospitality," said Lydia. Jonathan accepted her explanation but still held his vision on the two as he stepped towards the bedroom. When he was out of sight Lydia took Thomas's hands and placed them on her breasts. He was frightened and excited at the same time. He wanted to take her right there on the table. She would have not resisted the advance had he held the courage to do so.

Their rational selves stepped in and quelled the energy of passion for now. Jonathan entered the room holding a new pipe he had fashioned. He wanted to show Edward his handy work. Thomas left the house behind Jonathan but not until Lydia had blown him a kiss.

The hours of the afternoon rendered the sun to a point in the sky to signal it was time for weary men to find their way home. The day's work displayed salted meats hanging from rafters that would see the family through the winter months. One by one the men descended the hill. Each with their own thoughts, their own concerns, and their simple desires.

Edward turned to Thomas and asked, "Is everything okay son? You appear troubled about something." "Yes father, it's just that I have a lot to think about. Squire Andrews offer seems much more appealing to me right now. I long for a life that leads to discovery and adventure. I love words and the power they render when read or spoken. I honor you and your choice of the farm life, but I can find no desire within to do likewise," said Thomas.

"It's a good offer, one that has a secure future and much promise. If it is your desire to accept, then by all means go. If it doesn't work out, you can always return home. I will miss you on the farm when the work is too much for one man. But I can always hire one of the woodland people. Most of them at one time or another were farmers. Your love is with words and their arrangements. You were not born to be a farmer. Anyone can see that. I will be sad to see you leave as will your mother," spoke Edward to his son.

Edward placed his hand on Thomas' shoulder and said, "There was a time in my life when I too wanted something different. I loved to read as much as you do. Just know that love for another can bend the direction of a soul's desire. My plans, my path were changed by the sight of your mother. I would have surrendered any and all things just to be with her. We fell in love at first sight and still love each other as much as the day we met.

There were many flowers about in those days that were pleasing to look upon and wonder. When I saw your mother, I knew that she was the flower I wanted to pick and bring into my life. If you should be ever so privilege to feel the same, then my advice to you would be ask for her hand. But if this world should put something between you and her, then carry her in your heart forever. So that one day she will return to you. Love has no regard for time, and neither should lovers.

I sometimes wonder where I would be if I had not met your mother. What would my life be like, where would I be? Then I have to remind myself that life is not about endless dreams, fantasies or what if this happened or that. Life is about choices and the circumstances of those choices. Rejoice in those that give pleasure and rethink the ones that don't.

Life is about learning through all the lessons experienced. I'm not saying to give up those dreams which sing from the heart. They are the wind that fills your sail. They carry you through the storms that await you. I'm speaking of the curse of second guessing yourself.

That practice can lead to guilt and blame. They are the things that blind the heart and sow the seeds of sorrow and disappointment. Some of the woodlanders experienced such a curse. Yet they are our brothers and our sisters, our mothers, and our fathers.

The laws of nature require obedience dear son, never forget that. You cannot cheat nature and its laws. If you chose to sow the seeds of knowledge in life, wisdom will be delivered at the harvest," spoke Edward.

Thomas lifted his head to look at his father after his words. His eyes were filled with love as a tear or two rolled down his face. He tried to speak but choked up. He had never heard his father speak in such a manner before. Thomas raised both arms and placed them around his father. Edward took his son in his arms and held him tight. Thomas began to cry, and Edward followed. The love held within each spilled forward to render a love which knows no bounds and carries little or no expectations. "I love you father! I thank you for all you have given to me and mother. I will remember your words and carry them in life and in death," cried out Thomas.

The door of the Sonnet's home flew open and the light within pushed back the darkness of night. Diane's silhouette was framed perfectly in the doorway. "Where have you two been? Come inside and warm yourselves and I will feed you a working man's portion," said Diane. The two entered in peace, as they savored the words and care offered by a loving wife and a sound mother. The door behind them closed ending another day's witness. The moon's light now lit the countryside as the smoke from the chimneys lifted upwards to the stars of the heavens.

CHAPTER 19

The weeks passed one after the other. Trails of smoke from chimneys could be seen rising to clear blue skies. The beds carried many blankets now and the wood piles begin to wane. What crops flourished in falls air have been consumed or dried for soups. Winters here were lean times for country folk and town folk alike.

Thomas was now an apprentice. It became necessary for him to live at the shop because of the cold conditions. He had a modest bed in the shops work room. It had a fireplace that kept him warm at night. Squire and Rebecca slept upstairs in the living quarters.

The season of winter was especially hard on the homeless and destitute who sheltered on the outskirts of town. Such hardships could lead one to theft in order to provide food to survive.

The Rose' home was a place where mother and daughter alike were with child. Lydia was especially showing her condition. Jonathan was sure she was carrying a strong boy. One that could help him at work on the farm.

Mary too was beginning to show. The morning sickness had subsided. She was filled with dreams of family life. She was aware of Thomas's position with Squire Andrew. She hoped to encourage Thomas in his new trade. She dreamed of living in town away from the hardships and boredom of country life. Today she would face Thomas on his visit home and give him the news. Then she could begin her wedding plans with Lydia and Diane.

Jonathan and Lydia had spoken to Edward and Diane about Mary's condition. The plan was to inform Thomas on his visit home. They planned to take the midday meal at the Sonnet home to plan the needed arrangements.

This Sunday morning was a cold one to awaken to. Thomas rose from his bed and dressed. Squire had left bread and cheese along with some jam for his breakfast. He ate his meal and set out for the walk home. He knew the road home would be safer at the early hours of the morning. Today he would bless his parents with the money he'd earned. He was proud to be able to help his parents. He left the safety of the shop and headed home.

Thomas was making his way through town when he heard a door slam behind him. He turned to see Rebecca running from the back door of the Reverend's rectory. She was in flight distancing herself as quick as she could. She was without coat and scantily dressed. The door on the rectory flew open and the good Reverend Richard appeared. He was shouting out to Rebecca to return as he held her coat. The Reverend turned and saw Thomas observing him. He looked at the coat then at Thomas. He knew Thomas saw what had just happened. As Thomas stared at the Reverend, he too stared back at Thomas. Thomas and his family were not religious people and had often expressed their misgivings of the Reverend's teachings. Still, Thomas knew he had power within the community. So, Thomas turned away and began his journey home.

As he walked in the morning chill he thought of his mother's cooking and tried to imagine what she would have prepared for him. "Apple cobbler. Yes, I know that she will have some of her cobbler waiting on me when I arrive," he thought.

The long walk along the road was a peaceful one. Small areas of ice were forming on the edges of the stream. He caught sight of smoke rising in the air and knew home was a short distance away. This excited him and he became quicker in step.

He looked forward to seeing his parents and the home he grew up in. He missed his parents. He missed his mother's cooking, and he missed his bed. He was also missing the clarity of interaction of country people.

Living in the countryside one is surrounded in nature. Living in town one is surrounded by human nature. He found it to be a strange animal indeed. One offered clarity while the other offered bewilderment. He noticed how townspeople said one thing and did another.

Smiles were given on sight but fell away at passing. It seemed to him that people expressed what they thought others were expecting to hear, rather than express their truth. They could express indifference to one and reverence to another. People were more influenced by one's position rather than the contents of their hearts. He had believed that brotherly love ruled the world beyond his humble country life. This new reality challenged this concept. He was determined to learn all he could about it.

Thomas saw his father standing beside the road. In the cold air the smoke from his pipe was slow to rise. He was happy to see his father. Thomas expected to see a smile on his father's face. As he drew near but he could see his father had a careworn look about him. Edward reached out with one arm to embrace his son. "Come inside Thomas. Mother has tea and honey ready for us along with some apple cobbler. Let us warm our bodies and share in the weeks adventures."

The pair entered and Diane rushed to her son and held him tight. She kissed his cheeks and rubbed his hands to warm them up. "We are so happy to see you son. Thomas reached deep in his pocket and revealed the money he earned to give as a gift. "Here is something to help with things around the home," said Thomas with a sense of pride. Edward took the coins and stared long at it. He knew how much it meant to Thomas to play the role of provider. "I accept your gift Thomas and welcome you here today in a new light of understanding," said Edward as his gaze was still held on the coins. Diane stood enjoying the presence of family.

Diane was a loving soul. Kindness was her virtue. She was well thought of in the community. She was the daughter of parents who were artists. Her father was a story writer of historic figures. He was gifted at romanticizing the tragedies of history. Her mother was a minstrel. She loved poetry and often set the lyrics to music. Diane's mother would sing whenever the need presented itself.

There was plenty of love in the home but little sustenance. They were always able to get by as performers. Diane had her mother's lute and kept it in the corner of the bedroom. On a warm summers day, she enjoyed playing the lute under the shade of a tree.

"Come Thomas, sit and tell us of your time in town," said Diane. "I'm learning my trade and a good trade it is. I meet people who have traveled to far off places. Some come to the shop just to talk to Squire while others come to purchase books or stories that Squire carries in storage. Some even come to have their words put to the press so they can offer them as gifts or for profit. Squire lets me read from his collection. Some are very old about places and events that are much older than the books. There is another world out there and I want to see it all," said Thomas with the conviction of an honest politician.

"The Squire has been generous to me. He has sworn to teach me to become a master printer. He has also extended his generosity to include Rebecca's hand in marriage if I so desire. He offered to deed me his property so long as I complete our agreement.

I hope you agree with me when I say it is a sound future. But I must confess while such an arrangement is good for the body, I cannot find within me the fulfillment my soul desires to bring about true happiness. As for all, there is the life that is handed to us and the life we create from that. I seek your thoughts on this matter," said Thomas.

Edward and Diane looked at each other. They could see and hear a change in Thomas. His use of words had improved. His time with Squire and life in town was having a positive influence on him. Edward turned to Thomas and said, "We agree with you. Squire is being more than generous to you. It's a good agreement the two of you make with each other.

Everyone is given a life at birth from their parents and the support they carry. It's true that all grow from such an arrangement. Some continue to remain in its confines while others set out for new horizons. It's good to hear you speak your heart and seek counsel from those who love you so. That brings me to another matter.

The Roses are visiting us today for the midday meal. They bring some news with them that will give you some insights to the answers you seek. Your mother and I are aware of the news they bring. We think it best that you hear it from us first so that you are not overwhelmed at their announcement," spoke Edward. Thomas's eyes were wide open, staring back and forth from one parent to the next.

"Mary is with child, your child. Soon you will be a father and a husband. Your apprenticeship should provide you with the needed means to support them one day. For now, we must face the consequences of our desires but never to let go of our dreams," said Edward. A deep sinking feeling came over Thomas. He heard his father's words, but the magnitude was more than he could handle.

Diane took him by the hand and said, "It's okay. I know it is a shock for you. It would be for anyone. Mary's parents have come to terms with the matter and are at peace. There are arrangements to be made. Ones that require you to be responsible in every way. We will guide you and help you in planning. Do not be discouraged by life's plan for you. One day you will find the blessing in it all."

A loud knock came at the door. Muffled voices on the other side could be heard. Slowly Edward opened the door without looking at those who knocked. Rather his sight was fixed on Thomas. He knew what the outcome would be from the revelation about to be bestowed on young Thomas by his demeanor. One by one the Roses stepped through the door. First Jonathan, then Lydia and finally Mary. Once they were inside Edward closed the door. A deafening silence was about. No one spoke up. It was an eternity to Thomas as he stood before Jonathan and Lydia.

"Let's everyone sit down while I fetch some tea to warm the body and mood for our occasion. Please everyone sit," said Diane. The chairs were being drawn from under the table as each one sat in piety. Diane began pouring the tea as the room was held in silence. Thomas surveyed the faces of the Roses as they sat beside each other.

Jonathan engaged in light conversation with Edward. Mary was smiling at Thomas that reflected her content with things. Lydia sat quietly with her head down staring at the floor. The tension in the room was building for Thomas. He could hear his heartbeat in his ears. He felt numb in mind. From his mind's eye he could see Nathan, the guide from the streams pool. A great sense of relief overcame Thomas. He wasn't alone.

Nathan looked at him with caring eyes and said, "Fear not Thomas for this is your destiny. The child that comes to you carries a message for you. A message that that you will need as time turns the wheel of life. The child is an old soul that entered the arena of the mortals with you in ancient times.

There is another child of your lineage that is here also. Lydia carries that one in her womb. Both have come to walk with you in the realm of time and space. Fear not the morrows or what they might hold. Worry and anxiety will not change a single word in the Book of Life, not one single word. Embrace the moment dear lad for today is the first day of the rest of your life. Stand tall and never turn in fear. Live your life your way and not the way of others."

Thomas took a deep breath and became aware of his mortal surroundings. Diane placed a mug of herbal tea before all present and took a seat. "We have informed Thomas of Mary's condition. It is in our hearts that we as neighbors and dear friends can resolve whatever may arise here today. It would be proper Jonathan if you were the first to speak since you are the father of the mother to be," said Diane.

Jonathan turned to Thomas to look at him. After a brief moment of silence Jonathan said, "I think it best that Thomas and Mary be given the time alone to speak about their situation. After all, it is he and Mary who must decide the path that they will tread. I think it best that we parents excuse ourselves so that the two may have their own words with each other. Come let us step outside and let these two speak in private. One by one the parents left the house as their children looked on.

At the sound of the door closed, Mary spoke. "I'm sorry if this brings a heaviness to your heart Thomas. I'm aware of the difference of our ages of eight years. I don't feel that it really matters. I know that you must be feeling some ill will towards me. I don't blame you for a moment. I can tell you that I'm happy about the arrangement. I look forward to being your wife, if that's what you want. That is what you want? Isn't it Thomas? Do you want to marry me so I can care properly for our child and it's future?" spoke Mary in a slight pleading voice.

Thomas sat quietly reflecting on his emotions and what he received from Nathan. When he looked at Mary there was no fire in his heart for her. She was a lifetime friend and someone he looked up to in life. She was more like an older sister to him. He realized the gravity of the moment. He accepted the arrangement in mind.

"I will take you as my wife Mary and I will learn to love you as a husband should love a wife. I will work to give you and our child a safe living. Let us call our parents in before they freeze and give them our plans," spoke Thomas.

"Oh, thank you Thomas. Thank you for your words. I know that we can be a happy couple living as one," shouted Mary. The door flew open and both fathers tried to enter at the same time, then fell to the floor. "What! What is going on? Are you two, okay?" said Jonathan. The wives and children were laughing at the two lying on the floor. The laughter carried on until the two on the floor began to laugh at themselves.

Everyone settled back to the table and began their plans for a wedding and care for the child. Thomas and Mary were seated side by side. He took her hand as they listened to the parents going on with their plans never asking the young couple what they wanted. It was humorous for the young couple to witness.

CHAPTER 20

It's morning, and another day is born. Thomas rose from his bed and dressed. It was a long night with little sleep. The events of yesterday had shuffled the cards in the deck of life. The old cards had been replaced with new ones. A new vision and direction had taken the stage. The plot had been rewritten to accommodate the additional actors. The tethers of this world and its decrees were turning the wheels of destiny.

Diane prepared a celebratory breakfast for her son. She knew he would awake troubled from yesterday's revelations. She was sad for him and cheerful at the same time. She recalled how her own aspirations as an entertainer had been dashed in similar manner. It was her intention on this morning to support her son and send him off in good spirit.

Thomas entered the main room to see his father and mother waiting on him. Edward stood from his chair and pulled out Thomas' chair for him to sit. Once Thomas was seated his father kissed him on the head. "We want this day in your life to be one to remember. Last night you went to sleep as our son. This morning you awoke as a father and husband to be. This day is the beginning of a new life and a new path. How you perceive it is the way it will appear. We honor you son," spoke his father in sincerity. Thomas was moved by his parents concern and love for him.

Diane prepared the table with sausages, butter apples, eggs, and fresh baked bread. "Today we celebrate your good fortune and blessings. We support you along your path and those you love and care for. Let us remember this day for all the years to come and grow from the gifts it renders," said his mother.

Thomas began to quietly weep. He could no longer hold back the emotions or the tears that needed to be released. He cried for the love his parents shared. He cried for the boy that no longer dwelt within. He cried having surrendered his dreams for mortal desires. He cried because it was okay to cry. He cried until there were no more tears to shed.

The things that haunted his heart no longer troubled him. The tears had helped to dispel the fears and worry. He felt better about life and looked forward to what was to come. His parents were pleased to see him in such a way.

Together the family enjoyed the grand meal while Thomas shared stories of the world of printing and town life. He was excited about his apprenticeship. It was time for Thomas to return to town. He rose from the table and began to bundle himself for the journey back.

Diane came to him and gave him a hug and a kiss. Edward extended his hand to offer a handshake. He had never offered such a gesture before. Thomas' hand met his father's hand. For Thomas, it felt good. He knew his father was accepting him as an equal. Thomas was filled with pride and joy. Still, he reached for his father to give and receive a hug. Edward held the embrace longer than Thomas had intended. When they broke a tear was running down Edwards face. He was releasing his boy and embracing the man.

Thomas began the journey back to Danbury. Edward walked with him a little way. He was having a hard time letting go of him. Thomas could feel it. Finally, Edward stopped walking as Thomas continued. He watched his son until he disappeared from sight. Slowly he turned back to return home. He could feel the void within him and could not understand it. The love for another can deliver joy to sadness in a single breath.

Thomas was nearly to town when he saw a little girl appear from behind a tree. Her clothing was stuffed with leaves to insulate her from the cold. She cautiously approached Thomas with sad heavy eyes. She stood before not saying a word. Thomas knew what she wanted.

He was carrying a bundle that his mother gave him before he left. It was filled with dried meats, bread, and apples. Thomas looked at the bundle then at her. He extended it to her, so she stepped forward and received it. She gave Thomas a smile of gratitude and ran off to a place where two boys younger than her stood in wait.

She opened the bundle to view the prize before the others. They were excited and the boys began clapping their hands. One of the boys ran out to the road where Thomas stood. He stood at attention, then bowed before Thomas and blew him a kiss. He returned to the others and began to eat his fill. It gave Thomas cause for concern.

"Why must some starve, while others indulge beneath the heavens?" he wondered. "Why do we profess our love to a God and turn our backs on those of his creation? The church speaks that God, all merciful, rewards his flock and punishes the sinners, that they should suffer on earth and in the lower regions."

He looked at the three children still laughing and enjoying their prize. He asked himself, "Wherein lies the sins of these three? What sin did they commit that a loving God would have them live in the forest like animals? They express joy therefore they possess love. They laugh as they share so they are without greed. I must know this God before I leave this world. I must question his ways so that I may tell others."

Thomas was startled by a woman's scream. He turned in the direction of the scream and saw a small crowd of people huddled around a woman. As he drew near, he could see she was lying on her back with her knees flexed. There on her knees, at the woman's side, was Mildred. The woman was about to give birth and Mildred would deliver the baby.

Thomas stood in silence with his eyes in witness. Mildred was doing her best to calm the woman through her labor. Mildred looked up and saw the look on Thomas's face. She smiled at him knowing that she would one day be delivering his children also.

"Watch Thomas, watch and see the miracle of life bear itself before you," said Mildred in an angelic voice. Thomas watched as the baby's head appeared. "Hear she comes. Push one more time dear. Push with all your strength," said Mildred. The woman clenched her fists and let out one more scream. The baby's body popped out and Mildred caught it with both hands. The baby's warm body in the chill of the air caused steam to lift upwards. It gave a ghostly appearance which frighten some. Mildred was quick to wrap the baby in swaddling clothes to protect her from the cold. She placed the child to the mother's breasts to nurse.

The father of the child stood looking on as a tear ran down his face. Thomas recognized him. It was Jack Danbury and his wife Helen.

Their house burned to the ground some months ago. All that they had owned or cherished laid in ashes. Now they lived as woodlanders.

"Lilly, we will call her Lilly. The lilies of our garden is the only thing the fire spared. Therefore, no harm shall ever come to this child or the one that gave her life. This one will give us hope again and the promise of a future," spoke Jack as his loving eyes embraced mother and child.

He fell to his knees and embraced Mildred. He began weeping as a child while Mildred held him tight. Helen's hand reached up to touch her husband in his grieving. The child's birth was all it took for this man to let go of all the pain he had held on to for so long. It was a healing moment for them and all who witnessed.

Thomas was deeply moved by what he had seen. He was inspired and no longer held regret of his situation. Rather he felt a sense of purpose and a renewed clarity. Nathans words sunk deeper within. "This world is but a stage and we are the actors," thought Thomas. He turned himself towards town as the sun was rising above the trees offering warmth to the air and to his soul. He was close enough to town to smell the wood smoke from the fires that warmed the homes of this little piece of the world.

What appears as an insignificant event witnessed by these people living out their lives in this village located on an island of a small planet was anything but insignificant. To these people and their families that lived here, this was their universe, their planet, their earth, their island and their witness.

The infinitely vastness of space and time coupled to the infinitely smallness of a single life came from the one source. It can never be divided nor destroyed.

A single person's desires, passions and quests for love holds equal importance to the stars and the life that lives amongst them. All things great and all things small were cut from the same cloth.

The Oneness of Being declared it from the beginning. So here we coexist together in pursuit of the same thing. No matter the path be it high or low the destination will always remain the same for all creation.

CHAPTER 21

Thomas entered Squire's print shop. He was removing his coat when he heard Squire and Rebecca arguing. He wondered what it might be about this time. Rebecca had a habit of getting herself in trouble when it came to handsome men. It did not matter to her if they were married or not. Rebecca gave the gossipers in town plenty of subject to chew on. She cared little what other people thought of her. She was an independent soul in search of pleasure and gain.

Rebecca's mother died giving birth to her. She had been raised by her father who loved and adored her very much. Too often he gave her favor which led to a spoiled child that grew into a woman.

At a young age she learned how flirting can open doors that would normally be shut. She enjoyed the attention and the gifts of the dance. Beautiful as she was and as charming as she could be, there was not a man born that could hold her heart. She could never be satisfied by the fruit from just one tree. She preferred to dance amongst the orchard and taste the fruits of many.

Rebecca carried pockets that this world could never be able to fill. She would find no rest in this lifetime, no peace or closure. Rebecca was being Rebecca playing her role on the stage of life.

Thomas started a fire in the shops fireplace. The room had to be warm in order to spread the ink evenly over the printing plates. Thomas was preparing for the days labor when the door opened.

It was Agnes Hyatt. Each morning and at midday Agnes would deliver meals to the Beckett home. Squire did not cook nor did Rebecca. Squire hired Agnes to feed them well and that is exactly what she did. It was obvious to Thomas that that Squire had a light in his eye for Agnes as she did for him.

Agnes was a widow for some twenty years. She was an important figure in the community and in the church. She sang and led the choir each and every Sunday.

Squire once thought of asking her for marriage. He knew Agnes and Rebecca would never get along together. There was just too much difference between the two. She did not approve of Rebecca's behavior but held her silence because of her fondness of Squire. Agnes went to great lengths to gain favor and the eye of Squire Beckett.

Agnes asked Thomas to summon Squire as she placed the mornings fare on the shops counter. Thomas stood at the foot of the staircase to call out to Squire. He was waiting for a pause in the argument going on.

Agnes was trying her best to overhear what was being said. She held her breath so that she could hear better. "Did Andrew just yell out Reverend Richard's name?" thought Agnes. Rebecca was sobbing between her words. Agnes took a few steps closer to the staircase to hear better. Thomas stood there indifferent to the melee. It was a common event to the days witness.

"Squire!" shouted Thomas. "Agnes is here and would like to have a word or two with you." Then silence. "I will be right down," said Squire. The voices upstairs were now muffled. Agnes returned to her original position at the counter, awaiting Squire's descent from the staircase.

Squires bulky frame was heard as he took each stair one at a time. Squire appeared older than his true age. The trials of a single parent had taken its toll on him and his health. Still, he was a jovial fellow who loved people and intellectual conversations.

Many times, Agnes presented herself to Squire in a way to encourage him to ask the big question. She believed that she had the love in her to heal whatever was haunting Rebecca. The door to her heart was always opened to this pair. For now, the only way to show her love was through the meals she so carefully prepared. She wished for his love, and he longed for hers.

Two hearts held in silence from pointless fears. A place that dwells within many of hearts. A place where the "what ifs" rule over what could be. Where one wonders whether to hold the dice or roll them. To play it safe or risk losing the known for the sake of the unknown.

A soul such as Rebecca's rolls the dice every day. She is aware of the consequences and embraces them in joy and in sorrow. A soul such as Agnes holds the dice, always over thinking until she can no longer feel. Hearts held in bondage on both ends of the rainbow. One will know no peace while the other will never grow beyond yesterday.

"And a good morning to you Agnes and the hearty meal you present to us on this fine morning," said Squire. "Would you stay and break bread with us this morning?" inquired Squire. Agnes blushed from his invitation. After overhearing the argument, she thought it best to decline the invitation. "I will return at midday, maybe then we can share then Andrew, if that is alright with you?" said Agnes. "You do that, and I'll be sure to find a little summer wine to toast our friendship," said Squire. Agnes's heart sprang up hearing a glint of a possible proposal. Agnes was well aware that Rebecca was never home at midday. Agnes had not even left the shop before she started planning the midday meal. She was feeling happy in her own way.

Agnes was walking home when she saw the Reverend Richard walking about aimlessly. He appeared to be troubled about something. She wondered if it had something to do with the Becketts. No matter. She was still planning the event for later.

Diane Sonnet was dressed and ready as she stood quietly at the window waiting on Lydia's arrival. The two were going to town to arrange for their children's wedding. Edward had readied the horse and wagon for their journey. On the table behind Diane was an apple cobbler covered with a cloth. It was a gift for the Reverend. She hoped to purchase a pence worth of cheese once in town to couple the gift. Reverend was known for his fondness of sweet treats.

Meanwhile at the Rose's home Lydia and Mary were gathering their gifts for Reverend. Lydia planned on gifting a quilt made by her mother in the last year of her life. It seemed fitting to her to give up the possession of the quilt. It was a time of releasing the things of the heart. Painful as it may seem, surrender offered a strange sense of comfort.

Lydia and Mary left the house and began walking towards the Sonnets without speaking a word. Diane saw the two on approach. She wrapped herself with a scarf and blanket then exited the house. "It's about time the two of you arrived. We'll have a wonderful day together and enjoy the blessings of our efforts on this day," said Diane in a cheerful manner.

Diane's positive outlook on life was gifted to her from her mother. As her mother Hazel lied on her death bed, she took Diane' hand and said, "I, the actor at heart, am finally standing on the stage of life for my last act. I so want to be able to stand and take my final bow. I want to blow kisses to my audience, all those people I was blessed with in life. I want to hug every last one of them and tell them how blessed, how grateful I am for their love and their sharing.

Dear Diane, my only daughter, life is nothing more than a stage, a comedy of fools it is. We spend a lifetime searching for love, and all the while ignoring the love that lives within. But never mind, everyone eventually finds it. That's why we're here. I found mine. I did it by loving everyone I met, no matter the size of their heart.

There are only three things in life that matter. The love you have for others, the love you have for yourself, and the love you have for whatever brought the two together." Hazel gave up the ghost after her words. Diane always felt her mothers' spirit whenever she struggled within. She was feeling her right now.

Edward helped the ladies into the wagon one by one. He had never seen the three look more beautiful as they did now. He mounted the wagon and took hold the reins. But before he could give the command to the horse, he deepened in mind. It was then he realized the gravity of the moment.

The events of this day were about to change the direction for the lives of those present and the lives of those who were to come. Another fork in the road this life has offered. Another act written on the grand stage of life.

> Oh, what giant stone I do lie over my head,
> So that I may design my own truth instead,
> What is this thing called life and love?
> They say is heaven sent from above,
> I find my light in candles made of clay,
> To this very stone, I shall always stay,
> For I have no desire, therefore I can never fail,
> The dreamers they dream, yet they cry and wail,
> Their losses are many, far too many to count,
> They reach inside pockets that yields no amount,
> They speak blindly of a physician who offers peace,
> Yet they know not his name or the place where he sleeps

CHAPTER 22

The ride to town was filled with anticipation. Diane and Lydia went back and forth on the arrangements. They were as two school girls talking with no end in sight. Mary sat quietly listening to them while her imagination ran away with each proposition. This was a special time for her. She knew once she was on the other side of the wedding things would be different. She wanted to do her best to keep the marriage alive.

Mary knew Thomas' mind was always centered on possibilities and far off places. She was the practical one. She would have to take the lead in the relationship. It was good that Thomas was learning a trade. He would be able to give her and their child a safe haven one day.

The wagon was rounding the last curve before the road opened up to town. There stood three small children beside the road. The little girl was holding a cloth sack. Diane thought it looked just like the one she gave Thomas before he left the house. She wondered if Thomas was okay. Diane turned to Edward and said, "Go by Squire's shop first. I want to see Thomas before we visit the pastor."

Edward drove to the shop and Diane dismounted the wagon. As she entered the shop, she saw Rebecca doting over Thomas. "Thomas, I need to speak to you in private," said Diane as she looked upon Rebecca with piercing eyes. Rebecca was quick to read Diane's feelings about her. So, Rebecca began to casually walk from the room. She looked over her shoulder at Diane and said, "I'll be back Thomas once your mother leaves." Diane held her tongue but gave Rebecca a severe look.

"I have two questions for you, young man. First, how did those little ones in the woods come in possession of the sack I gave you this very morning? And second have you told Squire and Rebecca that you are to be married to neighbor Mary," asked Diane in a loud voice. Those waiting in the wagon outside could hear her every word.

Thomas could see that his mother was not pleased at all. "Mother I gave my food to the little ones because they were starving, and my belly was still full. I cannot stand to see anyone hungry. And no, I have not told anyone, and I won't until the arrangements have been made. The news will cause Squire some discomfort. He offered everything you see here, including Rebecca if I finished my apprenticeship. He is aware of Rebecca's reputation with the towns people. He believes that a marriage would help her reputation and a chance she might settle down," said Thomas.

"You are not marrying Rebecca! You are marrying Mary and you will care for her and your child! What you do or where you go after that is up to you. Soon you will be a husband and then a father. You have no quarter for either. They will have to live with me and your father while you work in town. Can you see where this is going Thomas?" said Diane.

"When I see Rebecca behaving in such a manner, I can't help but be upset. You will tell her of your situation, or I will," spoke Diane in a firm tone. "Yes, mother I will tell them," said Thomas. "We are off to visit the Reverend on your behalf and to arrange a wedding. I love you, Thomas. Please don't disappoint me," said Diane as she walked out the door to join the others.

The wagon pulled in front of the church, and everyone climbed down. The women casually walked towards the Reverend's home. Edward removed hay from the back of the wagon and fed the horse. He watched as the women were being received by Reverend Richard. Once they were inside, he was off to see if he could find work to raise income for the new additions in their home. He was a good carpenter and carried a good reputation for being honest and upright.

The women had no sooner entered the Reverend's house when Rebecca appeared from the back of the house. Diane's eyes opened wide, and her legs quickened to spring to a stance if needed. "We'll talk more Richard once your party leaves," said Rebecca as she stared down Diane. Once Rebecca was outside, everyone's attention turned to the Reverend with inquiring looks. She is a very disturbed child," said Reverend.

"Now tell me, what can I do for you ladies." Diane led the conversation informing him of the circumstances and what they required of him. Marriages such as this were common. The Reverend had joined many a soul in matrimony with similar arrangements.

"The misses and I have not been fortunate enough to bear forth a child of our own," said Richard. "By the way where is the Misses Rayburn on this day?" inquired Lydia. "Oh, she's off to a meeting this morning. Some of the town folk want to do something about ridding the vagrants in the woods. There's too much thieving going on. Those people must be driven away so that honest God-fearing folk can rest easy at night," spoke the Reverend as if he was speaking from the pulpit. The women uttered not a word. They just looked at one another. Some of those people he was referring to were friends of theirs that had fallen on hard times.

How soon can we arrange the church for a wedding vicar?' said Lydia. "Let me see here," as he opened a book. "The whole of next week is open. Just pick a day and I'll enter your names accordingly. The women discussed the possibilities and decided a week from Thursday would do nicely. They thanked Reverend and he thanked them for their gifts and kindness.

The women left in excitement and joy. "We need fabric for a new dress that will give glory to Mary's beauty on her special day," said Lydia. "Yes, let's go and find the finest of material in Danbury," said Diane. "I hope the two of you will include me in your efforts," joked Mary. "Oh Mary, we are so sorry. Yes, of course dear. It's your day and you dress. Please forgive us. It's just that we are so thrilled for you, we forget ourselves," said Lydia.

Thomas was at work aligning the press for a new printing. His mind however was focused on how he was going to tell Squire about his situation. The Squire was off to the same meeting that the vicar's wife went to. The Squire's position on the woodland people revolved more along the lines of rehabilitation and care rather than driving them away like cattle. Squire had a deep sympathy for those who were less fortunate.

Edward found work at the furniture shop on the outskirts of town. The resident carpenter had taken ill and was unable to work. Edward had a great sense of relief and wanted to celebrate his good fortune with a pint of ale at the town's tavern.

All seemed well in this little part of England. The day had been fruitful by anyone's standard. All that was left to do was to prepare a celebration for a life to come. It would include a union, a birth, a move and a blessing from above. The effects of which would have influence on more lives that could be counted. These choices, these decisions would carry on through many generations to come. Soul interaction would repeat itself a thousand times before a finality would be realized.

CHAPTER 23

Edward finished his second pint of ale. He lit his pipe and took a long draw. He was pleased with the good fortune of finding work that offered a wage. He entertained the thought of going into business for himself one day. He and Diane could move to town and live a little easier. It could give them more time to spend with their grandchild.

Lydia and Mary had narrowed their choice of cloth for Mary's wedding gown down to two. Mary was determined to make every aspect of the wedding special. Her dress would be the vessel for the departure from the old to the arrival of something new.

Lydia was doing her best to accommodate her daughter in fulfilling her dream. She wanted Mary to be happy and was concerned for her daughter. She feared Mary would suffer a great disappointment once the reality of married life set in. All the fantasies she created would one day come crashing down. Lydia gave up trying to be practical and thought it best to let Mary have her way.

This union of two people in marriage was not formed out of love for one another. It was born from desire and innocence. Social mores coupled with guarded reputation creating the acceptable recourse.

Mary cared dearly what others thought of her. How she looked and how others perceived her was important to her. Mary was not in love with Thomas, nor Thomas in love with her. Mary was in love with a perceived notion. She believed that marriage was the answer to solve the problems of life. It was an honorable escape from the doldrums of life she knew. The child within her was a second thought for now.

Diane rushed off to Squire's print shop to inform Thomas of their arrangements. She was walking past the Reverends house and saw Rebecca at the window watching Diane. Rebecca's lips were moving as if she were speaking to someone out of sight. Then Diane saw Reverend Richard step up to the window beside Rebecca. He was nodding his head yes to whatever Rebecca was saying. It disturbed Diane and caused her to stumble and nearly fall down.

Once she regained herself, she saw Rebecca laughing at her. Diane turned towards the window and began walking towards it. Diane was not going to be intimidated or laughed at. Rebecca saw the fire in Diane's eyes and decided to leave. She turned and ran out of the back door of the rectory. Diane continued her march towards the home while the Reverend watched.

She banged on the door as loud as she could. Slowly the door opened. The Reverend peeped around the door. "What was her business here?" shouted Diane. The Reverend was shaken by Diane's forwardness. "She came to discuss another matter. There is this matter which I need to discuss with you also," said the Reverend. "I'm not so sure about the wedding arrangement. Please have Lydia and Mary come by so we can discuss the matter further. I do not believe it to be fitting that a child conceived in sin by two sinners should be allowed to wed in God's house. It just would not be fitting now, would it?" spoke Reverend.

Diane gave him a look that placed him in a state of fear. She took a deep breath and released it. The fire that once occupied her sight was gone. She took a half step into Reverends comfort zone and said, "The date agreed upon is one week from Thursday, is it not?" spoke Diane in a softer voice. "Yes," spoke the Reverend. "Very well then. We will be in attendance with family and friends on that very date as we agreed. Have I made myself clear on the matter? Or do I need to add more clarity to what I just said?" said Diane. "Yes madame. You have made yourself truly clear" replied the Reverend. Diane gave Reverend a polite smile and withdrew herself from his home.

Diane's frustration over Rebecca was growing. She arrived at the print shop and opened the door. There stood Rebecca talking to Thomas. Diane made a quick step towards her. Rebecca turned to run away but tripped over her feet and fell down. Diane stood over her. "Who's laughing now, you little troublemaker," said Diane. Rebecca raised her arm above her face for fear that Diane was going to deliver more than words.

If you ever try to interfere with our family's life again, I promise you that you will live to regret it. Now get up from there and get out of my sight," said Diane. Rebecca crawled a few feet away from Diane, then rose to her feet. Rebecca brushed away the dust form her dress. She turned and walked upstairs to the living quarters.

Thomas was in shock by what his mother just did. Diane turned her attention to Thomas. "I have something to tell you son. I will speak loud so that everyone can hear what I have to say," said Diane as her eyes peered upward towards the living quarters. "You are getting married in the church a week from Thursday to Mary Rose, the woman you gave your seed to. She is going to have your baby and you are going to provide for the both of them.

I raised you to be responsible and son…you have bitten off a man's share of responsibility. You can be a printer if you like, or you can be a farmer like your father. Either way it's your choice and it matters not to me. It was your choice to bed Mary. Now you have to bear the burden of your actions. We as your family, will help you along the way. But you must fulfill the duties of a father and a husband."

Diane feel silent. She noticed that Squire had entered through the back door and heard all that she said. "That was well put Diane. You are upset as any parent would be. Your child is leaving the nest and the strings of motherhood are stretching like never before. I understand what you are going through. I wish I had sought your guidance when I was raising my daughter. Perhaps things would have turned out better for her.

Anyway, Thomas is welcome to stay and finish his apprenticeship if he so chooses. I'm happy to hear of the union with Mary. Her parents are fine people and filled with love. I hope to receive an invitation to the occasion," said Squire. "Oh, heavens yes. You and Rebecca both are most welcome," said Diane. "Then it's settled. Thomas will continue to work for me so that one day he and his family will be well cared for," said Squire.

The wagon with Edward, Mary and Lydia pulled up to the print shop. Squire greeted them and said, "Come in one and all. I have heard the wonderful news and I rejoice with you each and every one. Rebecca come downstairs child and wish our friends well. Bring my firkin with you," said Squire. Squire cozied up to Edward and the two began to talk. Rebecca gathered mugs and the cask of wine Squire called for. Slowly she descended the stairs and placed the items on the counter.

Squire drew each one a measure of wine as Rebecca handed a mug to each. "Let us lift our measure of wine and our measure of joy for these two love birds, who bless our lives with their youth and promise of life," spoke Squire as a father toasting his child. Everyone quietly lifted the mugs to their lips and began to drink in as many a reason.

One happy for his new position and wages. Another happy for a loving son. One happy for a long-sought dream to come true. Another sad for the loss of a lover. One in fear and anger bent on revenge. Another joyful for friendly unions. And one standing amongst the six connected to each present but never attached to any one thing. The path he walked belonged to him and him alone for now.

Seven souls stood at this one moment in time, this one place in space. Each believing and perceiving in their own perception derived by their view of life, or one borrowed from another. Each one invested in the collective effort, each one holing their own desires.

Time and circumstance will present each one an alternative viewpoint should they decide to carry it a ways. Some desires and intentions will become dust, some will become ashes. Some will forge diamonds and gold. Yet all were the precious lessons of life that gave light to the soul and lift to the spirit.

Perhaps the words of Solomon can lend clarity to the pursuits of mortal life. "For everything there is a season and a time for every purpose under heaven."

CHAPTER 24

Where two souls walk, some will remember, some will forget,
Whenever love lifts its wings, some will rejoice, while others weep,

The sun was peeking on the horizon announcing another day. Stillness filled this quaint little setting. The night was surrendering to the dawn. Soon the fire places would be burning sending smoke upwards signaling that the residents were at another day's journey.

Today and the days to come, were animated to bring a shift from what once was, to what will be. Children will become parents, parents becomes grandparents. All that was known embraced to the dawn of a new day. All beginnings received their births from endings, where some rejoice and others weep. There would be plenty of time for both in the dance of mortality. In this reality, the two walk together, hand in hand, in harmony and acceptance, visible to some, blind to others.

Diane was busy making plans for the wedding. It was a special time for her. Her only child was getting married and a grandchil on the way. She had a new daughter to share life with and Edward had a job to bring in more money for the family.

Edward was still in bed making plans for the day. He and Jonathan would ride their horses about the countryside. They would spread the news and invitations to family and friends for the wedding to come and other matters of importance.

Lydia was about her business of the day as Jonathan and Mary still remained in bed. She carried no joy of heart, no plans to inflame enthusiasm. Her emotions were repressed with opinions locked away, held in silence. Lydia was a mother and a wife. She would perform the duties of each in body but lacking in heart in these times of change. Deep within she wept without sound or tear.

Her mother had died from a roof collapse one night during a terrible storm. It led her father to become a drunkard from the loss. He could not support his daughters and abandoned them. Lydia was the oldest at fourteen. It fell to her to be the caretaker of her three sisters.

At times they lived on the charity of others. Other times they survived by begging. She would resort to stealing when their bellies cried from hunger. On occasions Lydia would sell her body in order to feed her sisters. Some of the men abused her while some assaulted her causing injury.

She learned how to numb herself from the pain suffered in those times of need. The memories of those hard times still dwelled inside her. There had never been an outlet given so she could heal the past. Except for that day at Chad's wake when someone stepped through the door and gave her a reason to carry on.

The salve that offered a measure of healing was the passion she felt for Thomas. His youth and innocence, the way she felt being beside him. It was like a single flame on a candle placed amongst the deepest of darkness. A single flame of light that gave hope that all things dark in life could be revived through passion.

Passion is the soul's way of fighting back. Passion which lives in the heart as nectar for the human spirit. The adoration for Thomas made that single flame visible. This feeling, this realization would see her through all the passages of life so long as she could foster their relationship.

Mary was drifting in and out of consciousness as she lied in bed. She knew this day and the next would be occupied with creating her wedding dress. Her special time had finally arrived. No thought or concern was given to the reality of marriage or motherhood. Mary's concern revolved around appearances, how she would be perceived by others.

She had always longed for a home of her own with family and position in society. This desire would be the author of her destiny, the script she would rehearse day in and day out. All she desired would come to her threefold. Yet there was one thing she forgot to add to her detailed list, happiness. The type of happiness that is generated from within rather than from outside. The type of happiness that is free from attachment and expectation.

Mary drifted back into slumber. There stood Chad, her brother, smiling at her with the warmth of love seldom seen. She cried out his name. Lydia heard her and stopped what she was doing and stood in silence. Jonathan was still in bed and heard it also. His eyes opened wide as he held the silence. Again, Mary cried out, "Chad!" She began to weep in deep sorrow.

Johnathan sat straight up in bed still in silence. Lydia became weak in her knees and had to sit. The three under roof began crying without reservation. The sobbing could be heard outside in the stillness of the dawn. Lydia wanted to run to Mary's room, but she was too weak to stand. Jonathan rolled over in bed and buried his face in a pillow to muffle his crying. In spite of the tears and wailing, the pain of loss and sorrow was gifting a healing this family so desperately needed.

These who join in sorrow also join in surrender. Surrender to the loss of temporal love for an everlasting love that knows no boundaries nor conditions. A love eternal that gave birth to the stars and our every desire. All who draw breath live in that single flame of a single candle that dances in the darkest of darkness.

Thomas did not sleep well last night. He kept peering with one eye open for the suns light to enter through the window. He was ready to start work since he could not sleep. Yesterday's scorn from his mother was still ringing strong with him.

Squire and Rebecca were not early risers. One of Thomas' duties was to build a fire in the shops fireplace to warm the home before those above awakened. He'd prepare hot water for the mornings tea then spend time reading the many books held in Squire' collection.

There was so much to life, more than he realized. He had imagined himself traveling about, seeing new things, and meeting interesting people. He loved reading about the adventures of others and their conquests. The thought of a domesticated life with its expectations and responsibilities felt like water cast upon a hot fire. He had no true feelings for Mary and he was aware she had little or none for him.

The light of Lydia's energy came to him. He could feel her presence. It gave him a deep sense of warmth and security. The passion held between these two reached far beyond mortal understanding or physical limitation. No matter what went on in the world around them or the measure of distance between them, this level of passion would never wane. He closed his eyes and could smell her rose oil. Something soft brushed against his face. He knew it was her. He could see her face in mind's eye. Her eyes running deep, her smile touching his soul. He never wanted to leave here. This love between the two circumventing the limitations of mortal mind.

As he sat there in the dark as the fire grew to yellow, then blue, then white flames. The light each gave danced across his face giving it a three-fold appearance. His eyes were held in a blank stare. His soul off to some place searching for balance and understanding. Searching for the hand of the one who occupied his heart.

Within he became still like a pool of water. A deep sense of peace came over him. Before he knew the warmth of his mother's womb, before he drew his first breath, he knew. He could see beyond the veil and the mystery of this thing called life. A broad smile came upon him as he reflected on what he was receiving. He was free of worry. Free from fear of the morrows. Fear, which is the illusion that delivers truth for all who stand against it.

Interpretation is beholding to conditions, beliefs and an ever evolving understanding. The purpose of it all is singular in nature. It is without direction or division. It favors no one thing over the other and possesses no senses. It is carried on the winds and will ever so be.

Eight days will pass and bring these to the ninth. On that day the foundations of the lives and the future of the same will be set to motion. One cause leading to the desired effect creating other causes and other effects. Some will rejoice while others weep.

The sun was now above the trees and hills that surrounded this little place under the heavens. Things were stirring as these mortals wake from slumber, dreams, and visions. The frost that covered the ground was surrendering itself to the sun's rays once again and to the cycle of nature, to the cycle of life everlasting.

CHAPTER 25

Edward saddled his horse and waited for Jonathan to arrive. The two men planned to ride the countryside offering invitations to the wedding to friends and family. Diane prepared food for the men and packed oats for the horses. Edward drew a measure of whiskey to help fend off the chill. Jonathan was on approach to the Sonnet home riding his horse. Edward mounted his horse and Diane handed the provisions for the trip. The two rode off together on their horses side by side. The break from their domestic routine was most welcomed. Their day would be spent on horseback visiting people. Some they had not seen for some time.

Lydia and Mary were busy inventorying the dowry to be presented on the day of the wedding. They were behaving more like sisters than daughter and mother. It was a good time for these two. They laid the offerings across Mary's bed. Mary's eyes were filled with splendor as she looked at each piece. The desire for wedlock and a new life was just a short time away. Her most longed after dream was unfolding around her. She was excited and filled with joy. This was her moment in the sun.

It was also Mary's time to learn what to expect from a reality born from change. The time of growth that no one can ever truly prepare for. The misdirection of good intentions and the errors that follow are the very life blood of climbing above one's greatest of expectations. It's the failures that take us by the hand to guide us to a new awareness not found in book or tales. Every new beginning carries with it its own ending. Today mother and daughter together dance as one in heart.

Thomas could hear the sound of footsteps above him. He knew that the next thing he'd hear would be Rebecca's footsteps descending the staircase with tea pot in hand. This was the routine six days a week. He wondered how she would receive him today after yesterday spirited conversation with his mother. Rebecca's foot touched the floor and Thomas turned to look at her. She was aloof and failed to acknowledge him. It bothered Thomas. He felt as if he had done something wrong. She quickly turned and ascended the stairs stomping her feet at every step.

The water was ready for tea. He called out to Rebecca, but she did not respond. "Thank you, Thomas. Rebecca will be right down," yelled Squire. Thomas could hear the two upstairs speaking to each other in low tones. Rebecca was arguing with her father in protest.

Then came the sound of her footsteps descending louder than when she went up. She walked over to the fireplace and took the pot. She gave Thomas a blank stare and turned towards the staircase. She stopped before taking the first step. She placed the pot on the stair and turned to face him. She took her dress at the collar and pulled the dress down to expose her breasts. She stood in silence as his eyes took measure of her beauty. "You'll never know what it is like to have these for your pleasure, but other men will," said Rebecca. She pulled the dress back to her collar and took to the stairs.

Diane ruled the day and Thomas yesterday. Today Rebecca would take back that control.

A loud knock at the door broke the hold of Rebecca's spell. Thomas opened the door to see a gentleman dressed in stately clothes. "Is this the business and residence of one Andrew Beckett," inquired the man. "Yes, yes sir it is. Shall I call on him on your behalf?" replied Thomas. "Yes son, that would be nice. May I enter?" "Yes, yes sir, please. Make yourself warm at the fire while I summon Squire. May I ask who has come to greet him sir?" asked Thomas. "My name is John Thorstrom. I've come to offer your Squire a business proposition."

Thomas took to the stairs stopping halfway up to gain Squire's permission to enter the living quarters. Thomas made his announcement and was allowed to enter to converse with Squire. Thomas returned to the guest and assured him that Squire would soon join him.

Rebecca came downstairs with holding a tray of hot tea and biscuits. "Please sir take rest while my father prepares himself for you," said Rebecca. "Thank you, child, I most certainly will," said John. "And where have you traveled from sir," asked Rebecca. "London, I'm from London," replied John. Thomas' attention perked up hearing him say London. He listened to every word that the man spoke. Squire was heard descending the stairs. Once he made eye contact with John, he stepped quick to shake his hand. "May we talk in private Andrew," asked John. "Of course, we can. Children go upstairs until we have finished our business," said Squire.

Thomas followed Rebecca up the stairs and was torn in two directions. He wanted to hear more about London and the business at hand. He also did not want to lose favor with Rebecca. Their time together could help to mend sensitive feelings.

CHAPTER 26

Jonathan and Edward had visited the homes of family and friends by midday. Their journey was more than just inviting those they knew to a wedding. Each visit revealed its own news. Some had been blessed with fortunate times, while others offered tales of sorrow. This was the way of the country people. They fought, struggled, and cared for one another. Hardships were a way of life and the very fabric of humanity. These people were born onto this world to make it a better place for those who would follow behind them.

Their last stop would be to Mildred's, the midwife and country healer. Jonathan was looking forward to the visit. As they approached her house, they saw her feeding her goats. Mildred looked up and caught sight of the two. She was wearing a look as if they were expected. "Relieve your animals and let them feed with mine while you come inside so that I may feed the two of you," said Mildred. The two men graciously accepted her invitation and entered the home with her.

Dried herbs and flowers hung from the ceiling of her quaint home. The smell of meat stew filled the room from the pot sitting on the hearth next to a warm fire. The table was already set for three. "Come warm yourselves by the fires light," said Mildred. Both men were glad to obliged her request. They were cold and beginning to tire.

Mildred took a loaf of bread and cut three hearty slices from it. She laid each piece in a wooden bowl and ladled stew over it until the bowl was filled. She placed each one on the table and invited the two journeymen to join her. The men sat quietly at the table and began to eat.

This was their first visit to Mildred's home. Her home was adorned with crafts that she had made over the years in her solitude. There were baskets with hand painted designs depicting the flowers of the forest.

Handmade bracelets and necklaces were carefully displayed on a shelf. She used them as gifts and items for trade. Some of the towns people visited her in secret to purchase her wares. No one dare reveal their association with her for fear of retaliation from the religious community. Some believed her to be a witch and a sorceress. Others saw her as a healer and a wise soul to be respected.

The men were familiar with both sides of her reputation. They preferred to judge the hearts of others through their own reason rather than rumor. Whenever there was a death or birth Mildred was not far away. Her energy always helped to sooth the nerves and comfort the weary. Country souls preferred to trust others through witness and reputation. They knew the rumored stories of others were only reflections of their own fears born from the weakness carried in their hearts and mind.

The last bit of stew was about to vanish as the men scraped their bowls. Mildred rose from the table and took a cask from a shelf. She drew two mugs of wine for her guests and placed each one on the table. Jonathan and Edward thought it was the best wine they had ever drank. Jonathan drank his and she poured him another. He was trying to work up the nerve to ask her some questions he had about the women in his life. He hoped the wine would help to relax his tongue and calm the nerves.

"Never have I ever tasted wine such as this. What is made from?" he asked. "It's made from wild berries that grow on the hills of Landon," replied Mildred. "How do you get the smoothness it holds?" asked Edward. "I use the water that's used to clean my goats," replied Mildred. Jonathan choked and spat the wine across the table. He was wiping the wine from his shirt as he looked at Mildred. Then he realized that she was having fun with them. The room broke out in laughter as Mildred poured each one more drink. "The recipe was my mothers. She always wanted to have a measure for those who traveled past our home," spoke Mildred in a quiet tone.

The men knew Mildred's mother. She was the fairest woman in these parts. Her beauty and her grace was sought after by many a suitor after her husband died. Mildred, as a young woman, had returned home one day to find her mother dead, lying naked on the ground. She had been raped and killed to conceal the identity of the assailants. Judging from the horse tracks there were at least four riders.

Mildred buried her mother somewhere near the house without a marker. She wanted to make sure that no one could ever find her mother again to cause her harm, even in death. Mildred still carried the weight of that day.

Later she became aware of the men who took her mother's life. They turned their eyes away from her out of fear and shame from what they did. Sometimes she would speak her mother's name out loud as she passed one of the men. Some would cease in step or start to cry. One uttered a threat towards her. Mildred held no malice for these men. She knew if she did, she would become as one of them, unable to forgive.

Her mother taught her that forgiveness was all that was needed for one to be free in mind and in heart. Her mother Rachael told her that if one casted a stone towards another out of anger, the stone would only return one day to inflict the same pain that was intended, times seven. Mother and daughter were close, one the teacher one the student.

Jonathan cleared his throat and said, "It would be our honor Mildred if you would join us to celebrate our children's wedding day." Mildred issued a great smile and relied, "Yes, I'd love to join you on that day of celebration." Mildred was blushing in front of the men and covered her face with her hand. She was moved by their hospitality.

"Also, I was wondering if you knew anymore about the women in my life? Are they okay? I mean are the children that are coming to us, okay?" asked Jonathan. "Yes of course Jonathan. The women are fine, and the children are all anxious to join everyone here. You have no worry my friend," replied Mildred.

"We best be on our way Mildred. Thank you for your kindness and your gifts," spoke Edward. "Yes, thank you Mildred. You are a saint to us and all those about the countryside," said Jonathan. The men mounted their horses and rode towards home. The day was getting long and the two were tired.

Diane and Lydia were sharing recipes with one another and enjoying their time as they put their plans in motion. Jonathan was giving a hog for the reception as part of the dowry. John Clayborne, the towns inn keeper had a pit beside the inn that was used for cooking meats.

Mary was anxious to start her dress. The material was laid out on the table and a deep silence overcame the room. Each one staring at the cloth and what it meant to each one. Diane was removed to her past. She recalled a time when her plans for the future took a sharp turn. She met a handsome man whose kindness and soft words she could not resist. Then came Thomas as the gift for that special evening.

Lydia also fell back to the past as she looked at the cloth. Her marriage was her escape from a life that beard little or no fruit. Jonathan was the knight that rescued her from her plight. He gave her love when she had none. He gave her hope when there was no hope within her. Those who have so much love always seem to find those who have so little.

Mary had her own view of the dress. To her, the dress was like a curtain that would open to reveal all her dreams and desires. A house in town would follow with servants. A husband successful in business to provide wealth and position. All these things she created in mind. It was her piece of heaven on earth, not to be denied.

These three gathered together to bring a dream to fruition for Mary. These three would design and create the finest dress possible. This dress for Mary was her coronation to a new life. For Diane and Lydia, it became a moment of retrospect. There are the plans you make for life and the plans life makes for you.

Out came the scissors, the chalk and measuring string to begin the long awaited task. The dress would hold the past, the present and the future rolled into every cut and every stich. Mother and daughter and mother-in-law to be, meshed as one as their chatter and love for one another filled the room.

At the print shop Thomas could hear Squire and his visitor offering their farewells. He heard the door close when Squire summoned him and Rebecca to join him downstairs. The two raced down to join him. Thomas knew by looking at Squire something special had happened.

"I have great news for you both. I, we have been commissioned for the printing of a book. A special book, the Bible. It will bring us a good wage. Enough to live a comfortable life once we have finished. It will be long hard work Thomas. You too shall profit from such a venture. Enough to care for you and your new family.

I must go to London to procure the needed supplies and sign the contracts. Thomas you will remain here and to look after things while I'm away. I promise you once we have filled the first stock of printing, you may accompany me to London," said Squire.

Thomas was excited from the news. So much so that he turned to Rebecca and gave her a hug. At first, she was shocked, then she joined in the celebration. "Father may I also travel with you to London?" asked Rebecca. "Yes, my dear, you may. Now I'm off to the tavern to have a pint or two in celebration. Thomas, I would ask you to join me. Will you do me the honor?" asked Squire. "Yes, sir I would love to share with you," replied Thomas. The two grabbed their coats and left for the inn.

CHAPTER 27

The eighth day arrived since the mothers visit to the Reverend Richards home to make arrangements for their children's marriage. The air was somewhat warm for a winters day. A gray heavy overcast created an umbrella of stillness over the land. The wagons of each family pulled to the front of John Clayborne's tavern and inn. John's two sons came out to help unload the wagons for their stay in town. Diane and Lydia directed everyone as to what went where.

Mary decided to visit Thomas at the print shop. Little did she know that Thomas was inside having his fill of ale with Squire. Lydia and Diane entered the tavern and saw the two seated together. It was obvious the two were celebrating something. The mothers walked over to the two merry men who had not noticed their presence. "And what do we have here Squire? Are you corrupting my son with strong drink and tall tales?" asked Diane.

"No, why no Diane. We were celebrating Thomas' good fortune. On the morrow he'll take the hand of the lovely Mary. Soon he will be a father. And once we fill our new contract, he will have the funds to build a future for them. We have received an undertaking that will profit the business and our pockets," replied Squire. This most certainly stirred the women's interest.

Jonathan and Edward entered the tavern with interest to the conversation the family was having and a hearty thirst for a pint. Squire ordered pints for the two men as all took a seat at the table.

Mary entered the print shop to find it empty. Then out of nowhere, Rebecca entered the room from the back of the shop. The heavy sound of a man's footsteps was heard. Then the back door slammed shut.

"I guess you're here to see Thomas, but he's not here. He and father are at the tavern sharing a pint. They are planning on our trip to London," said Rebecca in a condescending tone.

"I guess that man you were with when I entered, that left in such a hurry was running back to his wife," said Mary with a taunting tone. "Well at least he was a man and not a boy like your groom to be. You couldn't get a man to marry you, so you preyed on someone younger, who wasn't wise to your trickery," spoke Rebecca.

Mary took two steps towards her, and Rebecca followed by stepping towards Mary. The two stood in a face off. One waiting for the other to make the first move. "Here, here! What are you two doing?" yelled Thomas. "Squire sent me here to fetch you two. We need to prepare for the morrow. Has anyone seen the Reverend?" It was then that Rebecca alerted. Mary knew by Rebecca' reaction who the man was that ran out the back door. Mary stood there glaring at Rebecca. Rebecca was doing her best to stay composed. "Come on you two. They are waiting on us, "said Thomas.

The three entered the inn together. A crowd had formed at the main table. People were laughing and making one toast after the other. The Clayborne brothers entered, having placed the meat hog on wood embers for tomorrow's celebration. Mary and Rebecca had forgone their earlier dispute and mixed with all those mingling about. The conversations and measures of ale continued well into the evening.

Mary, Lydia and Diane inspected the kitchen where they would prepare the food for the reception. The pots hung from a rack attached to the ceiling. The fireplace was huge. There was plenty of space to cook all that was planned for the celebration.

Helen Clayborne, John's wife, showed the families to their rooms for the nights to come. New straw had been added to the mattresses with an extra measure for the honeymooners. Most were ready for slumber given all the excitement and drink. Squire and Rebecca left the crowd to go home. The townspeople were returning to their homes as the last remnants of sunlight were fading.

Thomas was the only one still seated at the table. The inn was quiet, and the moons rays were building across the landscape. He sat staring at the single flame of a candle. The flickering of the flame gave him a sense of peace. He didn't know why. It just made him feel good.

The last remnants of his youthful innocence and the dreams once held would be no more beyond this day. Tomorrow he'd stand to witness his bride as she walked down the aisle of a church alongside her father. A short walk down the aisle of a church to begin a long walk through the aisle of life.

No one really knows why we take these steps in life, only to say that all things under heaven must be witnessed, all things must eventually be embraced. There was never a beginning that didn't carry its ending in hand. No one could predict the difficulties that lie ahead in life. Only that they awaited the passing of time to bring into witness.

As the night carried on, the stillness felt earlier deepens. Snowflakes begin to fall one by one then by the thousands. Quietly they blanket the ground. The sound of each snowflake touching the earth sounded like whispering raindrops. One day ends and another arrives for embrace. Some will rejoice the morn while others will curse it. So, it is in this thing called life.

CHAPTER 28

Everyone except Diane and Lydia were still in bed sleeping off the celebration from the night before. The mothers were busy in the inns kitchen preparing the food offerings for the guests. Bread pans were filled with dough rising. A pot filled with dried apples was soaking in water and wine for pastries and pies. They were moving in harmony with one another about the kitchen. It was like a rehearsed dance recital. Without uttering a single word, the two poured their hearts into every detail and every effort. Soon the wedding party would be awake and ready for a much needed breakfast.

Mary was filled with joy. Her long awaited wedding day had arrived. All the disappointments of past romances were dashed away this morning. She imagined the people arriving to pay her honor on this day. The church procession, the ceremony and the reception to follow had been rehearsed hundreds of times before in her imagination. She pictured the life that would follow and what it would hold. She wrote the script of her life as she wanted it. If the other characters in her play stuck to the script, she would enjoy a life of bliss. If they didn't, she would rewrite the script to preserve her vision.

Thomas awoke in high anxiety. He felt as if he was riding a horse that had no reins or bridle. He had no control of the direction or destination. All he had was the faith that the horse knew the way. He searched inside for courage to see his way through this day. He was experiencing cold feet.

There was his obligation to Mary and the parents. He needed to fulfill the duty of a father and husband not knowing what those duties were. All this he knew to be true. All that was lacking was his heart and passion. He loved his parents and would never disappoint them. He knew he'd learn to love Mary and that it would come in time.

He lied there in bed still held by worry. His eyelids were becoming heavy as he drifted off to sleep. He was carried off to another reality that walks close to this one. He was walking on a great city street. Snow was falling around him that offered a deep sense of peace. He could see a figure of a man off in the distance. It was Isaac, his spirit guide. He quickened his step until he reached him. Thomas's spirit was lifted, and the worry was no more.

"Today you begin the destiny that was given to you. It's why you entered the realm of mortals. The first step will be your union with Mary and the experiences that will follow. Know that your children will be born three days apart. The first will come from the daughter. The second, from the mother. You will support both, one nearby, the other from afar. Your desire for passion will belong to the mother. Your duty to social conduct will be for the daughter.

This is the path that has been laid before you. You must learn to navigate the storms and the quiet seas of life. Some days will be filled with sorrow, others with joy. You will marry one and desire the other. It will feel as if you are being pulled in two directions. You will want to abandon one for the other then return back to the other.

The fondness and frustration from such an arrangement will give insight. The insight will in turn render an even plane to write the words to deliver the story and rhyme to open the hearts and minds of many. You will find no inner peace in this incarnation or the ones that follow. Only until you let go of the world around you, will you find the peace you so strongly desire. This path which lies before you is in no way meant to harm you or anyone else. It's only purpose is to challenge you so you may learn truth above all things. It is so for all of humanity my son.

There was a time when one side of the universe was filled with nothing but darkness. It called out to the light and the light answered. These are the two paths of a journey that leads to fullness. The light and the dark. Each one as important as the other. Yet by themselves they are nothing, like a tree that grows strong but never bears fruit.

The direction of the will and the objects of desire remain in a constant state of collapse and renewal. The beginning seeks it's end while the past seeks only the future.

It's time for you to return to your mortal reality and take the stage of life as the actor before your audience," spoke Isaac with his deep blue eyes and kindest of smile.

The snow around them became thick and the wind increased. The figure of Isaac was no more. Thomas quietly turned around to take a step when his eyes opened to see the room his body was in and the bed that held it.

The aroma of food cooking stirred his hunger. Thomas got up and dressed to join the day. He walked to the window and peered outside. It was snowing hard. The wind was swirling sending the snow in every direction. Just as it was when he left Isaac a few moments ago. The ground was covered with a foot of snow or more except where the pig laid roasting in coals buried under ground. He wondered about the invited guest. The snows storm and the depth would keep some or all away from the wedding celebration.

He walked downstairs to see some seated. The table held food for more than was needed. Lydia and Diane were pouring everything they had into this day. It was theirs to share with Mary. So much love, so much food so many dreams to fill.

Mary's wedding dress held the love and care of three who created its design. It held all things past and all things to come. And for Mary it was her coronation to a new life, a new manner of being.

The church would be decorated to honor the prince and princess as their vows were made. Nothing was left to chance. It was a special day for everyone concerned.

Mary saw Thomas coming down the stairs and turned to entered the kitchen. When she returned to the dining hall, she was carrying a tray full of breakfast fare. She placed the same before him and said, "This day I will always hold sacred in honor of our union as husband and wife. This child I carry is our child and our beginning. I vow to serve you both with my love and devotion. Enjoy this meal I have prepared for you, my prince." Everyone applauded her words as she wrapped her arms around Thomas and kissed him.

CHAPTER 29

Lydia, Mary, and Diane were beginning to prepare the food for the reception. They knew the weather would keep some away especially those who lived in the countryside. The townspeople were most likely the only ones who could brave the weather. Still the desire to prepare a feast for many still held its grip on them. So, they decided to go ahead with their original plan. Their joy of the celebration would override all rationality and reserve.

Edward and Jonathan were off to the stables to tend to the needs of their horses. They walked side by side in the swirling snow as the sound of crunching snow was made with each step. They too were sharing in joy for the day and its expectations. They joked in laughter and sounded more like schoolboys than men.

Thomas was anxious to pay Squire a visit. It was important to him that Squire was in attendance. The snow had not let up and he feared it would keep the good Squire away. Mary decided to go with him. She was anxious about Thomas being around Rebecca and her troublesome ways.

The two entered the winters snowy domain together holding hands to steady each other through the snow. They became playful as children. Thomas made a snowball and threw it at Mary hitting her on the forehead. Mary returned the gesture and before long the two had regressed back to their childhood. Mary threw herself backwards landing in the snow. She brushed the snow with her arms making a snow angel. Thomas stood watching her as the little girl inside her played to her hearts content. He had never seen Mary act so carefree and playful.

She began singing as her arms went back and forth making the impression of her wings deeper. Thomas was overwhelmed with Mary's display. He fell to his knees beside her, and she stopped singing. She looked up at him and lifted her arms to embrace him. He met her embrace and laid down beside her. As their lips pressed together Thomas rolled on top of her pushing her deeper in the snow. The energy of passion was building around them, nothing they had experienced before.

Everything about the moment, how they saw themselves, how they felt about each other was completely absent and without foundation. They were in a new reality, a truer reality held deep within each. Desperately they tried to hold each other tighter and kiss each other longer. As hard as they tried, their physical exchange could not deliver the intensity their hearts were held in. The two were falling in love.

The relationship was shifting. No thought of moral obligation or reputation was present. Precious and few are the moments when the world around you falls away and the light enters. Their thoughts were not held in regrets of the past nor anxiety for the future. They were present without time, without space. The roots of their souls were meshing together in single purpose. Wrapped around each other these two were, one in body, in soul and spirit.

Mary felt the child within her move. She opened her eyes and looked at Thomas with depth and conviction. The child within made its presence known, for it was not the binding of two but of three. Mary pulled Thomas to her and said, "Take me! Take me right now right here in the snow! I have to feel you inside me. Right now, in this moment so that it can live forever. I don't care who sees it. Just enter me and give me your seed once again. I beg you."

At first Thomas held her request in reserve. Then he saw the strength in her eyes, and he couldn't refuse her. He had to oblige her request. Thomas arranged himself atop her and prepared himself. As he entered her, he felt a rush overcome him. She looked at him as if held in trance. Her eyes were open held in blank stare. Her body held rigid and without movement. She was somewhere else in mind and spirit. A smile grew across her face as she gasped for a breath.

Thomas's thrusts became intense. She reconnected to the moment and kissed him exuding pure passion. The energy around them was swelling. Together they felt it, as it delivered a new elation. It continued to build as Thomas released his seed. The sexual fervor gave way to a spiritual essence.

The two were intoxicated with passion. Their bodies were shuttering. Stary eyed they were as lied beside each other in the frame of her snow angel. Faces came together until lips meet in delightful embrace. Thomas rolled Mary over on top of him as they held each other for the first time as lovers. They held the embrace as gentle snowflakes rained down on them.

A face behind a window from the inn had witnessed the display of the young couple. It was the face of Lydia. Her eyes fixated on the two lying in the snow. She felt the child within her stirring about as if to receive her attention. So much love in as many forms. One trumping the other out from desire. One was mending a heart while another was breaking it to pieces.

Confusing to the mind, confounding to the heart, this thing called love. True love, forever it be, is not built on obligation or arrangement. It has no bounds, no rules of engagement by which to abide. Neither can be found within its realm bridle or reins to guide its path. It does however possess a saddle, should you decide to ride along the journey known as life.

CHAPTER 30

Lydia and Diane were doting over Mary and her dress. All three were speaking at the same time with occasional moments of laughter. The magic of the wedding was taking hold of these three. The long awaited moment was almost here.

The men were busy shoveling the snow between the inn and the church. Their pipes were lit and filled with good tobacco for the occasion. They spoke of their younger lives and the times they had. Occasionally they'd replenish themselves with a nip of good whiskey to ward off the cold. Both were pleased with their children's arrangement. They would no longer be neighbors. They were family now.

The Reverend and his wife, Susan were decorating the alter per Mary's wishes. Reverend Richard obviously had his mind elsewhere. He appeared upset about something. Whatever it was it weighed heavy on his heart. Susan noticed a change in him in the last few weeks. Sometimes she'd hear him crying in the night. She tried to bring the matter up, but he refused to share his burden.

Thomas was sitting quietly by himself in the deepest corner of the inn. He was donned in his finest clothing. His leather shoes were shined, and his hair was pulled back in a ponytail and a red ribbon was tied at its base.

The morning's embrace with Mary was special for both. He believed their relationship was growing stronger with each passing day. Yet, it in no way had waned his feelings for Lydia. He loved both but in separate ways.

The men were entering the inn having completed the shovel detail. They stomped their feet against the floor to shake the snow from their boots. Helen Clayborne made herbal tea flavored with honey and a little wine for them. They walked to the fireplace and reached out to embrace the heat with their hands. They hadn't noticed Thomas seated in the corner.

"He'll make a good husband for your daughter Jonathan, don't you worry. His heart is true, and his mother and I raised him well. Mary is welcomed to live under our roof until such time Thomas can afford a roof of his own," spoke Edward.

"I have no reservation about his character or heart my friend. I know him from his youth as you have known mine. Thomas has the eye of a seeker. He will not be satisfied with country life or a stable trade to benefit one's family. He will seek adventure and new things that are not within reach from these parts. I fear we will one day see the backside of him as he follows the sun," replied Jonathan.

"Today we celebrate the union of our children and the life they have yet to live. I pray their lives are as fruitful as the love they bear for one another," spoke Edward. The men toasted the day with their tea and wine.

"Let the tea thaw your bones and I'll be giving you a swig of good Irish whiskey to heal what ails the body," said John Clayborne. "I pray that heaven follows them in life and rains down its blessings for those they love and those who love them. That they give no quarter to argument nor undeserved sorrow," spoke John as he raised the flask high. He took a drink and passed it to Jonathan. "May my only daughter find the happiness and peace she has longed for," declared Jonathan as he took a long drink. He handed the flask to Edward. "If they be true to themselves and each other trouble will never find them," said Edward as he took a long drink of his own.

Thomas stood from the table and walked over to the others. The fathers were surprised to see him. Each placed their hands on his shoulder and patted him on the back. Everyone said his name aloud. Then louder. Then shouted his name at the top of their lungs. "Thomas!" The flask of whiskey was passed to Thomas. This was his invitation to stand with the men.

He tilted the flask upwards and took his first swallow. It was followed by a slight choking and the lack of the ability to speak. The men gave gentle laughter to his display. Thomas laughed with them as the bonding of mortal mind continued.

These that lived day by day cherished moments such as this. The passion and love that arises from the mortal experience was the grandest of virtues.

At the church the hour of wed was nearly at hand. Thomas stood at the alter beside his father. Harriet Jennings was playing her lute and singing while daughter Emily played her flute. The few guests that were present were bundled in warm clothing and enjoying the music.

Diane, Lydia and the bride to be waited in the Reverend's home beside the church. Lydia looked at her daughter and said, "Something old, something new, something borrowed and something blue goes the story that brings luck and prosperity to all brides.

For something old I give you the bridal veil that I wore when your father took me to be his bride. She presented the same to Mary in a ceremonious fashion. Mary hugged her mother as she wiped away the tears. Lydia held her tight and kissed her cheek.

Lydia gently nudged Mary away from her to make the next presentation. She looked at Mary and said, "Now something new. Your wedding gown is your something new. It was cut with our hands, sown from our imagination, and fashioned to your will. This dress represents the transition from daughter to wife. One ending yielding to a new beginning."

Diane stepped towards Mary and reached inside her pocket for something borrowed. She removed a beautiful broach that she held with reverence. "This was my mother's given to her from her mother. She gave it to me on my wedding day. I have held it all along hoping to give it to my daughter one day. In foolishness I believed that day would never come. I was wrong. Today I stand before my daughter to honor her on her day.

You are to hold it for as long as you wish. Diane carefully placed the broach on Mary's dress and gave the broach a love pat as if to let it go. She gave Mary a warm smile and stepped away from her so she could admire the broach one last time. "It's perfect. I pray one day it will be passed down to another daughter, your daughter on her special day," said Diane as she held back the tears. She was recalling her mother and grandmother and the love they shared together.

Lydia stood beside Diane. She looked at Mary one last time as a daughter. She reached inside her apron and removed an indigo blue ribbon. She stepped to Mary and said, "Today Diane placed a red ribbon in young Thomas's hair before arriving here. Now I will place this blue ribbon in yours. When you arrive to your bridal chamber remove his ribbon as well as your own. Together braid the ribbons into one. There will be times when you fear something may come in between you and him. When it happens hold the braided ribbon and remember this day and what was given. Find your strength again and the fear will leave you. One day when you are old and gray you will look upon this ribbon with fondness. Now, it is time for us to join the others," spoke Lydia in tenderness.

Susan, the Reverend's wife, came into the room clapping her hands and said, "Okay ladies let us join the party at hand and begin this celebration, shall we?"

The front door of the church opened, and the light spilled in as it reflected off the snow cover. It created a glare which made the human figures standing in the doorway appear as shadows as they entered. Thomas held his focus on the glaring light as it dissipated once the doors were closed. There stood Jonathan chin up, chest out appearing more than just a father. Beside him stood the bride in her full gown and veil appearing like an angel. Her head was tilted downward as if held in humility.

As the two drew near to the alter, the veil revealed stitched daisies on both sides as the symbols for new beginnings. The fragrance of lavender was sweet as it trailed behind her. At alters cusp stood father and daughter. The Jennings women silenced their music. Mary lifted her head upward to see Thomas standing in awe of her beauty.

From one man, one is given to another. The one who loved her in birth to another who would love her in death. And so, weaves the story of life, of celebration and of loss. Each generation handing off the story lines to the next.

Reverend Richard began the ceremony. "Those who stand before us have professed their love before family and friends. Do those of you who have come to witness their union know of any reason why these two should not be joined together speak your mind now," spoke the Reverend. The congregation held silent. "Very well then," as he looked at Rebecca seated beside Squire. "By the power of God and the Crown's authority I pronounce these two as husband and wife. You may kiss the bride young man," spoke the Reverend in relief.

Thomas lifted the veil as if he were looking upon her for the first time. Her eyes widened and he felt his heart skip a beat. He took a deep breath and brought his face close to hers. She wrapped her arms around him holding tight to her bouquet. The two kissed and held the pose for nearly a minute. Rebecca sprung up from the pew and stomped out of the church before they broke their embrace.

The two released their hold and received applause from the guests as they started down the aisle. They thanked each one for their attendance and well wishes. Reverend Richard reminded everyone that the reception would commence at the inn.

CHAPTER 31

The bride and groom arrived at the inn for their wedding reception. The few guest that could attend filed in to share with the newlyweds. Some could not stay long for the journey home would be difficult because of the snow. The celebration was alive with everyone sharing in the celebration with plenty of food and ale for everyone.

The young maidens who dreamed of their own wedding one day clustered around Mary, much to Mary's delight. The maidens blushed with their questions and giggled at some of Mary's replies.

Gifts were left at the bridle table. Some were hankies tied together with ribbon holding coins. Handmade crafts for decorating the new home and one beautiful grapevine wreath left earlier from Mildred.

Squire Andrew stepped up to the couple and took the hand of each. He looked at them and said, "As long as the breath comes into me, I will always give you position and wage. You need not ever worry about comfort. I will sponsor you through life so that you will prosper together." Mary was comforted by his words and stepped closer to Squire. She gave him a kiss on the cheek and said, "Your generosity and kindness is the greatest gift we shall ever receive. I thank you sir for all you do."

"Thomas, I will give you three days leisure to consummate your marriage. Soon I will travel to London and make the arrangements needed to contract a publishing agreement of our liking. It should profit us well beyond our present position. I would ask you to keep an eye out for Rebecca while I'm away," said Squire. Mary perked up and said, "We'd love to look after Rebecca while your away. It would be our delight." "Very well then. When I return, we must be ready to work diligently. This could lead to other fortuity," said Squire.

A strange noise was heard from outside. Edward and Jonathan walked to the door to find the source. When Edward opened the door, he came face to face with Jack and Helen Danbury and the infant Lily wrapped in a blanket. They were shivering from the cold as others stood behind them. They were of the woodland people.

Edward and Jonathan knew the Danbury's well. Some years ago, each helped the other in building their homes. Jack was a gifted carpenter who loved to sing while he worked. Helen helped deliver Thomas when he was born. They were not strangers to anyone present. Now they stood before friends as uninvited guests to share in the celebration of their children's fortune.

"Come in! Please come in out of the cold you two and those who are with you. Please come in and join us," spoke Edward. Slowly the Danbury's entered and looked around at the people and the table fare on display.

Those who followed them entered cautiously. They were well aware of the towns people's attitude towards them. They huddled together for warmth but mainly from a sense of protection.

These people who lived in the woods were often blamed for things they had no investment in. Some of the church goers were convinced that God was punishing them for their sins. The Roses and the Sonnets knew that Jack and Helen had done no wrong. Perhaps the same could be said about the others also.

"Please join us in celebration and friendship to mark this day forever in our memories and in our hearts," said Jonathan. Lydia and Diane saw Helen and ran over to her. They hugged and kissed their old friend that had been away much too long. "Thomas, come over here and meet your godmother and godfather. She delivered you into this world. She was the first to lay hands on you," shouted Diane. Thomas approached the group when he recognized Helen. "I saw you that day on the road when you delivered your baby. I was there!" said Thomas. Helen laughed and said, "I hope it wasn't too much for you to see." "Oh no, I found it impressing," replied Thomas.

Helen Clayborne entered the dining room to see what the excitement was about. When she saw the woodland people, she immediately protested their presence. "Get them out of here!" shouted Helen. Diane was quick to calm her. "We have more than enough food for everyone, and the fire burns bright to give more heat than we need. Could we not extend our bounty to others who are in such dire need of nourishment and compassion? It's Mary's wedding day and they have come to share in the joy. I beseech you Helen, just for today, let us welcome our guests under your roof and in your blessing."

Helen stood silent as she looked at the woodlanders. In mind she was shifting her objection. Diane's plea had opened the gate of her heart. "They can stay but no one can lodge here for the night unless I get six pence for a bed," said Helen. With that said the group broke from their huddle. Some walked to the fireplace to ward off the cold while others stood before the buffet table.

The Clayborne sons entered from the side door carrying the roasted pig as the steam rolled off the carcass from the winter air. They carried it to the main table and sat it down for all to see. Never had such an animal received so much adoration than this one. Helen came from the kitchen carrying a large pot of boiled potatoes and other vegetables. She dumped its contents around the pig then placed a large knife and fork in the pig's hind quarter.

"Who amongst you men will do the honors of serving?" asked Helen. The men looked around at each other, but no one spoke up. "I will," spoke Jack Danbury. "I would consider it an honor to serve such kind people who have opened up their hearts to us."

One by one the line began to form at the table so each one could receive a generous portion. Adults and children alike began to open up to the fortune bestowed before them. The conversations were many, the laughter contagious as everyone took pleasure in company and food. It was more like a Christmas celebration than a wedding reception. Some were gifted with a new presence, while others were gifted with warmth and food. Everyone, rich and poor, healthy, and ill were all one in this celebration. Their stories of life were shared as each gained insight of the others point of view and witness.

Thomas took the hankies holding coins given as wedding gifts and gave the same to Helen Clayborne. "Here is the coin for those who wish to sleep here tonight out of the cold. You said six pence for a bed. Would two pence buy a nights rest on a warm floor?" asked Thomas. Helen looked at the offering he held in his hand and was moved by his charity. "Very well Thomas. I accept your offer. You have the good wit of business about you and a large heart. So be it son. So it be," as she giggled and walked away.

All things under heaven are possible. All things above heaven await one and all. There is no mystery to life, nor to love or creation. Mystery only exists for those who have not yet reached deep enough or far enough.

Hoist your sail when the wind favors you. Never look back on the past and its hardships in regret. They were the lessons that brought the wind to your sail and the opportunities you now witness at your feet.

All the stories had been exhausted amongst those who came to celebrate. The children were asleep with their heads in the laps of their parents. The wedding party had retired to their rooms. The heat from the fireplace was nothing but red embers rendering the last portion of its light. Not a pint of ale remained in cask nor scrap of food found. The crumbs scattered about, allowed the inn's mice to also partake in the celebration. It was a time for sleep and a time to reflect in dreams.

CHAPTER 32

Today's sunrise brings with it a new dawn for these families and a new direction for everyone it touches. The poor and homeless of the Danbury community awoke this morning on a warm floor. Their bellies did not disturb their slumber from being empty. For they had dined as kings and queens, princes, and princesses.

Edward and Diane have a new daughter, Jonathan, and Lydia a new son. Thomas has a wife and Mary, a prized husband with a baby on the way.

The aroma of food was still in the air as the occupants of the inn began to stir. Jack Danbury stoked the fireplace adding more wood to the embers. Helen was breast feeding Lily and humming a song under her breath. Her humming excited Lily as the little one held her eyes to mother. A gentle tear rolled down Helen's cheek and landed on Lily's forehead. Lily blinked then smiled at her mother.

Helen Clayborne rose earlier than normal that morning. She was so moved by Thomas' charity she decided to offer some of her own. She baked rolls, lots of rolls for the woodlanders to carry as they left. She stood by the door as they gathered themselves to leave. Some were sad to leave the comfort of the inn. Others accepted their plight and entered the cold air in embrace. Each had a story, their reason for this way of life.

Edward descended the stairs when he saw Jack and Helen huddled in one corner of the room, seated on the floor. They'd hope not to be noticed by the inn keeper to stay warm as long as they could for Lily's sake. Edward walked to the couple and Jack stood to shake his hand. Helens eyes turned upward at Edward as if looking for help or better yet a miracle.

Diane was coming down the staircase singing a song form her childhood. She was pleased with the wedding and the reception. She saw Helen sitting on the floor holding Lily. She ran over to the two and helped her up. "May I have the joy of cradling your little one?" whispered Diane. Helen nodded her head and Diane held Lily with the tenderness of care. Diane began singing her song to Lily as she danced and swayed across the floor. Lily would giggle and kick her legs at Diane's antics. Edward couldn't help thinking that this was prelude once Mary's child was delivered.

Helen Clayborne was in the kitchen clanging her pots and pans. This was the way she made her music. She was preparing a grand breakfast for the wedding party, a breakfast to remember.

Jonathan and Lydia came down together and sat with the others. Helen Clayborne and her son entered the room carrying a tray of food. They placed it on the table where everyone could partake in the offering. The tray was lined with portage, bacon, and loaves of fresh baked bread, and cheese. There were cakes topped with apples and honey. Tea was served with the meal as everyone busied themselves with food and conversation.

Lydia was staring off as she looked at Lily in Diane' arms. Lydia stood from her seat and walked over to Diane. Gently she took Lily from her and held the child to her face. Lydia closed her eyes and a great smile appeared on her face. She kissed Lily on the nose that made the baby giggle as she squirmed in Lydia's embrace.

Lydia sat down at a table away from the others. She was feeling motherhood all over again. She had lost two sons in death and a daughter to marriage. Holding the baby was a salve to heal some old and fresh wounds that she beard in her soul. She was tearing up and trying her best not to cry. Diane and Helen watched Lydia and moved to her to offer comfort. The three held one another as Lily looked on. Where love and compassion meet nothing else may enter.

Footsteps were descending the staircase. It was the newlyweds holding hands. They offered greetings to all as they sat down. William and Stacy Clayborne brought the couple their breakfast tray. It held fried pork, boiled eggs, cheddar cheese and cakes drizzled with honey.

Helen Clayborne entered carrying a pot of tea. She looked at the newlyweds and said, "Enjoy the first meal of the first day the two of you will walk together as one. Your parents are proud of you. You carry their prayers wherever you go. Give them praise for what they have given you and live in God's peace."

Helen's words touched everyone present. The men continued speaking strong words while the women doted over Lily as if all three were her mother.

The married couple had gone silent within. The gravity of their union was entering into a new realization. All the plans they made for their union had transpired. It was a grand success with a few pleasant surprises mixed in. "Now what?" they thought. They would have their three days to honeymoon. Mary would go off to live with Diane and Edward awaiting the birth of their child. Thomas would return to the print shop to work for Squire. "What then?" they thought.

The meal was nearly completed. The newlywed couple stood and hugged everyone still seated. Helen Danbury asked the couple if she could have the remaining boiled eggs so she could give better milk for the baby. "Yes, please take all the eggs and whatever else you want," said Thomas.

Lydia jumped up from the table startling everyone. "Jack and Helen, you are coming home with me and Jonathan! Yes, that's perfect. You can move into Mary's room. That way you and the baby can have shelter from the winter. We can work something out in the spring. Jonathan, you need help on the farm with Chad passing away. Yes, that will work well, and Helen can help me when our child comes into this world. Yes, that's how it will be," said Lydia as she paced back and forth still holding Lily.

Edward and the others stood with their mouths open at Lydia's display. Lydia never gave them a look. She wasn't concerned with what anyone thought about her decision. To her it was a forgone conclusion. "I'm going upstairs to pack. Jonathan, you get the horse and wagon ready. We're going home and Jack and Helen are going with us," spoke Lydia as she raced up the stairs.

Everyone returned to what was left of the meal. Helen filled her purse with the eggs. Jack and Jonathan left the inn to ready the wagon. Edward followed them as he too prepared to leave. The families were leaving earlier than planned. No one held the mind to challenge Lydia or her plans. Thomas and Mary donned their coats and set out for Squire's to pay him a visit before he left for London.

Everyone was gone from the dining table except Helen holding Lily. Helen was struggling as Lydia's words were sinking in. She wondered what could have moved her to decide the things she did. No one objected her or even dared to.

She looked down at Lily. Lily was smiling at her mother and gave her a tiny wink as if she knew something that had escaped the awareness of the adults.

Something that could not be pointed at or held in hand had entered and intervened on behalf of another from a place called love.

CHAPTER 33

The group assembled outside the inn. Hugs and well wishes were exchanged with a few plans mixed in. One by one they mounted their wagons to begin the journey home. Nothing would ever be the same for these people. Everyone had a new beginning to embrace as they crossed another threshold of mortal experience.

A young man lied beside a beautiful woman on her bed on a day not so long ago. The innocence of his youth coupled with developing hormones brought him to discover the pleasures of physical exchange with another. All of which brought everyone present to this point in time and space together.

The wagons were moving off to their respective homes. The snow was melting as fast as it fell opening roads once impassible. Thomas and Mary watched them as the wagons were nearly out of sight. Lydia stood up in the wagon, turned around to look at the couple holding a blank stare.

Thomas felt his feelings for her rise up. Lydia appeared to project that she was leaving but it was not goodbye. He would always remain in her heart and she in his. The way of the world and the way of the heart would fight many battles before this journey of life was completed and a rightful ending written.

Thomas and Mary started towards Squire home walking in silence. The sky above them was clear and the suns light was melting the snow and ice giving the day a look of transition. As they approached Squire's home, they saw Stacy Clayborne loading Squire's wagon for his trip to London. Squire saw the couple coming and ran out to meet them.

"There you are. And how are the newlyweds this fine morning? Are you ready to go to work Thomas? Are you ready to have the sound of coins jingle in your pockets?" inquired Squire. "Yes Squire, I am ready for the task. If only I could travel with you to London," said Thomas. "You will Sir Thomas, you will soon enough. But first we must make our mark on those who possess such wealth that they find us worthy. Come, let us enter the shop so I can show you what must be done while I'm away," said Squire.

The three entered the shop and joined Rebecca who was listening to the conversation from the doorway. Thomas and Squire went into the back of the shop while Rebecca and Mary remained in the front. They gave each other a cold hug and sat for tea. Rebecca poured each cup and passed one to Mary. They stared at one another sizing the other up.

"So, what is your plans as far as your living conditions?" asked Rebecca. Mary was not pleased with the present arrangement of living with Thomas's parents while he spent six days in Rebecca's company. She knew Rebecca was baiting her and she did not like it. "I'll be staying with Thomas's parents while he prepares for our future together," replied Mary as she smiled at Rebecca.

Rebecca was well aware of Mary's situation. She wanted nothing more than to goat Mary. This was Rebecca's game. "Well, I want you to know that while you are away living with his parents, I will look after his needs while he sleeps in the shop. I promise to take good care of him," spoke Rebecca in a teasing tone.

The smile on Mary's face fell away and was replaced by a sinister look. Rebecca returned the gesture by giving Mary a pleasant smile. Rebecca knew she had Mary right where she wanted her. Rebecca stood from her chair and gently began to rub her belly and looked at Mary. "Why you never know. There might be more babies going around besides yours and your mothers," taunted Rebecca.

Mary's anger went from passive to full blown rage. She rose from her chair and grabbed Rebecca by the hair and the two went crashing to the floor. Rebecca was screaming for help while Mary was attempting to remove Rebecca's head from her shoulders. Thomas and Squire entered the room to see the two engaged in full combat. Thomas tried to pull Mary from Rebecca, but Mary wasn't letting go. When he pulled on Mary, Rebecca's head came with her causing more pain. The harder Thomas pulled the tighter Mary held on to Rebecca's hair. "Alright you two! That's enough! Mary let go her hair right now and stop this before you injure the child you're carrying," yelled Squire. Mary heard him and released her.

Rebecca was still screaming and kicking. She turned toward Mary and thrusted her knee into Mary's stomach knocking her breath away. Mary panicked because she could not speak or breath. Once her breath returned, she began weeping without pause.

Thomas held her in his arms to shield any further assaults form Rebecca. Squire reached down and lifted Rebecca from the floor. "Upstairs daughter. You go upstairs and do not come down until I tell you so," said Squire.

Rebecca's face carried no remorse for her actions. She was wearing a look of satisfaction. As Rebecca stood at the staircase she turned and looked directly at Thomas. She gave him a smile then a wink. He knew Rebecca would always have power over Mary. She would also have power over him. Thomas feared for his wellbeing under Squire's care and direction. He feared dismissal from his position since blood runs thicker than water.

This single event would bring about an outcome no one could have ever predicted. This moment was in the hands of the potter and his wheel as he crafted the clay into form. The wheel of life spun round and round never revealing what fashion the clay would become. Who could know? "No one," spoke the voice of destiny as it lurked in the shadows of what is to be.

Thomas held Mary as she continued to weep. She was curled in a fetal position holding her womb. He felt compassion for his bride as he gently stroked her hair. It helped to her to calm, and the crying ceased. "My belly hurts where she kicked me," whimpered Mary. "If you can get up, we can return to the inn and you can rest until you feel yourself again," replied Thomas.

Squire was moved from the couple's display. "I want you both to go to the inn until I have spoken to Rebecca about what has happened here. I apologize for this shameful display. I trust you are well enough to make it back to the inn Mary?" inquired Squire. "Yes, I'm sure I'm okay. Thank you for your concern, Squire," replied Mary.

Once at the inn Thomas opened the door to allow Mary to enter. His arm was around her as Mary held her belly. "Here, what's this I see? Mary why are you in pain child? What has happened?" asked Helen. "Mary and Rebecca took to argument and tussled about. Mary was kicked by Rebecca and she's still feeling pain," replied Thomas. Helen dropped her broom and came running to Mary. "Here child sit and take rest while I get you some buttermilk. It will help ease the pain and settle the nest that lives in you.

If the likes of Rebecca Beckett shows her face here, she'll kiss the wrong end of my broomstick. I'll clean the very floor we stand on with the dress she's wearing while she's still in it," proclaimed Helen. She went to the kitchen to fetch the buttermilk.

The front door of the inn opened. Squire stepped through wearing a troubled face. He walked over to the couple with caring eyes. "How are you, Mary? Are you feeling any ease at all?" Mary nodded her head, yes.

"I've decided it's best to take Rebecca with me to London to live with her aunt for a while. Since the ruckus she confessed to some things that are very disturbing. One that I'm afraid best not revealed until some changes have taken place.

For now, the shop and living quarters are yours to use until my return. I only ask that you use Mary's room for sleeping and partaking in marital practice. Thomas, you ready the shop as I showed you before. I will return in a few weeks. Then we will start at our trade. Together we will show all that we are the publishers that can deliver the goods! God's love to the both of you."

Thomas watched as Squire walked through the inn and opened the door. The bright light from the sun and its reflection from the snow, turned Squire's form to a shadow figure. Just like when Mary and Jonathan entered the church.

"How many doors does one person open in a lifetime? How many thresholds are crossed that never return one back to the same? Do the doors of life bring about change to render one to glory and another to defeat? Is not one person's glory set through the defeat of another? Who or what decides which? Is it chance or the toss of a coin?" thought Thomas. Perhaps tomorrow will tell.

CHAPTER 34

Yesterday's wind blew the first breath of spring across the landscape. Some of the wild flowers of the field were poking their tiny colored heads above the blades of grass. They appeared like little trumpets announcing the coming of spring as they awoke from their winter's nap.

The woodland children took notice of springs arrival as they played in the fields. The girls were picking flowers to make bouquets to make as gifts to one another. Some even imagined their wedding day as they fashioned the bouquets with the grandest of care.

The boys were running about pretending to be soldiers fighting in gallant battle. They held sticks in hand and fought as if they were swords. If outnumbered or defeat appeared certain, the swords became blunderbuss, and a few volleys would render them the victors in battle.

The woodland birds were singing new songs of love to attract the fairest of the females. It was spring, a time for renewal, a time to make amends. All to support the cycle of life and prosperity for all held in witness. The realm of nature revealing time through observable events as they evolved.

The woodland children and the birds held something in common. Neither had a pocket to hold a single possession from one moment to the next. Their reality, their livelihood was dependent to the present moment, free of worry or strife. To them, this day, every day, was written for life and carried in heart.

A similar story was held in another great book of life. A rabbi informed his followers that access to heaven could only be given to those who had no pockets, no worry, or earthly concerns. The entry to heaven was made through the mind and heart of a child.

Some believe that access to heaven is achieved through ritual, creed, and obedience to dogmatic practice. Such practice is void of passion and internal inspiration for some.

One must ride the rainbow in all its colors from one end of the spectrum to the other. Only then can final rest be realized and held in heart for evermore.

Squire's arrival was long overdue. He was sending letters keeping everyone informed of the progress being made. He'd hope to arrive back to Danbury within a week. Negotiations were going slow due to commerce and civil unrest in France and Germany.

All the while, Mary had remained in town with Thomas at the print shop. The news of Squires return meant that it was time for her to take up residency at the Sonnet home.

The couple hired Stacy Clayborne to deliver Mary to the Sonnet home. Mary packed her belongings carefully. She wanted everything to be as proper as possible. She would miss her life in town but looked forward to being with Diane. She admired her and her concern for the precious things in life.

Diane had gone to great lengths in preparing the home for the new arrivals. She kept Edward busy preparing everything to make Mary feel like their home was her home also. The furniture in the house had to be rearranged three times before Diane was satisfied. She was looking forward to being a grandmother and having a daughter under roof.

The couple mounted the wagon with all Mary' belongings aboard. Stacy turned the wagon and set it towards the Sonnet home.

Thomas's mind was on Squire's business in London. He constantly worried about the work Squire spoke of. He was counting on the wages to advance his family. He was also thinking of Lydia.

He wondered if things would be different between, he and Lydia given the elapse of time since they last saw each other. The closer the wagon neared the homestead, the stronger the wonder grew.

The Sonnet's home was in sight. Diane was alongside the road waving at them on their approach. Diane was so happy to see them. She clasped her hands together and pressed her lips tight as not to cry from joy. Finally her daughter had come home to roost. Soon she'd have a grand baby to love and care for.

She ran to the wagon stopping it before it could come along the house. She reached upwards to Mary and helped her down. She cried out when she saw how much Mary was showing. She embraced Mary with hugs and kisses while engaged in conversation. She shuffled Mary to the house without acknowledging Thomas or Stacy. Thomas stood up in the wagon as he watched the two disappear around the corner of the house. He stood in disbelief of what happened.

Diane reappeared from the corner of the house. "Hello son. Be a good son and bring Mary's belongings to the house. Put them in your old room," shouted Diane as if Thomas were deaf. "We'd better do as she says or else, we may never hear the end of it," said Thomas to Stacy.

They carried Mary' belongings in the house and delivered them to Thomas's old room. Thomas was surprised as he entered his room. It had been painted white and the walls were decorated with care. Mildred's wedding gift wreath hung over the headboard. Beside the bed was a rocking cradle for the new arrival. Edward made it special for mother and child. The reality of fatherhood was coming into Thomas' focus. Excitement and fear all rolled into one emotion.

Diane walked in the room with Mary. Mary cried in joy seeing the room look so charming. She went straight to the cradle and rocked it back and forth as if the baby were already in it. Mary turned to face the others in the room. She was overwhelmed with joy. The reality of her situation was deepening for her also. Never had Thomas seen his mother so wrapped in joy and love. Never had he seen Mary as beautiful as she stood before him right now.

There was a special light in the room not visible to the occupants that gave off a silvery white glow. Wherever two or more gather together in the awe of love the light appears and bestows its blessings.

The cradle of destiny lurked quietly in the shadows of their witness. There is nothing in the journey of life that is haphazard or dependent on luck or chance. All things are chiseled in stone and all things of creation can be found within. It's all there, the beginnings and endings, the sorrows and joy. Each one drank from the same chalice of life.

Mary stepped to Diane and placed her arms around her. She held Diane with the deepest of love. Diane returned the same and the two began to cry a little. It was too much for Stacy and he left the room and then the house.

"Oh, what spell is this we call love. Where spoken or written word fails to transcend its power or its mystery? From what cloud above, does this thing called love fall to earth? Be it to strengthen one who lies in defeat? So, I will yield to its nature and its sight it bears on me. Therefore, to what I cannot conquer I must surrender to completely without reserve or hesitation," thought Thomas as he slowly moved from the room.

Mary and Diane left the room and made their way to the table in the middle of the kitchen. Thomas was already seated. The three sat quietly mulling over their thoughts. Edward entered the house breaking the silence. "And how is my son and daughter on this fine day before us?" he spoke. He hugged Mary first then walked over to Thomas and placed his hands on his shoulders.

He rubbed his shoulders and said, "It's a proud time for me on this day and all to come. I've watched you grow from a seedling to a strong oak. You bless your mother and me with the child Mary holds in her womb. Soon I will wear the mantle of grandfather. I can't tell you how strong that sits with me. I love you both. Mary, I remember the day you were born. You had a full head of hair and eyes ever so blue."

"Your words honor me sir. And the cradle you made for the child to come is a welcomed gift. I will always cherish it," said Mary. "Please child, call me father and sir no more. You are my daughter. Your child is my child for it carries the flesh of my flesh. Before this child can sing, Diane will have lavished it and you with more gifts than one could count," replied Edward.

"Oh! The baby just kicked me! That hurt. She must have heard you. Wait! How do I know it's a girl? Oh, dear Lord, could it be? Oh, how I have prayed for a daughter to hold and cherish," spoke Mary as she looked at those around her.

Diane was thrilled to hear Mary's words, trying desperately to restrain her enthusiasm. "A daughter comes to my door and brings me a granddaughter? How more blessed could one person be?" she thought. Diane had never felt such joy in all her days. "We are family today because of the treasure you hold within you Mary. Soon the little one will open its eyes to this world and all of us will be there to greet the child. Have you chosen the child's name yet?" asked Diane. "Yes, mother I have. If it's a boy his name will be William. If it be a girl, we will call her Lucille. It means light in French. Diane clasped her hands together and pulled them to her face to once again restrain her excitement.

There was a knock at the door. Edward opened it and there stood Jonathan and Lydia, Jack and Helen Danbury and Lily. The room was filled with greetings, hugs, and kisses. Mary made her way to Lydia. Both were showing the grandness of pregnancies as they stood beside each other. Mother and daughter managed an embrace and kiss which everyone applauded. Little Lily was smiling and pointing at the two giving some sort of baby talk at the top of her voice. It had everyone laughing which encouraged Lily to continue.

Diane was ready to burst when she walked to Helen with her arms open to receive Lily. Helen went to hand the child off when Lily reached for Diane while kicking her feet. Diane held the child to her shoulder with her eyes closed swaying back and forth.

Lily looked at Diane and offered more baby talk. No one knew what the child was trying to say. Diane just pretended to understand the child. Lily ceased her talk and reached for Diane's lips. She pulled on them trying to make Diane talk. Diane was so moved from the little one that she began to tear. One by one the tears began to roll down her face. Lily watched as each one roll down Diane's face. Lily leaned her face to Diane's and gave her a kiss. All noticed the exchange between Diane and Lily and were moved by it. Lily loved the attention, and everyone was ready to give her all they had. The child had the attention of the room because the child had touched into the love each held within as it spilled outward to the room.

The women began preparing the meal to celebrate their union and the strength of family and friends. The men took turns holding Lily, much to her delight. The women started singing an old Gaelic tune they learned from their mothers. Everyone was participating in the gift of sharing and the gift of life. It was a time and a place to remember.

CHAPTER 35

The morning found Thomas waking in the print shop of Squire Andrew. He had left home yesterday with Mary in good hands. The good Squire was due back any day now with supplies and news from London.

Thomas wondered if Rebecca would return with him to Danbury or remain in London. He knew her presence at the shop would only bring about trouble and worry to Mary. He would miss Rebecca' energy and attention she gave him. No one ever experienced a boring day if their path crossed Rebecca's. In spite of her rebellious spirit, there was something very special about her. Something she held inside herself for no one to see.

He prepared hot tea for the mornings start and would eventually have his breakfast at the Stagg Inn. He so enjoyed Helen Clayborne's care and cooking. She took a shine to young Thomas and the innocence of his nature. Helen cared for young Thomas the way a mother cares for their child.

For reasons unknown, the stars were realigning to create a mesh of new understanding. The stars shifted as did the hearts of pilgrims who walked the earth. Scattered they were across the planet in every land and in every language. Their light appeared as fireflies on a warm summer's night. From above their lights appeared as one connected in common purpose. The stillness in their heart had been awakened. They were bringing a new light to the world as promised in the beginning. Many more would follow them in time to carry the will of all that is.

Thomas entered the Stagg Inn. The air was full of the aroma of Helen cooking. He could hear her singing from the kitchen. She was a lover of life and a lover of family. To her, all were family. "I hear you son. Sit and warm yourself by the fire while I finish your meal. It will be good times when Squire returns with pockets full of coins for all to share," bellowed Helen.

Thomas removed his coat and sat beside the fireplace. His mind wandered off as he contemplated his future. He was aware that all roads to fulfill his desires would come through his association with Squire and the print shop. He wanted more than an honest living and family to care for. What he wanted could not be found within the confines of Danbury. The realization gave him worry.

Helen entered the dining area carrying enough food for two people. She placed it before him and sat across from him. "That breakfast should last you well into midday," said Helen. Thomas looked on her with gratitude and smiled.

"You're a man now Thomas and soon to be a father to Mary's baby. The will of the Lord you have, Thomas. I can see it all around you. You won't be long for us here in Danbury. One day you'll leave to seek what you cannot find here. Oh, you will come to visit us, you will. But never to stay. You will walk two paths in this life. One of need and one of desire. There will be much to gain and much to shed.

If you listen to your innermost voice, you will never be lost. It is the compass that lives in us all. If you listen to the voices around you, you will fall away from the things that are precious to mind and heart in this life.

Always be kind, even to the dark ones of life. They too must fulfill their journey as it was written for them. Walk in kindness and you will never have to look over your shoulder.

Beware of the beauties and their ways. They will come to drink your wine until it is gone, but never to work in your vineyard to produce more.

You will go far and remembered for your words that live in you. They will not know your heart or your thoughts. Nor will they know who you loved or who loved you. Only you will know, and only you will carry the rewards and burdens of your choices.

You are the testament of your life. It is you who will sow the seeds of today that brings the harvest of the morrows. You have been awakened, never to fall back into the dream of illusion and its play on the mind. Pave the way for others to follow so they too may find the light within.

Now eat and walk from here with your eyes opened to face whatever this day brings forth," spoke Helen with the light of a soothsayer.

Thomas ate as her words were sinking in. He was unaware Helen held such insight. Helen excused herself and returned to the kitchen. He was ready to begin another day with her message at heart. He finished his meal and prepared to leave. He opened the door and turned toward the kitchen and said, "Thank you Helen for all you give and all you do. God Bless." Helen did not respond as she usually did. Thomas thought she had left the kitchen to fetch more wood, so he left.

This would be the last time Thomas would see Helen in her usual way. Her son Stacy will soon find her crumbled on the floor of the kitchen still holding a wooden spoon in her hand and without breath.

Thomas entered the print shop with the savvy of a man ready for success. He serviced the printing press and did the sweeping. There came a commotion from outside. There was the approach of horse's hooves and the creaking of an old worn out wagon. "Squire!" thought Thomas.

He rushed out the door in a hurry. He tripped over his own feet and fell to the ground. Squire let out a loud string of laughter at the display. "Miss me did you young Thomas? And this is the way you greet your benefactor? Come here lad so I can see how much you've grown since I left." Thomas regained himself and stepped humbly to Squire. "Come closer Thomas for I have missed my apprentice and my young friend. He hugged Thomas as a father would hug a son.

"I have wonderful news that will offer a new shape of things to come. Come see the contents of the wagon and the future it holds. You and I will be busy for the weeks to come. Careful we must be about our business, not to speak too loudly. There are those who would bring harm to our souls and our bodies if they knew our business at hand," spoke Squire in a soft tone.

Together they viewed the contents. There were stacks of paper bound in leather. Enough ink and type to print a hundred books. There were binding materials to produce books rather than the pamphlets he was used to. There was a case with type of decorative designs and insignias.

"What is this Squire?" asked Thomas. "It holds all that we need to print and make the books from. It is our future and our fortune dear lad. We are going to turn your living quarters into the book binding area. You will take over Rebecca's room permanently as your living quarters. She will not be returning anytime soon. Her affairs are in London now with my sister Kate.

You will accompany me to London once we have filled the order at contract. I will introduce you to our benefactors. It is important that you become a figure in this endeavor. There will be times when you will make the deliveries to London without my guidance. So, unload the wagon while I visit Helen to settle the bill for the care, she gave you," spoke Squire.

Thomas did as Squire requested. He gathered up his meager belongings and took them upstairs to Rebecca' room. He could feel change in the air. His sleeping arrangement had been elevated. Thomas laid across his new bed and found it comfortable. It was kind to his body, and he took joy knowing this was his to sleep on.

He heard a noise and thinking it was Squire, he sprung from the bed to his feet. He looked up and there stood Helen Clayborne staring at him. At first, he was startled. 'What brings you to the shop Helen?" asked Thomas. "Do you remember what I told you about this morning at the inn?" replied Helen. "Yes, yes I remember Helen. The words still ring with me," replied Thomas.

"Good! I'm going away for a while. How long I don't know but I do know that you and I will see each other again. I love you Thomas, like a son I love you. You be a good husband and father to your children.

You be a good provider for Lydia and her children too. She will need your support when Jonathan leaves this world for the next. And most of all Thomas be good to yourself.

There will be those who will come to you pretending to befriend you. Their hearts are filled with deception and corruption. They come to steal your gift and profit from it. Listen to their words carefully and you will know their hearts. They walk with the dark ones.

Travel on the wind Thomas and never look back. They are calling me to go with them. I must go now. Goodbye dear child. You will always live in Helen's heart." As quickly as she appeared she disappeared.

Thomas wasn't sure what had just happened. It was almost like when Chad appeared to him, but he was asleep then. Thomas ran down the stairs to catch a glimpse of Helen. He looked in every direction, but she was nowhere to be seen. Thomas ran towards the inn thinking she would be there. He rounded the corner and saw people standing outside the inn. Some were crying and holding each other.

A chill came over him. Something was wrong. "What happened?!" he thought. He could hear John Clayborne yelling and weeping from inside the inn. Thomas stopped running and slowed his approach to the inn.

He entered the inn and saw Stacy holding his brother who appeared to have collapsed. Thomas thought he was about to cry and didn't know why. Slowly he walked to the door that led into the kitchen. He saw John on the floor holding Helen in his arms. He was rocking her body back and forth. He kept calling out her name as he wept without end.

"How could Helen returned so quick to the inn and suddenly die?" he wondered as he looked upon her lifeless body. He looked up and there stood Helen's ghost staring down at John holding her body. Then she looked up at Thomas and smiled. Without moving her lips, she spoke to Thomas and said, "This is why we are here, to build love from within and nurture the growth that comes through the trials of life. We weep because we believe that it was lost with a passing. Love never dies nor do we. It lives on and so do we."

Helen turned her back on Thomas and joined some friends that were waiting on her. She turned back towards Thomas and gave him a wink carried by the warmest of a smile. She returned to her friends and the group slowly disappeared through the wall.

Thomas turned to exit the room. He knew John had to grieve the loss alone. He entered the dining room and saw some of towns people offering comfort to Helens sons. He stepped outside and asked if anyone had seen Squire. "He's off to fetch the Reverend and his wife to aid John in his loss. Then he was going to find Jack Turner to prepare a grave for Helen' body," spoke a voice from the crowd.

Thomas spotted Squire stepping behind the rectory. He called out to him, but Squire continued. Thomas raced to catch him, but Squire had disappeared without a trace. Thomas decided to return to the shop thinking he might find Squire there.

Thomas was nearing the shop. He saw a man dressed in a military uniform. He wore a red coat with gold stitching. His slacks were grey with a black stripe down the side. His boots rode high, almost to the knee. He had the look of an educated man in manner. His horse was one of the finest Thomas had ever seen. The man began knocking on the door of the shop.

"May I help you sir?" asked Thomas. The man turned and looked at Thomas still bewildered from the latest event. "Surely you are not the purveyor of this establishment that I was told about, are you?" asked the soldier in a condescending tone.

"No sir I am not. I am the apprentice to this shop. Squire Andrew Beckett is the purveyor sir," replied Thomas. "Very well then, where might I find the Squire, apprentice?" asked the soldier "I couldn't rightly say sir. You see there has been a death at the Stagg Inn at the towns center. It was the owner's wife of many years. Perhaps you will find the Squire there" replied Thomas.

"Very well. I had planned on lodging there for a period anyway. Tell me apprentice, how will I know this Squire?" asked the soldier. "He's a tall man sir with a full belly and caring eyes," replied Thomas. "If I miss him, please inform him that I have a business proposition for him in the crowns name. Do you understand apprentice?" asked the soldier. "Yes sir, I do understand," replied Thomas. The soldier mounted his horse and rode away towards the inn.

Thomas entered the shop to put away the supplies Squire brought from London. A knock came at the door. It was Jack Turner, the towns handyman. "How much wood will you be needing this week, Thomas?" asked Jack. "A rick will do just fine Jack. Please don't bother bringing any inside. We are going to rearrange things as soon as Squire returns. I hear tell you are digging a grave for Helen?" "Yes, my oldest son is digging her resting place as we speak. A nice spot we chose for her too. There's room for John when he's ready to join her. I'll deliver the rick tomorrow or the next if we don't hit too many rocks digging the grave," spoke Jack.

Thomas walked Jack to the door and saw Squire approaching. His face was down, and he was wiping away tears. He had always been close to John and Helen. Helen was his cousin on his mother's side. Squire placed a shilling in Thomas' hand and said, "Go to the inn and fetch me a firkin of ale. Leave the shilling in John's pocket without saying a word."

"There was a man here to see you. I think he was a soldier," spoke Thomas. "Yes, I met him and heard his proposition. I told him I needed time to grieve my loss and he understood. So run along and fill my request. I cannot bear to undergo what must come with a sober mind and heavy heart," said Squire.

More people had gathered at the inn. Some were admiring the soldier's horse that was tied to a post outside the inn. There were small groups of people about going inside and out. Some came to honor Helen and offer their sympathies to John. Others were huddled in selecting a new wife for John. They were the towns matchmakers.

Thomas felt their efforts were disrespectful given that Helen had yet to be buried. But that was the way of these townspeople. Whether it be the arrow of cupid or the good intentions of sound people, John would need a wife and the boys would need a stepmother. There is a time for every purpose under heaven.

CHAPTER 36

Yesterday's wake for Helen was visited by most in town and some from the countryside. This morning was quiet and somber. Some were gathered outside the inn to join the procession to the cemetery. Some gathered at the gravesite awaiting her body. The woodland people waited near the cemetery amongst the trees. The funeral procession was about to begin.

Edward built a proper coffin for Helen. The coffin held her body as it rested on the wagon. John and his sons held each other one more time before stepping outside to take the walk behind the wagon that carried the body of one, they so loved and cherished.

An assembly formed waiting on John and the boys to exit the inn. Two members of the Rosenheim family came to play music for the procession to the cemetery. Patti played the flute and sang like an angel. Her brother Thom played the lute. They began playing their songs as friends and family waited on John and the boys.

John, Stacy, and William left the inn together and joined the others at the wagon. They were met with empathy and kindness. Soft conversation and gentle weeping were the only sounds about. Edward stepped to the horse hitched to the wagon. He took hold of the halter and led along the road to the cemetery.

Patti and Thom continued their music as they followed the procession. When the cemetery was in sight, Patti began singing in her angelic voice. Some wept while others sang along with her.

The wagon came to rest at Helen' resting place. It was the final destination for Helen on her mortal journey. A deep silence came over everyone. Not a bird could be heard singing and the wind fell silent. Patti turned to the crowd and said, "Father, accept this one who gave to those who had not. This one, who never spoke a foul word against another. This one, who's heart is as yours. We send our love to her and graciously hold the love she gave to us, Father. Count her among the angels. Then we can say we know Helen Clayborne when we too arrive at the gates of heaven. This we ask, nay we pray, of you, as your children, Father." Once again, a heavy silence ruled the moment.

The Reverend Richard began to address the crowd by clearing his voice. He was moved by Patti' words and felt his preparation deeply lacking. He gave a testimony about Helen' life and read a passage from the Bible. One that had been given before at other funerals. Some listened to his address while others were still holding to Patti's words.

Thomas realized that if words were to connect to the listener, they had to be inspiring and invoke inspiration. The right words spoken in the correct manner could move the direction of one or of many. It had to be received from something within.

The stranger dressed as a soldier was quietly moving about the crowd, speaking mainly to the young men. Afterwards he moved towards the woodland people that were watching from the cover of the trees. Some recognized him and turned away and disappeared. Whatever he was up to it was causing concern from the gatherers. No one dared question him. His appearance in uniform and the saber that clung to his side was intimidating enough.

The procession was breaking up. Most everyone would be attending the reception at the inn. It was an important part of every funeral. It was a way to offer the last of condolences and to celebrate the miracle of life.

A buffet table had been set to feed everyone in quick fashion. Diane, Lydia, Helen Danbury, and Mary were ready to serve and greet all who came to share in the life of Helen Clayborne. They planned to serve everyone just as Helen did with generosity and a smile.

John and his sons were seated at a private table. The ladies of the church stood by to serve their every need. The ladies were protective of the Clayborne men. They made sure no ill will or harsh word fell to their ear on this day. As with all assemblies in town, there were plenty of rumors and gossip going around.

Reverend Richard and his wife worked their way through the crowd. He stepped to the table where John, Stacy and William sat. "May I have every one's attention please," asked the Reverend. John nodded his head yes. "The Lord gives, and the Lord takes away. Let us not hold our hearts in deep sorrow or regret for this one. But let us rejoice in her service to us and those in heaven. Helen walks with God," spoke Reverend. John thanked him and offered a blessing.

A feeling came over Lydia as she was serving the last of the crowd. Her eye searched the room and there sat Thomas holding her in a stare. She gave him a warm smile and he returned the same. She felt flattered by his attention. Occasionally they repeated the exchange.

The reception was over, and most had left. William and Stacy collected the remaining food while their father went upstairs to rest. The food was placed in a pull cart used to bring wood inside. They pushed it through the front door and headed for the woodlanders and their camp. The townsfolk gave them disapproving looks. They did not approve of charity for the rift raft of society. But they held their tongues out of respect for Helen and John.

The brothers were near to the camp when the children came running to meet them. They followed alongside the cart like little soldiers protecting the kings' jewels. One by one the adults stepped forward. Some held desperate looks on their faces, while some held a glimmer of hope. Still the smiles and excitement of the children was contagious enough to lift the lowest of hearts.

There were the sick and elderly who looked on but could not walk to receive a portion. The adults had each child carry food to them before anyone was allowed to eat. These souls were poor in possession but rich in caring for one another. The elders among them came forth and gave an equal share to each member. It was a good day for these woodlanders and their families.

Helen would be very pleased of her sons and happy for the woodlanders. This was the spirit of Helen Clayborne on earth as in the heavens. Her charitable nature coming through her two loving sons that look after those in need.

Thomas was saying his goodbyes to family. He and Mary took privacy where they kissed and hugged each other. He felt her swelled belly as she pressed against him. "Soon Thomas, soon we will hold our child in our arms. We will rejoice in the birth together as man and wife," whispered Mary. "I hope it be a girl. If not, then I hope it be a boy. Either one will do," joked Thomas. Mary laughed and the two walked to those waiting.

Thomas helped Mary mount the wagon as she sat beside her mother. Both showing their way with child. The glow of their beauty crossed all limitations of mortal conception. Thomas stood in awe. Then both women looked at him and smiled in unison. The miracle of life and the miracle of love held to a single moment for the witness of one in a span of seconds that would be etched in soul for eternity.

Squire called out to him breaking the spell. "We best be going. We have work to do Thomas." Thomas bid farewell to everyone and turned to join Squire. The two were walking when Squire began talking to himself. Something about losing touch with a daughter and the passing of Helen. Obviously, he was trying to give himself comfort from some personal torment. Thomas recalled Squire appearing upset having seen someone standing among the woodlanders at the gravesite.

The two entered the shop and surveyed the supplies brought from London. "Tomorrow we begin our work. God's work it will be. Best you get rest and take meal from our stores if you become hungry later," spoke Squire in a humbling tone. He ascended the staircase and retired to bed. Helens passing had been hard on Squire.

Thomas climbed the stairs and retired to his new room. He fell back on the bed and was ready for some rest.

He turned over on his side to enter sleep with thoughts of Rebecca. He fell deep in sleep to enter another reality in another place not so far away.

He was standing before a building he recognized as belonging to Isaac, his spirit guide. He opened the door and saw Isaac writing in a large book. "What is this book you write in sir?" asked Thomas. "It's your book Thomas. It is your book of life in the planet world and in other worlds as well," replied Isaac. Thomas looked at the book and its writing. He did not recognize the print yet there was something strangely familiar about it.

"How far back in time does it go?" asked Thomas. "Time? Oh, I see. You speak of the measure of solar events in respect to its trek across the sky. So, I'll answer your question as best I can. The book began its birth before the measure of time, before the measure of space. The writing held within contains all that is. All things are ever present within all creation at every moment. Even when time and space are no more the book will continue to record.

On the table by the front door, you will find a lit candle. Take the candle and walk to the door that's behind me. There is a long hallway on the other side of the door with doors on both sides of the hallway. You may enter any door you chose as long as it carries an odd number on it. Do not enter a door with an even number. You're not ready to see what it holds. I will be here when you have seen enough. Once your return, blow out the candle and place it back on the table," said Isaac.

Thomas did as Isaac spoke without uttering a single word. He stood at the door and looked back at Isaac one last time. "Whenever you're ready Thomas," spoke the guide as he continues to write in the book. Thomas reached for the handle and pushed the door open. He was startled by something that quickly moved from sight once the light entered the hallway. He entered with eyes wide open searching the limits of light from the flame. He held the candle up to see the numbers Isaac spoke of. Deeper into the hallway he walked. He wondered what was behind the doors of even numbers because of his curious nature. The doors all looked the same except for the numbers posted on each door.

The door numbered nine appealed to him. Whatever was behind the door was calling to him. Gently he opened the door and stepped inside. He took a few steps inside when the door closed behind him. He was startled but not afraid.

There was a window on the opposing wall. He approached the window and peered in. There was a bright blinding light coming from within. He could hear children laughing and adults talking. Occasionally he could make out movement in the light, but no sense of form could be reckoned. The lights energy put him at gentle ease. A face came close to the window, and eyes appeared looking at him. The being's energy was warm and all knowing. The effect caused Thomas to feel free. He was overcome with waves of love.

He heard a familiar voice from the light. "It was Helen!" he thought. "Thomas, is that you son? Is it my favorite son?" exclaimed Helen. "I'm here in the light dear boy! I'm in the light with all the little children. They are the ones I fed from the back of my kitchen. The woodlander children! They have all come to give me their love for what I did for them! Oh Thomas! Can you feel their love? Can you share in their joy?

Charity Thomas! Go back and tell them, charity. Charity and good will is all that is needed to heal the past! Tell them child. Shout it out from the rooftops! Tell John and my sons that I love them and that I'll be visiting them in their sleep. There is much work to be done there and here dear son."

Thomas couldn't hold back the tears any longer. He went to his knees and wept for joy from the light and the gift it held. He wept in sorrow for the blindness of humanity and its appetite for greed. He wept in joy for the contact of one he loved so much. He wept as a child. He shifted himself to sit on the floor to regain his sense of self.

He stood as he wiped away the tears. He faced the window, but it was silent from within. Helen was gone and so were the little children. He turned back to the door to leave. He stepped over the threshold and felt something inside him was missing. He felt lighter and sure of himself. He continued down the hallway to make his exit. He blew out the candle, placed it back on the table and turned to Isaac.

"What you saw, what you heard, must come through you in thought. Mortal man cannot grasp the concepts of the other worlds and their influence on the plane that holds them. What is required of you is this. Be open to the blessings of the heavens. Let the light shine through you so it may reach the minds of the masses in this generation and the generations to come. Go in peace Thomas and follow the heart of charity and good will," spoke Isaac.

Thomas felt someone pushing on his back. It was Squire. "Wake up young man and come to meal. We must do the work to open minds and hearts. If our pockets be with coin as a result, then all the better we shall be. Now rise for there is much work to do," heralded the cheerful Squire.

CHAPTER 37

Thomas and Squire sat in silence as they ate their morning meal. Thomas could see that Squire was elsewhere in thought. Squire took a deep breath and released it. He looked at Thomas with a heavy eyes and said, "We have a contract with a group of financiers who wish to have Bibles printed. So many Bibles that there is a Bible for every man woman and child. I don't have to tell you how sensitive such a project as this can be. What with all the trouble between the Catholics and the Protestants going on.

Thomas, I can't stress this enough. We can never reveal the whole truth of our work. Men, good men have been punished or executed because they sought the truth and desired to spread the word over the land.

We must work quietly and long hours if we are to complete the task. Speak not to anyone, not even your family to the nature of our work. The trees have eyes, and the clouds have ears. If someone asks, we will tell them that we are printing reference books.

I will teach you how to bind the books we print. Once we have produced forty and two books, we will be on our way to London. We will be paid in note that we can exchange for silver. I received an advance so I could purchase the materials we need to print these Bibles. I also arranged for additional supplies to arrive in a few weeks.

"What kind of Bible are we printing Squire?" asked Thomas. "One that will turn this world upside down.

The church has strayed from God's truth and wisdom. Men of greed and wrecked souls have taken over the pulpit meant for truth seekers and true believers. It was always meant for the shepherds to tend to the flock. Not the flock tending the shepherd. A mockery they have made of the gospels and its revelations.

They hide the truth with their dogmas and creeds. They lead the lambs to the slaughter rather than to green pastures. They make war with one another and once they conquer their foe, they turn on each other to begin another battle. To speak against them openly is to attract their wrath and persecution.

One day there will be one that will rise against them to expose their falsehoods. These books we are about to make will be the beginning of that uprising. Voices must be raised against their tyranny and deception.

Let us descend our noisy staircase to begin the work. Let us pray that our work raises a greater noise across this land. What say ye Thomas? Are you up for the task?" asked Squire. "Yes Squire. I will take this task to heart and give it my best," replied Thomas. "Then let us begin," roared Squire.

The two stood in the shop surveying the work area. Together they planned how they would begin and the process to follow. They turned to look at each another and in doing created a bond that would see them through this moment and others to come.

The days passed one by one. The two were making progress in the printing and enjoying each other. Squire kept Thomas entertained with his stories of London. Most of Thomas's questions had been asked at least a dozen times before. Each time Squire was more than happy to give a variation of the same answer.

The front door of the shop flew open and slammed against the wall. The noise startled Thomas and Squire. It was Edward, Thomas' father. "I have some good news son! Mary has begun her labor. It will do well for you to leave here and travel home with me. You don't want to miss seeing your child enter this world," spoke Edward in excitement.

Thomas was excited and in a state of shock at the same time. He wasn't ready for this. He didn't move or utter a word. His eyes were held in disbelief. Squire and Edward could not help but laugh a little at Thomas as they recalled their first time.

"Mildred is with Mary and your mother and Lydia are there to help her. They sent me to fetch you. Mildred said the child was waiting on you. Hurry, there is no time to waste!" spoke Edward in his excitement. The two left the shop and jumped aboard the wagon. The horse started towards the house without Edward touching the reins.

"Once the child is born you will never be the same. The things you now hold precious will change once you see the child. Your mother and Mary are like mother and daughter now. The child will be well looked after and cared for. Dear God, I pray it be a girl and fit to receive the love that awaits her," said Edward as he looked upward to the sky. Edward kept on talking without any response from Thomas. Anyone observing the two would think that Edward, in his gentle hysteria, was the father of the child.

The wagon pulled alongside the house. Thomas heard screaming coming from inside. "It's time Thomas. Hurry, you don't want to miss it!" yelled his father. Thomas sat glued to his seat. "Get down from there now! You're not the one giving birth! Mary's the one doing all the work," yelled his father. Awkwardly Thomas dismounted the wagon and stepped towards the house like an elderly man.

Mary let out another scream. "Where's Thomas! Is he here yet?" yelled Mary. Thomas heard her and quickened his pace. So much that he tried entering the home without bothering to open the door. He fell back and landed on the ground. He was quick to get back up and recover from his spill.

He opened the door and yelled, "I'm here Mary! I'm here!" He ran to the back room and there she lied on the bed. Diane was on one side and Lydia on the other. Mildred was on the bed kneeling as she waited for the child to enter the world. "Come here Thomas and see the crown of your child's head as it enters the light. Slowly Thomas stepped behind Mildred. His knees weakened and he had to catch himself on the bed-post. "That will be enough Thomas. You go back to the kitchen and wait with the men. We will call you once your child has arrived.

Let's not hold this up any longer," said Mildred as she moved closer to Mary. "Push one more time Mary. The child is ready. Push one more time and let out a scream so loud that the towns people can hear you," shouted Mildred. Mary gripped Lydia' and Diane' hand. Mary lifted her head, took a deep breath, and let out a scream that sent chills down the backs of the men. Then silence. Then more screaming but this time it was from Lydia and Diane. "It's a girl! It's a beautiful girl!" Then joyful crying.

Edward and Jonathan looked at each other in relief. They too were happy it was a girl since the women so longed for one. Mildred held the child as Diane and Lydia cleaned her for the presentation to the new mother. The child was wrapped in cloth and placed beside Mary. Mary was weak and could only smile as she looked at her daughter. "The child must suckle Mary. Give her your milk so she will grow strong like you," whispered Mildred. Lydia assisted Mary and the baby began to suckle.

Diane stood watching. She was holding back tears as she watched the scene play out. Diane had a daughter and a granddaughter. It was the grandest of gifts anyone could ever receive. Her heart was filled with tenderness and new found love. Diane was present in her heaven on earth.

Lydia knelt beside the bed and wept. She stroked Mary's head giving comfort to the new mother. Mary looked at her and said, "I love you mother. We have a new daughter to raise together." "Yes, we do daughter. She's a beautiful baby. Just as beautiful as you were when my eyes first saw you," replied Lydia.

Mildred finished the task of midwife. She stood at the bedside as she rolled her sleeves back down. She looked at Mary and gave her a smile. "This one came from the upper heavens. She carries a message with her. The white light angels walk by her side. The sword shall be her testament and the message she brings her will never be forgotten. Raise her in love and all things under heaven will praise you. Now rest. You did well," said Mildred.

Diane and Lydia looked at each other hearing Mildred's words about the child. They did not understand the words but held them in reverence. Mildred's guidance and service was never questioned. She had earned the respect and reverence that was afforded to her.

Mildred walked to the door to leave and saw the men sitting at the table. Jonathan stood and stepped to Mildred. He handed her a cloth sack which held coins and said, "I want to gift you today, Mildred. You mean so much to all of us. Your guidance in these parts makes life a little easier for all of us. God bless you Mildred for all you do."

Edward stood and approached her. "You know I'm a carpenter and a good one at that. If you need repair of your home, I am here to make the repairs needed at my expense. It's time we support you for all you give without mention of payment. Thank you for your presence today. You stood stronger than any man present. God bless," spoke Edward in complete humility.

Mildred bowed her head in silence. She lifted her head and looked at all three men and said "I'm grateful for the coins and I'm grateful for the repairs. I am in need of both. Such charity that comes from the heart never goes unnoticed on high. You honor me with your gifts. I will return later and check on the child and the new mother. I will take my leave and pray that this home is blessed always with love."

She left and set out for another visit elsewhere. An elderly family member was about to leave this world for the next. She would be there to guide them across and give comfort to the family in their mourning.

"Let us celebrate the arrival of our newest family member and drink to her prosperity and health," declared Edward. He took three mugs and a cask in hand. He stepped to the door to go outside. Thomas and Jonathan followed. They gathered under the shade of a tree and sat on the ground. Edward poured the mugs with whiskey and made a toast. "These times in life are made to remember that family is the backbone of all communions, be it for God or be it for country. The bond of family is why we pray, how we laugh and what makes us cry. Today we welcome this one. Soon Lydia will give us another reason to celebrate. We three bond together here in this moment as we grow in number and in heart. Cheers!" The mugs came together rendering a clank. Each brought the same to their lips and drank.

"To life and to death and all in between, I lift my drink to those who I lost and to those I have gained," spoke Jonathan. Again, the three lifted the mugs upward but the clank was louder this time. Each reflected on the passing of Jeremy and Chad Rose.

The voices of men could be heard from deep in the forest. "Lumbermen," spoke Jonathan. "They seek good timber for the building in London. They pay in coin and leave what's left for firewood. It's a good business for them and us.

Jack Danbury is working amongst them. He knows the forest from his days living in them before the fire. They pay him well. Helen tends to the cooking in camp for the men.

They hope to build their own home from the profits they earn. I'm giving them a plot of land to build on. They deserve another chance at life. They are good people and strong in heart," said Jonathan.

159

Diane stepped from the doorway to join the men. "Thomas, it's time to say hello to your daughter. Are you ready son to receive her into your heart?" Thomas stood up and faced his mother but could only nod his head. He followed her back inside the house and followed her to Mary's room. Diane stepped to one side to allow him to enter first. He stepped cautiously as he peered into the dimly lit room. He did not want to disturb the child or Mary.

Mary lied there in peace wearing a smile as she looked at him. Slowly he stepped towards her and the baby she was holding. He knelt beside the bed and took Mary's hand. He kissed it, then kissed her on the cheek. "Say hello to your daughter Thomas. Her name is Lucille. This blessing I hold is my light and yours. Come closer and see the beautiful blue eyes she has been blessed with," cooed Mary. Thomas moved closer to see Lucille. A feeling came over him. He felt humbled and small in Lucille's presence. He had never seen anything as beautiful or more precious than her. He was overwhelmed and began to weep softly while he continued to kiss Mary's hand.

Lydia moved towards Thomas and said, "Stand Thomas so I may hand you your daughter. You need to feel her magic. She brings her light to all of us." Thomas stood and Lydia reached for the child. Mary was pleased with her mother' gesture.

"Are you ready?" asked Lydia. Again, Thomas could not speak so he nodded his head. Lydia passed the child to him, and he held her gently. She opened her eyes and looked at her father and the child's magic entered his soul. He was elated and nearly frantic. Thomas felt like any father who looked upon the first born. Proud to be a father and clueless as to what it means.

Lydia moved towards Thomas to receive Lucille back. She could see that he had taken only a few breaths the whole time he held her. He brought her to his face and gently kissed her. He looked at Lydia with heavy eyes in puzzlement. She took the child and returned it to Mary.

The witness in this world has a way of directing one to a direction where no map or chart shall be given. The tugging in one direction, while one's eyesight is set upon another. The soul and its expectations will always hold conflict with the world around it. A teacher once said, "Render unto Caesar that which is his and likewise for the one who gave Caesar life."

"Must one concede to the circumstances of the day and take pleasure with the lesson it renders at night in slumber? Are there two masters which must be served in order to break the bonds of slavery, free from expectation or mortal desire?" thought Thomas.

The stage of life was set. The script was written with many rewrites to its credit. The characters know their roles. There is witness to the story and the lessons to be learned. A new concept born from casting away the old for the new. And so, it is, in this journey called life.

CHAPTER 38

Mildred returned to the Sonnet's home as promised. She brought with her a clay of honey she received from the family she last gave comfort to. The honey would help Mary to regain her strength. The pollen came from fruit trees about the countryside.

Mildred found Mary and Lucille asleep and chose not to disturb them. She asked the women to put the honey in tea and have Mary drink it three times a day.

Lydia was feeling tired and wanted to go home. All the excitement had taken its toll on her. Edward offered to take her home in the wagon and she accepted his offer. He and Jonathan went to the barn to hitch the horse to the wagon.

Diane told Lydia to send Jonathan to summon her as soon as she began labor. She would rush to her to be by her side. Lydia was pleased to know that Diane would be there to see her through the labor. Neighbor helping neighbor creating family beyond blood or heritage. All who carry breath are family.

The men entered the house to help Lydia to the wagon. They chose to seat her at the rear of the wagon, so she didn't have to climb up to the seat. Jonathan sat beside her, while Edward drove the wagon.

Lydia placed her hands on her belly and gently rubbed it to give comfort to the child within. She knew it would be soon by the way she felt. She looked back at the Sonnet home and saw Thomas standing there beneath the tree. She waved at him and gave a smile. Thomas returned a long wave until the wagon was almost out of sight.

Mildred exited the house and stood by Thomas as the wagon was about to disappear. "Three days will pass, and your second child will be born from Lydia's womb. Your child will share his life with Jonathan's child. The two will grow together strong as two oaks. They enter this world together out of love for each other and the love they share for their parents.

This is the life you chose Thomas. Neither curse it nor run from it. Fear not the unknown nor turn from it. The days of tragedies live to build character not to destroy it. Seven times you will be called upon to give with empty pockets. Seven times you will succeed. Three times your world will crumble around you and three times it will be resurrected. Embrace each day as you have embraced this day with the little one called Lucille," spoke Mildred in prophetic manner.

Thomas never moved or spoke a single word in response to Mildred's words. She placed her hand on his shoulder and said, "I will return in three days to deliver your child and Jonathan's child. Please be present when the moment comes. Both children have sent their desire to see their father's eyes when they arrive. Your parents plan to witness the birth so you can join them. No one knows that two await to enter together as they have so many times in the past.

Mary and Lucille need you now. Go to them Thomas and know that all things under heaven are blessed." Mildred turned away and entered the trees to return home.

Thomas quietly entered the room where mother and child rested. Mary's eyes opened and she extended her arm to beckon him to her side. He walked to the bed and laid down beside her. He placed his arm around her and pulled her close so he could embrace her lips.

"I have good news to share with you Mary. Squire has tendered a contract that will line our pockets with coin and the good things that come with it. Eventually we could afford to live in town. Do you find it good news Mary?" asked Thomas.

"Yes Thomas, that sounds wonderful. When will it be possible?" asked Mary. "A few months or so, I believe. There is a trip to London which must happen for the delivery and receive payment," replied Thomas. He kissed his bride one more time and they drifted off to sleep.

Jonathan helped Lydia from the wagon. The couple thanked Edward for the ride as they entered the house. Lydia went straight to her bedroom. She was exhausted and quickly fell asleep.

Jonathan heard voices coming towards the house. It was Helen and Jack's voice. They entered the home with Helen carrying a pot filled with fine stew in one hand and the child Lily in the other. Jack was carrying wood for the fire place. Jonathan shared the day's events with them as a storyteller would speak. The Danbury's were amused with his antics. They laughed and cheered with the good news of Lucille's birth.

Helen went to Lydia' room to check on her. She saw Lydia sitting on the edge of the bed. She seemed disturbed about something. "What is it, Lydia? What's wrong?" asked Helen. Lydia looked at her as if she had seen a ghost.

"I'm carrying twins. I fell asleep and they appeared to me in a dream. One is stronger than the other. I saw them both sitting on a limb of a great tree. They were happy and teasing each other. They called out to me, and I spoke back to them. They appeared ageless. There was a beautiful silver light surrounding them.

They asked me if I was ready for them to enter. I told them I was ready. I felt their love for me, and I wept tears of joy," spoke Lydia between sniffles. Helen moved closer to Lydia as the baby Lily tugged at her cheeks. Helen was moved by Lydia's revelation. Helen knew not to discount what Lydia saw. She too had seen things in dreams that came true.

Jonathan entered the room carrying a hot cup of tea for Lydia. He felt a strange energy in the room when he entered. He looked at Helen and Lydia and believed it to be of motherhood.

Lily and Lucille had blessed their lives with new beginnings and new possibilities. Soon others would enter to join them.

The feminine energy and its influence on this world reigns supreme in the eyes of creation, for she was given the name Eve, for she was the mother of all things.

CHAPTER 39

Three days had passed since Lucille was born. Mother and daughter were doing well. This day would deliver two more children to these pilgrims before the sun could shed its last ray of light.

Helen was preparing meals for the Roses and the lumbermen in the forest. Lydia was fast asleep with Jonathan curled around her. She felt a sharp pain go through her which caused her to sit up in bed. "What is it my dear?" asked Jonathan. "A pain went form my lower back down my leg. It's gone now," replied Lydia. "I'll fetch you some tea. Lie here until I return," spoke Jonathan. He rose up from the bed and dressed for the day.

He entered the kitchen to see Helen hard at work. Jack was seated at the table holding Lily in his lap. Jonathan poured some tea and sat at the table. Lily looked at him and giggled. It made Jonathan laugh which made Lily giggle even more. The two went back and forth laughing at each other as it soon became a game.

"Quiet you two before you wake Lydia up," snapped Helen. Jonathan made a grim face at Lily in response to Helen. It made Lily laugh louder. "Jack, do something with your daughter," said Helen. "Shall I put her outside?" replied Jack. Helen stopped what she was doing. She pointed the wooden spoon she was holding at him. "I can do more with this than just stir beans. Would you like me to show you this morning before you get started? said Helen in a calm manner.

Wisely Jack lowered his head as did Lily. Jonathan was amused with their antics and laughed at the two. Everyone was in on the laughter. Helen was laughing the hardest. She plopped the spoon into beans hard enough to send some flying in the air landing on her face. Jonathan and Jack saw it and broke out in hysterical laughter. Lily joined in not sure why or what they were laughing at.

Helen continued preparing the food to nourish all those she cared for. She tended three pots while baking bread. The morning and midday meal for the Rose's would remain. The remainder of the food would go with her to the lumber camp.

Her heart and soul were in the work she did. The generosity afforded to them by the Roses was what they needed to get back on their feet. Cold nights sleeping on the ground with empty bellies would be no more. The Danbury' would succeed. They would rebuild and they would prosper as never before.

Jonathan took porridge and tea to Lydia. He entered the room and saw she had fallen back to sleep. He dared not wake her, so he returned to the kitchen.

Jack and Helen were preparing to leave for the day. Jonathan felt blessed to have them there in the home. Helen was good for Lydia. Jonathan followed them outside as they mounted the wagon and watched as they drove away. He turned to go back inside and saw Mildred walking towards him. He knew why she was coming. He knew today would be the day.

Mildred approached and said, "Please do not worry for the day. All things will come naturally without worry or unneeded concern. At days end you will be a father again. You will profit in heart and soul once the sun enters dusk. I need you to summon Diane for me. Tell her to bring Thomas a well to help with things. Now go."

Jonathan did as Mildred asked. He ran for a few minutes then slowed to a walk. He was happy, and he was frightful. He wanted to laugh, and he wanted to cry. He stopped in the middle of the road and went to his knees. He closed his eyes and clasped his hands together to pray.

"I am grateful for my life and the lives of those I love. I am grateful to be a father for it has enriched my soul. Three were born to me before this day approached. Two strong and loving sons left me before I could deliver all the love, I had for them. One of beauty still stands with me as she brought another soul to our hearts.

I say these things because I have something to ask in the deepest of respect. Please do not take this one from us before we have enjoyed all love has to offer. We could not bear another loss. Our hearts are still heavy from the past. Give us the courage to live and grow as one," spoke Jonathan in earnest.

Jonathan finished his prayer and continued on to the Sonnet home. He knocked at the door and Diane opened it. "You're here to tell me Lydia is ready to deliver. Am I right?" asked Diane. Jonathan shook his head yes as he entered the home.

"How are Mary and the child?" asked Jonathan. "They are doing well. Thank you for asking," replied Diane. "Oh, Mildred asked you to bring Thomas with you when you came," said Jonathan. "You go along back home, and Thomas and I will join you soon," replied Diane. Jonathan left and turned towards home.

Mildred entered the house and stepped quietly to the bedroom. Slowly she peered into the room. There sat Lydia in bed. Her eyes staring directly at Mildred's image. "Tell me. Tell me Mildred about these that hold their weight inside me. Tell me about them. I saw them both in sleep. They seemed to know me, yet I did not recognize their faces. Tell me Mildred who are they?" asked Lydia in a low tone.

"They are those who chose to enter this world through you and your energy. The two children each have two hearts for they were conceived in body by two fathers. One will take breath from the one you love. The other will take breath from the one that bears your passion.

The female child has chosen the name Judith. The male child has decided that his name shall be Liam. Both carry the love for their fathers and you. They bring with them the gifts of joy and happiness.

The love you share with Jonathan is strong like an oak that can bear the strongest of storm with little or no harm. You will be the strong wife for him. He is in heart for your love. The two of you are bound together by something greater than you will ever know.

The love you feel for Thomas is as uncertain as the wind. It comes and it goes, never knowing from which direction it came or where it will go next. Thomas will give you a lover's delight. There is no earthly bond between the two of you, therefore you are free. Free to express and feel the depths of passion and love.

At times you will be torn between the two, to hold one and cast the other away. Would you love one more than the other? Could you love one child over the other? I think not. You will need the love and comfort of both before your journey is over.

Practice never to slight or reject one over the other. Rather you will have to learn to accept the two as one. Both men love you as you are. The children enter this world through you because of the love they have for you. Should strife ever enter you from this arrangement, just know that it's from the imaginary realm of fear. Not from the love that brought all together," spoke Mildred in heartfelt manner.

Lydia sat motionless. She drifted from consciousness to a place where Mildred's words could be held in her soul. Mildred stepped from the room and walked to the kitchen. She added a few pieces of wood to the fireplace to make ready the hot water. She reached in her pocket and took out two pieces of twine and a sharp knife. She placed each in the pot. She gathered some odd pieces of cloth about the house to help with the delivery. She sat at the table and waited.

The front door opened and in walked Diane, Thomas, and Jonathan. Mildred rose from the chair and said, "Diane, I will need your help in delivering these two babies." The room became still. "I knew it! She's carrying twins!" exclaimed Jonathan. He turned to Thomas and held him firmly by the shoulders. "It is a wonderful thing that today we both will be fathers. It's the finest day of my life. Come let us take strong drink to celebrate." "Not now," said Mildred. There will be plenty of time to celebrate. First, we must welcome our new arrivals with a sober mind and steady hands. Would you agree Thomas?" asked Mildred. "Yes, I think it best. We shall wait," replied Thomas.

"Diane, I need a strong broth for Lydia. She will need to regain her strength as soon as possible. The berthing of the twins at her age will take its toll on her. Here are some herbs to add to the broth," said Mildred.

"Thomas you and Jonathan gather myrtle from along the road. Take the new growth from the trees and harvest as much as you can. Boil the limbs using the water from the spring behind the house. Take a mallet and mash the limbs while they are still hot. It will make a poultice to help heal her wound and relieve some of the pain she will carry after it's over," spoke Mildred as if she were a military commander. The men left the house to do as she instructed.

Mildred entered the bedroom to sit and wait for Lydia to begin labor. The time progressed along as did the labor. Mildred stood from the chair and walked to the bedside. "They're coming. Your children are ready to enter. Lift your hips dear so I can slip this blanket roll under you. These two are in a hurry. They are arguing over who will enter first," spoke Mildred in gentle laughter.

"Diane, I need you now," called out Mildred. Diane came into the room to see Lydia in labor pain. The contractions were closer together. Diane took her hand and said, "Breathe Lydia, breathe." "She's crowning. This one has a full set of hair. Give me one more hard push Lydia. That's it! It's a girl!" exclaimed Mildred. Lydia tried to see but was still too weak and in serious pain. Mildred took the twine and tied the cord. She laid the child down just as the second was crowning.

"This one has a head full of hair too and he's not waiting! It's a boy Lydia! It's a beautiful little boy," said Mildred as she held the child up so Lydia could him. "See the life that came from your passion and give praise," said Mildred. She tied off the cord and laid the child beside his sister.

Mildred lifted the daughter and said, "See the child of your love and devotion. This one carries the heart of a lion. She came not to this world to accept the life it had for her. She came to change it," said Mildred as a heralding angel. She cut the cords and placed each child at Lydia's side. Lydia was glowing with love and joy. A state of bliss known only to those who bring life forward for all to partake in. Diane looked on with adoration and solace.

Mildred turned to Diane and asked her to bring the men in to see the newborns. Diane found the two outside sharing a mug of rye. "It's time to see your children Jonathan. They want to see their father. You come too Thomas. Please be gentle when you enter the room. Lydia went through a lot and is having a great deal of pain. She is weak and needs time to rest," said Diane.

They entered quietly as they walked down the hall and stepped into the room. They stood in awe at mother and children. "Oh, come in you two. Stop staring and come to the bedside. They won't bite," spoke Mildred. They did as she said. Tears began rolling down Jonathan's face as he drew near. It took all he had to keep from crying. He didn't want to disturb the babies in any way. He went to his knees and whispered, "I love you my dear sweet wife." All Lydia could do was smile at him. She held him with her eyes while a single tear ran down her cheek. He leaned into her and kissed the tear before it could escape her face.

All children upon arrival are the product of love, be it strong or be it lacking. From love they are given, to love they are received and for love, will they search the world over. They search in yonder and over there as they dance the dance. For true love and affection can only be realized from the dance. No one should ever be disappointed by what was learned or what was lost. It was all a part of the dance, the dance called love.

Thomas quietly left to tell Mary about the twins. He knew the boy child was from his loins. He held his silence of tongue and emotion. He was pleased the twins were well and were cradled in the love of two wonderful people. He would return home to fetch Mary and Lucille. He knew Mary would want to see her new brother and sister. His and Lydia's secret would be forever held in silence. If the truth was ever revealed it would only serve to hurt those they loved.

Jonathan sat quietly in a chair in a daze as he watched Lydia and the angels she held to each breast. Mildred was cleaning up while Diane stood ready to grant any and all requests Lydia or Mildred might have.

Mildred was about to leave and walked to Lydia. She took hold her hand and said "Today you have been blessed from on high. Your choices in life are sewing the tapestry of your witness. Be strong in the days to come and remember who you are. For these two have entered here for your love and your guidance.

Love those who love you and those who turn their backs on you. For they do not see with your eyes, nor can they see the depths of your heart. Only you have that ability.

Forgive all who tease and ridicule you for they only dictate their destiny in time to come. The passion you bring to this world stirs the poet to take hold script and pen to hand. Stories to come shall inspire to give hope to all human endeavors from every corner.

Love the poet, love the man. Dance within the emotions and bring light to all that ails. Do this and you will know heaven and earth alike."

Mildred turned to Diane and said, "I will finish the poultice before I leave. It should be changed regularly until the bleeding has completely stopped."

Then she turned to Jonathan still in a daze. She stroked his head until he looked at her. He smiled and took Mildred's hand. He kissed each finger then the back of her hand. She returned the smile and left the room.

Mildred finished the poultice when Thomas and Mary entered carrying Lucille. "Your brother and sister are waiting on you Mary. They're two beautiful children and I'm sure they would love to meet their cousin. Your parents await you child." Mary took Lucille with her while Thomas stayed with Mildred.

"Oh, don't worry Thomas. It all works out. It always does. Just be true to your heart and live in the day and not the morrow. What we truly feel cannot be spoken in its full truth. It is too difficult for the mortal to perceive for any long periods of time. Love is the mortar, life is the brick. Together they build the stairway to heaven," said Mildred in kindness.

Soon the sun will set on this little corner of the world. When it rises again on the horizon nothing will be the same. The realm of change weighs heavy in this valley of souls. Busy as bees these souls commit as they gather the pollen of days to render the harvest of honey for the next life' journey. Be it ever so, for king and pauper alike.

CHAPTER 40

Some say the wind carries change. Others point upwards to the sky and claim it is written from above. While some say nothing changes. The only thing that really changes is the way it's perceived.

The publishing of English language Bibles was intended to bring about just that, change. Its goal was to allow the common people access to the scripture with an open mind void of religious influence and doctrine. The perception and meaning of the stories held within would be left up to the reader.

Free thinking and open minds can present a threat to the powers of the church. It was the reason the work of Squire and Thomas needed to be secret. There were mercenaries about the land to stamp out resistance to the church's authority over the flock.

The financial backers of the project foresaw Rome's efforts to put down the resistance. So they contracted printers all over England and Europe to make it difficult for them to locate every printer or to locate every Bible. There had already been a number of Bible burnings across Europe. The idea was to flood the land with Bibles, more than could be consumed by the flames of a tyrant.

Squire and Thomas were nearly finished with the publishing of the forty and two Bibles contracted. For Squire the satisfaction of completing the work early gave him a sense of purpose. For Thomas each working day that passed was a day closer to seeing London and all it had to offer. The tides of change would enter their lives once again once the work was completed and the wagon loaded for the journey.

Susan McGuire, the towns seamstress married John Clayborne seven weeks after Helen's passing. Helen and Susan were best friends when Helen walked the earth. Susan looked after John and the boys to help them through their grieving after the funeral. She was of good heart and mind.

The Stagg Inn was in a state of change. Industry in London was growing at a rapid pace. Investors combed the countryside looking for resources and land to harvest and develop. The rooms were rented out continually. The dining room was so busy that John had to hire more people to cook and serve.

Thomas's father, Edward was busy with his trade as a furniture maker. Some of the investors brought family and others with them in their ventures. They made good customers for many of the shops in town.

Diane and Mary, besides spoiling Lucille, tried their hand as entrepreneurs. They expanded their garden to supply the inn with fresh vegetables, eggs, and poultry.

Commerce was growing in and around the town of Danbury. The sleepy little town was waking up and embracing the changes that come with progress.

It was also good for the woodlanders. Some had steady employment and were able to purchase the things they needed. They spoke of building their own homes and improved shelters as they grew.

Lydia was busy raising the twins. She believed Liam would be her protector as he grew in body and strength. It was evident that he was of Thomas and Judith was of Jonathan. She loved each one the same, careful never to slight one over the other.

The child Judith clung to her father whenever he was near. She would fuss if he tried to put her down or hand her off to someone else. She loved her mother and adored her father.

Jack and Helen Danbury were busy building their new home. Jack's work with the lumber company had afforded him with plenty of building material. Jonathan gave them a parcel of land to call their own. They were filled with a new promise of life. They started a garden for food and winter stores. Lily enjoyed the garden and imitated every move her mother made while working there.

These people worked hard and never complained about hardship or the lack of anything. Together they had realized that worry and complaint had no influence on change. They embraced the nature of acceptance and welcomed the changes they faced in each day. They were humble and grateful for the day, for their lives and for family, be they blood or not.

One by one the days came and went. The wheels of life turning without end. Each day delivering change and its fruits. Time moves on without a whisper or tap on the shoulder. A time to be born and a time to die. A time to laugh and a time to cry. A time to accept and a time to ask why.

CHAPTER 41

The freshly printed Bibles were ready for delivery. Each were carefully wrapped and packaged to disguise their identity and loaded in the wagon. Squire and Thomas were packed for the journey to London. It was all Thomas could do to keep his composure. The excitement was building for both. Squire was filled with a deep sense of satisfaction. The Bibles would arrive before the agreed deadline. It meant a handsome bonus for both.

Squire was confident in Thomas ability and devotion to his work. He knew he could depend on him. Squire decided he would seek another contract. This time he would seek more Bibles for press and more money. It was a good time for all printers across the land.

Diane, Mary, and Lucille were at the shop to send the two off. They provided enough food for six or seven days even though the trip only lasted three. The well wishes, kisses and hugs were exchanged in earnest of heart. Thomas was excited about the trip yet sorrowful to leave has family.

The wheels of the wagon began to turn as the wheels of change followed alongside. No one here would ever look the same to Thomas once the events of the future had unfolded into his awareness. The young Thomas that rode the wagon and held the reins would not be the same one returning home.

The two were well outside town, when some of the woodlanders stepped from the forest with their hand extended in need. Thomas reached behind him and took two loaves of bread Mary had wrapped for them. He tossed the loaves to a woman standing with three children. She caught them and curtsied him with her head bowed in gratitude.

"I don't know why you think you have to give something to someone every time they hold out their hand. We will need that bread before our journey is through. Now we must go without," said Squire. Thomas looked at him and said, "Then we will know what it is like to go without as they do. Only our ordeal will be for the measure of one meal. Theirs will most likely be a lifetime," retorted Thomas. Squire spoke not a word in protest.

It was time to look for a place to camp for the night. There were common places along the road for camping used by many. Squire preferred not to use them because they were also known to thieves. Squire chose a place that offered good shade and water a good distance from the road.

A modest fire was built and the two sat eating their meal. They spoke of the things to come. Money, position and most of all, a new experience. Thomas listened to every word Squire spoke about London. He enjoyed forming a visual image in his mind. The two retired as the last flames of the fire slowly dwindled to embers.

The second day began with little thought of Danbury and its residents. Their sight was set on the road before them with anticipation building with each turn of the wagons wheel. Every mile that fell behind them saw parts of them falling away.

The soul knows from within that new things can only be embraced once the things of old are shed. So that one may see with different eyes. Otherwise, all things appear the same. Vision is dependent on perception.

Time and space are the taskmasters of all journeys for humanity. It's said that the gravest of errors anyone can make is to stand against its will, to resist the path or deny the knock at the door. All things desired are delivered. The manner by which they arrive is held in silence.

For the settler Squire, all he ever desired or wished for would come to his witness. For the pilgrim Thomas, all things new and unknown would call to him from a distance held beyond the stars.

Another day's journey traveled, and another camp made away from the road. On this evening the camps fire was at the center of the universe for these two. They ate by its side and repeated the same stories as the night before. But for Thomas it was as if he were hearing them for the first time. As the flames dwindled so did the stories. He was having trouble sleeping. He wished the night away in his dreams as the stars moved across the sky. Tomorrow's sunrise and the suspense it held would shift the tide of reckoning for the things to come.

Morning came and Thomas was quick to break down their camp and load the wagon. The two mounted the wagon and Thomas took the reins as usual. He snapped them for the horse to move. The horse took off and Thomas went flying through the air to land flat on his face. In his hurried way he forgot to hitch the horse to the wagon. "Let's try that again shall we Thomas?" spoke Squire. Thomas got up and brushed himself off. This time he hitched the horse to the wagon. He mounted the wagon and took the reins again. He cautiously snapped the reins holding them loosely just in case.

CHAPTER 42

The wagon, its crew and cargo were nearing the great city of London. The tops of towers and buildings could be seen from where they were. Thomas was ready to put the horse to a faster pace, but Squire protested.

Squire was busy thinking how he could improve the shop to take on more work. He'd need more help and perhaps another press. Future contracts were dependent on quality and quantity. Timely delivery was also of importance. He would need a larger wagon and more horses to pull it. He was excited about growth and prosperity.

Thomas had no such thought of profit or business. His was open for whatever came across his path. He wanted to soak up every image of every event. London was his oyster, and he came with a healthy appetite.

They were meeting people along the road that appeared very different from those he left behind in Danbury.

At home people dressed according to how they made a living. Here, people were wearing layers of clothing made of bright colors and strange fabric. Some had something on their faces that made them appear as ghosts.

A group of young men began mocking them as they passed by. "Make no mind of them Thomas. They are vagrants of the worst kind. If it were night, and there were but few witness about, they would rob us of our wares, our coin and possibly our lives.

Once we have traveled a little further, I want you to turn toward them to see if they follow us," said Squire. Thomas waited a while then turned to look at them. "One follows us as the others still hold where we first saw them," said Thomas. "Good. We may be able to lose him once we enter the city and are in the crowds. Don't look back anymore Thomas. We want him to be lax in his duty to the others," said Squire.

"Most likely he's scouting for the group. They would rob this evening should our cargo present a profit for them. We'll be taking our Bibles straight to John Thorstrom once we enter London. There will no cargo for them to steal lest they decide to steal the same from John," laughed Squire.

"We'll take our lodging at the Downey Inn. There we will have a hot meal and drink to fill our bellies until we can eat and drink no more. Tomorrow we will go shopping for clothes. We must look the part, or no one will take us seriously. Impressions are very important in business. You have to spend a little to get a lot," spoke Squire to his upcoming apprentice.

"Allow me to take the reins now Thomas. The streets of London are busy. It's easy to get lost here, and I don't want anything to go wrong," spoke Squire. He drove the wagon until they arrived at John Thorstrom's print shop. The two dismounted the wagon and stretched their legs.

They entered the shop and saw twenty or so men moving about as busy as any group of men could be. The clamor of the presses and the talk between each crew was something to witness. They had perfected an assembly line approach to their printing. Squire and Thomas watched with great intensity.

"Thomas go to the wagon and bring me the first bundle of Bibles," said Squire. Thomas hurried out to the wagon and removed a bundle from the wagon. He glanced across the street and there stood the man who followed them. He was leaning against a building watching Thomas. Thomas took the bundle inside and handed it to Squire.

"The man that was following us is standing across the street," reported Thomas. "I see. Be kind enough to give the man at the desk the bundle while I address the young man across the street as to his intentions," said Squire. Thomas did as Squire said and handed the bundle off. He went to the door to watch Squire as he spoke to the young man across the street. Thomas saw Squire reached inside his pocket and handed the man something. The man tipped his hat to Squire and walked away. Squire returned to Thomas.

"We won't be bothered anymore from the likes of him. I paid him enough so he could have his own good time without the others. It's a matter of business Thomas. The thief needs money by which to prosper. He will always chose the path of least resistance. Offer him one and he will take it. He will report to the others that we held books in possession. There is very little profit in stolen books and not worth the risk," said Squire.

"Hurry Thomas. The wagon needs to be unloaded so we may hold the fruits of our labor," chuckled Squire. Just then John Thorstrom stepped outside from the shop. "Excellent work Andrew Beckett! I'm very pleased with your work and the speed with which you delivered the same. Come, let us go inside to settle our business and strike some new contracts for all to profit from. Your boy can finish unloading."

"He's not my boy John. He is my business partner and one day a co-owner if I can keep him home after he's seen the sights of London," replied Squire. "Very well then. May I shake your hand young man and my apologies should I have offended you in the slightest," spoke a humbled printer. "No sir, no harm, I'm happy to say. I'm honored to shake your hand and meet your acquaintance," replied Thomas.

John and Squire went straight to John's desk. The two became engaged in heavy conversation and laughter. Thomas continued to unload the wagon. His enthusiasm after meeting John and viewing his shop had his head spinning. "Sir Thomas of London, printer to the Crown of England. Purveyor to the finer things of life," as he teased himself in thought.

The wagons cargo was now the property of John Thorstrom. Squire was given a fat envelope that went straight to the inner pocket of his jacket. The men shook hands and Squire stood to leave. He turned and looked about for young Thomas.

There he stood in awe of the display of the print shop of John Thorstrom. At home he and Squire spoke of good thing to eat and the latest gossip while they worked. These men spoke only of work. They were like bees on a hive. Each knew their assignment and each time it was completed in a series of fashion. The efficiency was amazing to watch.

"Come Thomas. Let us take lodging to rest our bodies and wash away the dust we collected along the way. We can find other travelers there that speak about their lands and its ways. London is a place where all who seek treasures and good fortune travel to. Some leave with sacks filled with coins while others leave with only the clothes on their backs. It's a matter of sharp mind and quick wit in the arena of commerce," said Squire.

The two mounted the wagon and started for the inn. There were crowds stirring about in the busy streets. Some appeared strange to Thomas. Some had dark skins or wore funny hats. Some had slanted eyes with long braided hair. They spoke strange languages and grouped together when they walked. There were beautiful women dressed in gowns that spread wide from the waist.

They had arrived at the inn. A young boy came running up to them and asked, "Shall I board your horse and wagon for the night sir?" "Two nights," replied Squire. "Very well sir. Shall it be hay for the horse or oats and barley?" said the boy. "Oats and barley if you please and sixpence for your efforts." "Thank you, sir. I'll tell my master of your desire and generosity," as the boy took the horse by the bridle and led it away.

The two took their bags and started for the front of the inn. They were stopped by two women. Both were beautiful and flirtatious to the weary travelers. The fragrance of wild flowers was about them.

"You two look like you could use a good time with the likes of Frances and me. My name is Milly and if there's one thing I know, it's how to make a man glad he's a man. What say you men? Is a good time with two good lookers on your bones?" asked the tall one. Frances moved closer Thomas. She heaved her breast up to his face to create a hefty cleavage, then bounced her breast a few times scaring Thomas. She smiled and winked at him. Thomas was completely surprised by what was happening. He turned to Squire and looked at him for some explanation or guidance.

"Not now ladies, not now. Perhaps when we have refreshed ourselves and washed away some of the dirt of a long journey. I must say you are a charming pair, and we are flattered by your offer," spoke Squire. The ladies bowed before them and turned to walk away.

"These are the ladies of pleasure Thomas. They give their bodies for coin to anyone who will pay their price. The church people speak strongly against them while the same indulge in their flesh behind closed doors. They are called prostitutes. I prefer to call them mothers and daughters who provide for their wellbeing and the wellbeing of those they love. It's the way of the world my son.

Always offer kindness at the beginning of every engagement. If it be accepted, then offer more. Our engagement with them was one of business. They sought a wage for a service. We did not accept or decline the offer. We merely offered a possibility to their proposal. They were satisfied with our response then excused themselves to offer their trade elsewhere. Judge not another for the life they lead.

The two entered and walked to the counter. A young woman greeted them with a warm smile. "How may I help you?" she asked. "We seek lodging at your inn for two nights and a proper bath for us both." replied Squire. "Shall it be one room or two, sir?" she asked. "I think two. My snoring would keep my friend awake all the night," replied Squire.

A boy stepped forward and offered to carry the bags to the room. Squire accepted his offer and gave him a pence for his pocket. As they stepped away from the desk, the young woman gave Thomas a wink and a smile. Thomas returned the smile and followed Squire.

"We have some of the finest dinning in London when you're ready to eat gentlemen," came the voice from behind the desk. Squire turned at her and said, "Yes you do child. Some of the finest in all of England I would say."

Once they arrived at their rooms, Squire said, "Thomas take rest until they come to get you for your bath. Take a change of clothes to wear afterwards. Either give your clothes you wear now to whomever wants them or dispose of them. We'll go shopping tomorrow for better clothing. It's important to look like proper businessmen." "I will do as you say sir and thank you for all this," replied Thomas as he entered his room.

Soon a knock came at the door. "Sir your bath is ready. Are you ready? came a voice at the door. "Yes, I'm ready. Allow me to gather some things," replied Thomas. He opened the door and the girl from behind the counter stood there to escort him.

He followed her down the stairs and out the back door of the inn. They entered another building where he saw seven bathtubs in a line. Three of which were occupied by one male and two females. His escort, seeing the look on Thomas' face said, "It's alright sir. This is commonplace here. The Romans were the designers of such practice.

Where are you from?" "I'm from Danbury," replied Thomas. "Danbury? One of our cooks is from Danbury. Helen is her name. You'll have to meet her. She is a lovely sort, always looking after everyone. "What is her last name?" asked Thomas. "I don't know. She never said. She's working tonight. You can meet her then. Your Squire knows her well. He is fond of her, and they spend time together whenever he visits London," replied the maiden.

"My name is Thomas, Thomas Sonnet. What is your name?" "Well Thomas Sonnet, my name is Catherine, Catherine Dubois. My father and his brother own the inn and a few other things in town. I work here along with my two brothers and a cousin," she replied.

"Your Squire paid for you to receive the first water for your bath," said Catherine. "What do you mean, first water?" asked Thomas. "The bath you will be having will be fresh water from our spring out back. After you have finished your bath, we will sell the same water to someone else for less money," answered Catherine. "I see. Shall I prepare for my bath in front of you?" asked Thomas. "I could turn away if you'd like but the others will have full view of your back and front side. It's up to you," replied Catherine. After hearing her he awkwardly disrobed and stood before all to see.

To his surprise he did not feel embarrassed. He was pleased with a new sense of freedom. It truly was something different. The display fueled his growing appetite for adventure and discovery. It was a time for new things, new ways, and a new perspective.

He stepped into the tub of warm water and a sense of pleasure overcame him. He released the weariness of the trip and his bladder. He sank in the water until it was at his chin.

"Here is a brush and soap to wash with should you chose to wash you self," said Catherine. "Is there any other way to wash myself?" asked Thomas in sarcasm. "Why yes, there is. Should you choose, I can wash you clean. Your backside especially," responded Catherine in a return sarcastic manner.

"Then please, wash me and wash me well. Wash away all the dirt and the discouraging times I've endured in my short life. Use the brush to scrub away all my errors so that I might stand with the strongest of this land. Use this water to rinse away all the self-doubt that resides within me. Do this that I ask, and I shall make you queen of all of England. What say you, young maiden?" spoke Thomas. He had everyone in ear shot waiting to hear what Catherine would say. "I say you're full of donkey dung and we have not the number of chamber pots to carry it all out of here. What say you of that sir?" joked Catherine. "I say, I am inspired by your wit and your sass," replied Thomas.

She began to wash Thomas while singing a Celtic song about a prince who searched for love. She started at his neck and shoulders using the washcloth to message him. Thomas closed his eyes and took in the moment. It felt good to release control and all inhibitions to another.

She took to washing each arm with extreme care. She would place his hand under her armpit to extent the arm fully as she stroked it back and forth. At times she would shift her body so that his hand touched her breasts. She took the cloth and rubbed it against the soap until it was covered. She began washing his chest by rubbing the cloth in small circles and enlarging the rubs. Then her hand moved to his stomach to continue the bathing.

She brought the cloth to his chest, then back down. She continued the action and each time she'd go a little higher and a little lower until the cloth was held between his legs. Her fingers danced from under the cloth as his enthusiasm grew in size. Her hands glided downward on his legs then back up. She continued the bathing much to his delight.

"That should have you clean and ready for whatever comes your way, Thomas," said Catherine with a smile and a twinkle in her eye. "Yes, I suppose you're right. I must say I really enjoyed the bath. I never knew something as simple as bathing could be so sensuous.

I think I'll try it again before we leave, given you be the one to bath me," replied Thomas. "I would love to have the opportunity once again. Perhaps you would enjoy the same privately in your room sometime," suggested Catherine. "What? You could bring a tub like this to the room?" asked Thomas. "Oh no, no. I would wash you with warm water and soap as you lied naked on the bed. It's best done in the light of a single candle. You let me know when you feel the need and I will fulfill it," spoke Catherine in seductive manner.

CHAPTER 43

Thomas dressed in clean clothes with Catherine in attendance. She took a comb and combed his hair pulling it back to form a ponytail. She removed a red ribbon from her pocket and tied his hair. She placed her hands on his shoulders, turned him around and said, "You look like a proper gentleman now. Welcome to London Thomas. I hope you enjoy your stay with us."

"Thank you, Catherine, for your hospitality and kindness. I never imagined such a time as this in my expectations of London. To this day I will always remember. I arrived this day to London open to whatever it would bring. So many things crossed my path. Yet, to have one as beautiful as you, offer such care to me, a stranger, touches my heart. The depths of which I cannot measure. Please take meal with me this evening, I beg you. I wish to know more about you and London," said Thomas.

"I would love to dine with you, but my presence is needed in the kitchen and at the tables. My father would not allow me to take such leave of my duties. Perhaps we could arrange something else. I could enter your bed this evening," said Catherine. Thomas wasn't sure he understood her intention. "That would be nice I must say. Perhaps we could meet later and make some plans that would suit us both," replied Thomas. "As you wish," responded Catherine. The two parted ways and Thomas went in search of Squire.

He heard Squire's familiar laugh and found him seated with others at a large table. Squire saw Thomas coming towards him. "What's this I see? Why Thomas you look lifted from last I saw you. What damsel has cast her spell upon you to have you appear as a prince? Tell me, so that I too may seek out this one to issue me under such a spell," joked Squire.

"Thomas, please join us. I want you to meet these men of commerce. Everyone, this is my apprentice and business partner. He is not from my loins but he as a son to me. He comes from good stock, fine parents and good up bringing," spoke Squire. Thomas sat with them as those seated, greeted him as one.

"What do you think of London Thomas? Does it suit you?" asked one of the men. "I'm taken back from all I have seen. I am enjoying myself and long to visit this great city as often as I can," replied Thomas.

The men continued their conversations of commerce and the developing trends. Some seated were also printers in the land. Thomas became the student as he listened to them. They discussed the risks in publishing Bibles for the common man to read. There was a campaign to suppress the availability to the written word. Some were being threaten while others had closed their shops.

The Catholic church was at odds with the Protestant stance of individual rights and free thinking. The Catholic Church sought to bring all under the rule of Rome and the pontiff. The rebellion would not be a peaceful one. Not only for England but for all of Europe and beyond.

The publishing and distribution was being funded by a silent group. No one was sure who they were. There was plenty of money to go around to flood the land with Bibles. The truth held within the text had been suppress for centuries by the orthodox churches. The European continent held the graves of many spiritual pilgrims who spoke out against the practices of the church.

It was believed that a flood of Bibles across the land could inspire others to rebel. So many that the church couldn't persecute them all. Free speech and the free press were the only things standing between freedom and tyranny in the eyes of some.

Thomas was listening with ears wide open. These men and their views were part of a reformation that was sweeping across Europe. Thomas felt privileged to be in such a presence. Hearing the different viewpoints going back and forth across the table was priceless to him. It was a time of reform. A time to open new doors and embrace literature, art, and the education for all.

"Is anyone ready for another pint? How about you Thomas?" came a voice beside the group. It was Catherine. "Why Thomas, you know this fine lass, do you? So, this is the source of your new appearance.

Excellent choice. Tell me my dear, did you capture this one in your net or did he woe you with his poetry," asked Squire. Thomas was embarrassed by Squire's words but tried not to show it.

Catherine looked around the table and said, "Oh, I would have to say that I had my sight on you Squire but because you turned from me, I had no choice but to choose Thomas in your stead." Everyone laughed at her wit coupled with her charm. One man fell backwards in his chair from laughing so hard. Squire was the loudest of them all. He was trying to stop but couldn't. He motioned to Catherine to bring drinks for everyone around the table.

Catherine soon returned with pints of their finest ale, cheese, dried meat, and bread for everyone. As she went to leave, she placed her hand on Thomas' shoulder brushing it as she stepped away.

When she was out of earshot, Squire leaned towards Thomas and said, "Be careful with that one Thomas. She is a fair lady indeed. She is sought by many a suitor who are patrons to the inn. Some carry jealousies on their sleeve and are quick to scuffle. Let your desire for her be private. There are many eyes about that watch her and who she is common with. Best to save one's heart for one more subtle in nature."

Thomas looked about the room and saw a man sitting near the bar. He was giving Thomas a long stare. It made him feel uneasy. Again, Squire leaned into Thomas and said, "That one is a ruffian from Ireland. He's known for his quick temper and bad behavior when he's drunk. Best not to provoke him. He loves to make a spectacle of himself as he beats down men. Keep your eyes away from his stare. Soon he will lose interest in you and return to his whiskey."

Squire was well known at the inn. He was known for his kindness and generosity to all who worked there. Never had he ever squabbled about price or service. He was known for tipping the workers often for the comfort and care they afforded him.

Thomas decided to step outside and take a stroll. He wanted to take in some of the sights while Squire had his bath. He saw a small crowd gathered around a man perched on a stool. He held a paper in one hand and held the other over his heart. He stepped closer to hear the man's words. Everyone standing before him seemed pleased by what he was doing.

He was reciting a poem about love. He spoke in dramatic form as the words left his lips. He would turn one way, then the next as his words dripped of weeping for a love felt, but never held. Then at the last of his performance, his voice lifted as the words came sowing the seeds of hope of one day seeing her again in the light of heaven.

The crowd applauded his performance, and he took many a bow in return. Thomas was impressed with the way he brought the poem from the ear to mesh with the heart by using body movements to accentuate the message.

A lady of wealth and position stepped towards him and took a coin from her purse. She pressed it in his hand as she spoke to him. He was excited hearing her words, and he kissed her hand in return. The onlookers had walked away. The poet was admiring the coin as he picked up his stool. Thomas was still standing there admiring the man.

"May I help you, young man?" asked the poet. "Forgive me for staring. It's just that I've never heard poetry spoken in such manner before," replied Thomas. "Where are you from? You don't sound like you are from here," asked the poet. "Danbury sir. I'm from Danbury," replied Thomas.

"I know Danbury. I used to travel with a troupe of actors. We traveled about the countryside offering our plays for food and lodging. We were in Danbury many times," said the poet. "I saw a few of them myself sir," replied Thomas. "What brings you to London?" "Books. I work in a print shop in Danbury. We delivered some books just today to John Thorstrom print shop," replied Thomas.

"Do you think my poem is worthy of the ink to publish it?" asked the poet. "Yes sir, I do. But reading the same would never do it justice. You could write a story around your poem. That way the reader could feel your joy and your pain," replied Thomas. "Could you write such a story around the poem as easy as you let on?" asked the poet. "Yes sir. I believe I could," responded Thomas. "Well, I must know more about you. I have an errand to perform for the shilling given to me. Once I'm free, I could meet you somewhere. Where are you staying?" "We are at the Downey Inn," replied Thomas. "I know the place well," spoke the poet.

"By the way, what is your name?" asked the poet. "Thomas, Thomas Sonnet," he replied. "My new friend do you know what sonnet means in

Italian? It means little verse or poem. My name is Colton, Colton Quigley. It's my pleasure to welcome you to London and all its treasures."

They agreed to meet at the inn later in the day in hopes forging a new friendship. Colton the poet went in search of his lady benefactor. Thomas the storyteller went in search of another treasure.

CHAPTER 44

The light of day was dwindling. The streets were less crowded now. Thomas was ready to return to the inn as he reflected on the events of today. Over and over in his mind he relived each one again. Each time he was elated in spirit. He was approaching the inn, when he noticed a small group of women speaking to every man that walked by.

"There he is," spoke one of the women. She approached Thomas and said, "How would you like to saddle me and ride me all the way home? I like you young ones. You're quick to find your oats, you are. How about it doll? Do you have a quid in your pocket to share with Lizzy?" Thomas was startled by her forwardness. She smelled strong of rose water, but her words were like thorns that would injure if one got too close. He walked past her without saying a word. He was relieved once inside the inn.

The Downey Inn was crowded with people seated at the tables and the bar. He had never seen such a sight before. Desperately he searched for Squire. He could hear his bellowing voice over the crowd noise. "Squire!" shouted Thomas. "Over here Thomas. I'm over here," shouted Squire. Thomas made his way to the sound of his voice.

There sat Squire with some of the men from the afternoon and others who were arguing about something. He sat beside Squire and listened in to the stories going back and forth across the table. There was one at the table that appeared suspicious. He listened to the conversations but never spoke. His ears were doing all the work as he seemed to be making mental notes.

Spies were everywhere in London. Good information could be sold for more coin than a month's wages. There were spies of industry, spies of the crown. Trust is a word, not a practice when it came to position and commerce. Success relies on information. The better the information, the heavier the coin.

The conversations became relaxed once the food arrived. Catherine, along with other family members, were serving the men. She took the first plate and sat it down before Thomas. Thomas enjoyed the attention and the looks he was getting from the men seated. "Here, what's this? The first plate always goes to the one that pays for the feast. Thank you, Thomas, for your generosity," joked Squire. The men laughed but Thomas wasn't so sure if it was a joke.

John Thorstrom was amongst those seated. "Relax Thomas. It is my honor to pay the bill for all the hard work given. What we do here today can change the world as we see it. Education, knowledge, and exploration is what is needed if we are to ever change the face of the planet. Look at the progress being made all around us. The press is making knowledge available to thousands more people than ever before.

One man's idea can be printed for others to build on. One idea leading to another idea and another. Held forever on pages between binders. One man can speak a truth that is heralded for its content. If the man is killed, then the truth and its revelation dies with him. But if the revelation is printed and the man is killed the truth lives on forever. This is why we do what we do. There is no limit to what printing can do. Our trade is an honorable one. We are the keepers of the word. We will not let the repression of the church to dictate what we can print and what we can't. You, Thomas are young enough to see how the printing of Bibles you and Squire delivered will change the landscape as we know it," spoke John as a true patriot.

Thomas was impressed with John's words and the devotion behind each one. He never thought about the work as a printer in such a way. Books could be the light bearer that the world was waiting for. Others seated at the table took John's words to heart.

One man rose from the table. He lifted his mug and said, "I traveled here today as many of you have. I too delivered the Bibles as contracted by John. My pockets weigh heavy with coin as does yours. I had hoped my return home would be spent listening to the sound made by the jingle of those coins. After hearing John, I think I shall be listening to words spoken here tonight over and over again as I make my way home.

I believe when I'm at my shop setting the type and pressing the ink, those same words will be reminding me of something greater than coin or position. I hope others here do the same. Here's to John Thorstrom for all his work and all his care that he gives freely without obligation. Gentlemen I ask you to rise and lift your drink high for our host. John Thorstrom." All the men, except the quiet one, stood and toasted John. Others added to the toasting until everyone was seated again.

The evening wore on. The crowd was no more. All that was left were staff and a few of the guests still seated. "Come Thomas. It's time for us to retire for the day," said Squire. The two ascended the staircase together. Too many years and too much ale required Thomas to help Squire with his walking. "Good night son and thank you for helping me." Thomas watched Squire open the door and disappear to the darkness. Thomas turned to his room and opened the door.

A single candle was lit in his room. There lied Catherine across his bed as the soft light of the candle sent its rays flickering across her body. "I wanted to be with you tonight, Thomas. I know we hadn't the chance to agree on my proposal from earlier today, so I decided to present myself to you in this way. If you want me to leave, I will do so with a heavy heart. If you want me to stay, I promise to make it a memorable night for us both," spoke Catherine in an enticing tone.

She extended one arm towards him to invite him to her side. He stepped to her and extended his arm to hers. Their fingers rolled around each other's as the energy between them grew. She gave him a gentle tug to join her on the bed. He stood before her and began to remove his clothing as he did when he prepared for his bath. Only this time she watched him with different eyes. He stood before her as the light of the candle continued to dance its rays about their bodies adding a greater allure to the moment.

Catherine went to her knees while still on the bed. He stepped closer and the two embraced. Lips met in fury. Hands quickly caressed across each other's body in exploration filled with excitement and pleasure. The kissing was so intense each had to gasp for breath. She pulled Thomas down to the bed landing on top of him without breaking their embrace. They rolled over on one another several times. He broke away from her lips and placed his hand to her breasts, gently caressing each. She lied there looking up at him to view his approval.

Their passion gave pause, and their hearts fell to silence. Eyes still held themselves in embrace as the two slowed time in order to taste the fruits of passion. He brought his lips to hers as she wrapped her arms around his neck. He entered her gently as she held his face. Their eyes were darting back and forth as the fervent passion was returning. The only sound in the room was their breath as they reacted to each other's love making. Slowly the two rocked back and forth with eyes still holding their embrace. They were nearing the summit together. They were feeling the energy building around them. Their eyes widened with each passing breath. They were one step away from euphoria and held their breath. They exploded in ecstasy together with passion still building taking them beyond the summit. His back arched lifting his face away from hers. Her arms left his neck and took hold his back. She pulled him to her as they released the sounds of pleasure. Their bodies went limp as lied beside each other.

They continued to kiss each other as their bodies exchanged each other's sweat. He began stroking her hair as she looked at him with deep green eyes. The two drifted off to slumber holding the other. The last light of the candle sent its ray across the room and was no more.

Morning came and Thomas awoke. Realizing where he was, he turned to see Catherine, but she was no more. He rolled over and closed his eyes thinking about the night before. Then a loud knock at the door that startled him. He shot out of bed and stood by the door. "Thomas are you up?" shouted Squire. "Yes, I'm up. Let me get dressed and I'll be down," replied Thomas. Thomas relieved himself in the chamber pot and washed for the day. He was dressed and heading down the stairs, careful not to trip on the way down. The evenings tryst with Catherine left his legs a little shaky.

He sat beside Squire feeling taller, stronger and a part of something grand. He could feel the wind at his back. He was no longer consumed by task and outcome. He was thinking about possibilities and the opportunities that go with it. The mind of a created was shifting to that of a creator. The power of a word and how it can affect the mind, heart, and direction of one or many made him feel alive.

Catherine walked lively to their table carrying a platter of sausages, cheese, and fresh baked bread in one hand and a tea pot in the other.

"What a pair I have the honor of serving on this fine morning. I trust everyone had a sound sleep from evenings end," as she winked at Thomas. He smiled and was slightly embarrassed.

"That reminds. Thomas did you injure yourself in some manner last night? I heard yelling coming from your room," asked Squire. "No sir," replied Thomas. "I think it was from a nightmare or something like that." Catherine giggled and said, "Well, I've heard it called many things before but never a nightmare. Was it a nightmare Thomas?"

Now he was embarrassed. He hung his head and said, "No I don't believe so." Squire looked at him, then at Catherine, then back at Thomas. "Oh, I see. Well, I guess the sound of yelling is the same for pleasure as it is for pain," spoke Squire as he smiled before taking another bite.

All obey the desires of the body and the desires of the soul. Yet spirit lacks desire and carries no map or plan from which to learn. Quietly it observes the plight of the mortal on its journey through life. At times its whispers enter to offer blessings in moments of rejoicing and times of grave sorrow. To wipe away a tear or offer salve to an old wound from a battle fought long ago.

The jubilee awakens those who still sleep under the heavens and the stars. A great light comes forth bringing love for all mankind, slave and master, mother and child, father, and son. One lost lamb of a hundred found, and so the shepherds work is done. To this destiny and its completion are the footsteps of the mortals and of the souls of those who came before these in witness. Those who walked in the darkness for the sake of the light.

CHAPTER 45

Thomas and Squire stepped from the inn on to the bustling life of Downey Street and the heart of London. Cargo wagons from afar lined the street to sell their wares to own a part of the prosperity offered here. Food vendors were at every corner sending wafting savory aromas to spark hunger. Street peddlers were calling out to passersby to purchase their offerings. Minstrels walked the street singing songs of love and despair. Musicians played were the crowds gathered. They lived on the generosity of onlookers. These busy streets were filled with purpose and desires. Thomas was absorbing every moment. He took great delight as a child would at the site of so many new things.

"Come Thomas. Let's find some proper clothing for you. I wish to offer you another lesson in the world of commerce. It's not enough to produce a quality product. There is so much more to it," spoke Squire as they strolled along the streets. Squire was stressing the importance of first impressions and the art of barter. How one's clothing speaks before the first word can be spoken. The manner in which a person presents themselves to others is of most importance.

Impressions carry a great deal of weight and so can the coin carried in one's pocket if done correctly. It was important to sell yourself before the product or idea. "Charm the women with flirtations and compliment. Then they will steer their husbands in your direction. If you dare sleep with one, that too will attract their husbands to you but for reasons that will render no coin or future in your favor. Shake a man's hand firmly, look him in the eye and he will respect you. Shake a man's hand and it feel his limp, bless him and walk away," spoke Squire.

Thomas listened to every instruction Squire gave. The good Squire taught him the art of printing and book binding. Now, he was teaching Thomas the art of commerce. "Please teach me all you know Squire. I wish to be as quick witted as you in knowledge and stature," said Thomas with sincerity. "Such is my intention, Thomas. One day you will come in my place. When my body is worn and my bones can travel no more, you will represent our interests here in London.

First, we must make a proper gentleman out of you. When that day comes you will dress as a prince and speak as one. It's all about the act. Act the part and all else will fall into place. We are all actors Thomas on the grand stage of life.

Here we are Thomas at one of London's finest haberdasheries. Once we enter it's important that you not become overwhelmed by what you see. If the shopkeeper see's that on your face he will ask a higher price. If you appear indifferent, he will ask a lower one. Understand?" asked Squire. "Yes Squire, I understand," replied Thomas.

As they stepped inside, they were met by a charming Irishman. He was wearing a green tweed suit with bright orange hair and a beard to match. Thomas had never seen anyone with orange hair before. "How may I help such fine looking gentlemen on this beautiful day," he asked. "First impression," murmured Squire. "We are here to see if this establishment carries a suitable line of clothing for my friend," spoke Squire in an indifferent tone as he looked around the store. "I'm sure we can accommodate whatever need you have sir. Allow me to show you some items that just arrived only yesterday. I'm sure your friend will find them acceptable," said the clerk. "Lead the way sir. We have business elsewhere. We have no time to tarry," said Squire.

The clerk took them to the back of the store away from the stock at the front. The clerk having seen what Thomas was wearing thought it best to take them to their least expensive stock on hand. Squire recognized his play and planned to use it against him.

"We have everything for the farmers and the dukes. Have a look around and decide what is a proper fitting for your friend. I will check back with you momentarily," said the clerk.

Thomas went about looking at the clothes one by one. They all looked good to him. They were of good material and void of tears and stains. He imagined himself owning several sets. Squire took no interest in the clothes he was looking at.

Soon the clerk returned and asked, "Have we made a decision on what you'd like to purchase today?" "I think not. I'm looking at these and see they are used clothing. We did not come here to your haberdashery to buy the clothes from the backs of others sir. I could have found better from the street vendors I passed on the way here. Why do you insult us with such direction sir? I was told by respectable people that you were one of the finest in London. Did they speak falsely to me sir? asked Squire.

"I am sorry sir. I misled you and your friend. Please allow me to make amends that would be satisfactory to your liking sir," replied the clerk. "Allow me to summon our seamstress so that she can fashion a suit that would be fitting for such a handsome young man." He stepped away from the two and soon returned with a woman at his side.

"Gentlemen, this is Mary our seamstress. She will fashion you a satisfying array of clothing to your liking," spoke the clerk. "A most agreeable arrangement, I'm sure. We are pleased with your offer. And how much do you expect in price," asked Squire. "Why sir only a few shillings over our cost, I assure you. I pray that you will share with those who recommended our establishment of our hospitality and accommodations to your needs," replied the clerk. "I will do as you request sir. Your proposition is most acceptable," replied Squire. "Mary, please attend to these gentlemen and give them your best. Won't you?" said the clerk as he stepped away. "Come with me young man. I need to get your measurements for a proper fit. Then you can pick out the cloth that suits you," said Mary.

They walked to the tailoring room where long tables held partially made clothes. Stacks of material filled the shelves attached to the wall.

"Nichole? Nichole come dear. We need to measure a young man for a suit. It was a suit you wanted, right?" asked Mary. Thomas nodded yes.

"I only ask a coin or two for my apprentice. She has fallen on bad times, she has. Poor thing, they left her on a church step when she was born to have the sisters look after her. She was raised in an orphanage with a bunch of other little crumb snatchers. She ran away when she had the chance and wound up here. The owner took pity on her and gave her a room to live in. She's been here some seven years now. She kept the place swept and clean in the beginning. Eventually she learned how to cut the cloth and sew the likes of whatever the customer wanted. She's as good as any in London I tell you," spoke Mary to the two.

Nichole? Did you hear me dear? We have work to do. I need you in here dear. Come out and meet the generous gentlemen who come to benefit us."

A hand appeared to one side of a curtain covering a doorway. It pushed the curtain to one side and out stepped a young woman with long blonde hair and eyes bluer than the sky. Her skin was the color of milk. She walked with her head down, her eyes fixed on the ground before her. She stood before the three, curtsied and bowed her head displaying the manner of one who spent in lifetime in servitude.

Squire was moved by her manners and her innocence. He smiled warmly as he watched her. Thomas had never experienced one so humble. She was a woman of beauty. Thomas felt something familiar about her but did not understand it. "I'm pleased to meet your acquaintance gentlemen," she spoke in a low voice.

"What my dear drove you to be a seamstress as your trade," inquired Squire. "It was out of necessity sir. I needed a place to live and eat. They were kind to me and took me in," replied Nichole. "I am of the understanding that you are in need of finance. How could one of so little means have a debt to bear. Please tell me if I pry out of curiosity," said Squire.

"I receive favors and teachings from those who work here. Sometimes my labor here is not enough to pay for such things, so I create debt," replied Nichole. "I see. And what is the price of this debt, if I may ask?" replied Squire. "A single quid is her debt," spoke Mary sharply at Squire. "Very well. Consider her debt cleared. I will square it with the owner when I leave," replied Squire. "I can take that for you sir. You see the owner is not here right now and I'm one of a few here that can be trusted," replied Mary. "I see. Here is the quid for the ransom placed on her shoulders. And I offer another quid to pay for any other debt that may occur in the near future," replied Squire.

Nichole raised her head to look on Squire and thank him for his generosity. Her face came into view and Thomas was smitten. She too felt something when she looked at Thomas. An awkward moment arose as the two stared back and forth at each other trying to say something, but no words came.

Finally, Thomas asked, "Have we met before?" "I think not sir but once I had a dream. Someone who looked like you came to me. He told me wonderful things about life. He said the two of us had shared in another place and in another time held in the grasp of love. He promised to find me again one day and take me away from hardship. He said his name was Thom, I think. Yes, it was Thom," she replied. "I'm Thomas, Thom is short for Thomas! Was I the one you saw in your dream?" he exclaimed.

"I think this exchange has gone too far for the two of you. A dream is just that, a dream. Would you believe a dream held a prevalence to the matters at hand? I think not children. Fantasies and wishes have no place in commerce or love," spoke Squire.

"Mary, I beg you, show us your cloth so we may employ your services to do our bidding. Measure him for pant, jacket, and vest. I think three shirts will do well to finish your trouble. Make your stitch strong as a horses back and craft the fit well. When he is asked where such fine clothing may be found, he can tell them it was from your hand," spoke Squire as he leaned into Mary with a smile. She accepted his flattery and returned the smile. "Thomas when you have finished meet me at the tavern across the street. All this talk has parched my throat," said Squire as he turned away to leave.

"Come Thomas. You pick the cloth, and we will do the rest. Nichole get the measure string from the drawer so we can begin," spoke Mary. Thomas selected a fine gray tweed for his suit. "Oh, you'll be happy with your selection. It comes from a reputable merchant and his family in Dover. It will repel the dampness and hold its color much longer than other cloth," reported Mary.

Nichole stepped up to Thomas standing just inches away from his face. Her blue eyes spoke from the heart. The exchange about the dream was still alive in spite of Squires dismissal. They stood before each other feeling a connection having no history in this lifetime.

"Give me the lad's chest size Nichole," requested Mary. Nichole raised the string and wrapped it around Thomas' chest without breaking her vision of him. "How many knots Nichole?" "Forty and two," replied Nichole. "And his waist?" "Thirty and one," replied Nichole. "What of his inseam child?" Nichole still held Thomas in her view. Slowly she went to her knees. Carefully she placed one end of the string to his groin and the other end to his heel. "He's a thirty and two Mary," replied Nichole. "Now his sleeve if you please." It be between thirty and thirty one," replied Nichole. "Thirty one it is. And his neck dear. What about his neck?" asked Mary.

Nichole stood inches away from him as she placed the string behind his neck. She pulled on the string until their lips met. She closed her eyes and kissed the prince. He was on fire inside. He reached up and put his arms around her as he returned the kiss. They held the kiss as long as they could. What is his neck … alright you two that will be enough. I want his neck size dear, not how long he can hold his breath," said Mary. "He's a sixteen," replied Nichole as she kept tugging on the string for another embrace. "Alright, there it be Sir Thomas. Two days pass and your suit will be ready for you. Nichole see the young man to the door, won't you? And don't forget to come back. We have plenty to do before the day is through," said Mary.

Nichole took Thomas by the hand and led him to the front of the store. The couple turned to look at each other as she placed her hand behind his neck. "May I take one last measure before you walk away Thom?" asked Nichole. "Yes, of course you may," replied Thomas. She brought her face close to his as her eyes shifted back and forth at his. She pressed her lips against his. His arms wrapped around her and held her with care. It was a moment held from a time passed. In body they were strangers. In soul they were not strangers. They were lovers and the best of friends.

Their lips parted and she looked deep beyond his eyes. "I knew it. My measure was to see if the fire I felt for you equaled the fire that lives in you for me. It was. So much so that I would leave this place right now and walk with you. We would embrace every sunset and at every sunrise as one in heart and soul. Every day I would drink from your cup and you from mine.

If you walk out the door without me, we will remain prisoners held in a world built of circumstances and consequence. We can break the chains of bondage together right here, right now. Or will you return to your Squire to defer our freedom for another day, in another lifetime? Either way I shall weep, one out of joy or one out of sorrow," spoke Nichole from the heart. A single tear rolled down her cheek. She could see the answer in his eye.

A sinking feeling overcame Thomas. She was right about what she said. She possessed nothing, so there was nothing for her to lose. She was free to walk away and follow her heart. Thomas admired and envied her position.

Yet his duties were to those who depended on him to fulfill the agreements of the past. Their futures, their prosperity rested on his shoulders. The fruits of desire and passion held in contrast to the duties of obligation and dependency. The two perplexing life at every twist and turn.

Nichole looked at him and said, "Should you ever change your mind, you can always find me here. I will wait for you Thom. I will wait for you as long as it takes. Nothing in this world can hold me from what we feel at this moment. Nothing. I'll wait for you, I will,' said Nichole. She turned and walked back to the sewing room as her heart was weeping.

CHAPTER 46

Nichole's image were still burning into his memory. Everything about her. Every word, every look, and every step she took etched to his book of life. Heart strings were tugging at him to return to her embrace while his feet carried him towards the pub.

Thomas saw Squire seated towards the rear and took a seat beside him. The bar maid brought him a pint of ale as Squire had requested. "How many days do they need to finish your clothes?" asked Squire. "Two days," replied Thomas. "Then we shall tarry longer than expected. No complaint from me. How about you?" said Squire. "I could stay here for weeks if you'd be willing," replied Thomas.

"Tell me Thomas, what was the most important thing you observed across the street, besides Nichole?" asked Squire. "I don't know what you mean," replied Thomas. "The art of barter young man, the art of trade. They would have been happy to sell used clothing as new stock at a high price. Everyone in business has an angle and at least two follow up angles should one fail. Never pay the asking price. Otherwise, your reputation will suffer. Businessmen respect a good trader who uses his wit.

At home I'm the only printer. John Clayborne owns the only inn in town. Because there is no competition, we are not bothered with price dickering. Here in the grand city, there are many printers and many inns. All are trying to be the best deal at a best price. Success in business is measured by the profit of your work be it coin or be it in reputation. Finish your pint and I'll show you another side of London.

Thomas was quick about the pint and the two entered the bustling streets of London. Squire hailed a passing carriage and they climbed aboard. "Where to my lord," asked the driver. "We wish to visit the River Thames area," replied Squire. "Very good sir. Do you want the scenic way or is your business one of importance?" asked the driver. "The scenic route will be fine. It's my friends first visit to London," replied Squire. Thomas was taking it all in and grateful for the experience.

Thomas saw a man appearing to sell boys to others for a price. Squire assured him that wasn't the case. He explained that they were chimney sweepers. The chimneys of the homes needed to be cleaned to prevent a fire from starting and burning everything to the ground.

He watched as two men fought in the street. They wrestled each other to the ground and rolled around. One of them took a knife and cut the others throat. The injured man lied bleeding on the ground gasping for breath. No one rushed to help him. They walked past the man without even a look. The carriage went by the man lying on the ground bleeding. Thomas stood in the carriage to look down at the man. He looked up at Thomas and outstretched his arm to plead for help. Thomas was furious in heart because no one would help him.

"He was a thief and a bully to those here. No one will help him. He'll be lying in a paupers grave before the sun sets," said the driver. "Justice is better served with words rather than knives," said Squire. The driver continued on the way without offering a response.

The carriage was nearing the river district. The crowds of people grew larger the closer they traveled to the Thames. Some they passed by were dressed in stately clothes. Their walk was more like a prance. The men bowed before the ladies and the ladies gave curtsy to the men. It appeared like a dance to Thomas. "Prim and proper they be Thomas. Make no mistake. They seek profit in status and position. You will never find one with knife or dagger. But they will, in their own fashion, stab one another in the back. Climbing the social ladder of London is not for the faint of heart," spoke Squire as he gazed upon them.

The minstrels followed close to the socialites as did the opportunist. Each shared an interest in earning a coin for a service or favor. Profit was the center theme here. Be it in the form of wage or the fickleness of love.

A man was at the corner of a street standing on a wooden crate making proclamations. He held a book in one hand as he spoke to the crowd. He spoke of the sin of man and hells fire damnation for the unbelievers or those who turned their backs the church. He was shouting to those who passed his way. Two women stood before him quietly listening and accepting his teaching. Others mocked him as they passed him by.

Thomas was taking it all in as the student. He was in the grandest of classrooms. Everyone he came in contact with were the faculty. Processing every witness, every word, every action, and reaction. London was having an effect on everything he ever believed in.

Squire realized that the Thomas that left Danbury would not be the Thomas that would return to Danbury. He knew Thomas would never be satisfied at home. He has the heart of an explorer. He would prefer to live in a tent so he could move on to the next adventure rather than live in a mansion that held all the treasures of the world.

Thomas turned his attention at a group of onlookers applauding one of the minstrel' acts. There stood Colton Quigley in the middle of them soaking it up. "I know him!" shouted Thomas to Squire. Colton caught sight of Thomas and waved at the carriage and rushed over to it. Squire recognized Colton from the previous plays he attended while in London. He also knew that he was a ladies' man who took strong drink on occasion.

"It is of good fortune to see you once again Thomas. Squire, it's good to see you also. I had no idea the two of you were connected. Please come down from your carriage and join us. I wish to introduce you both to some of the cast that will be performing this evening at the theatre. I do hope that you can attend," spoke Colton in pleasant manner. He helped both men dismount. Squire paid the driver and he pulled away.

Colton began introducing the two to the troupe as they walked alongside the socialites. Thomas was enjoying the venue and its pleasantries. He imagined himself being a member of the cast for tonight's performance.

Some of the troupe were receiving a coin or two while others received notes of invitation. The notes gave address and dates for private affairs. The opportunities would sometimes lead to steady work be they poets or musicians.

Squire had purchased poetry from some members of the troupe in the past. His late wife was a poet and wrote many a stanza. It was her work that inspired him to be a printer. He printed every one of them. He had small book of them he kept at his bedside in Danbury.

Squire enjoyed these people. They gave him the attention that he loved. They were free spirits and they so reminded him of his late wife. Once the introductions had ended Squire invited everyone to Engels Pub located at the river's edge. He received cheers from the troupe as some of them ran ahead of the others. They entered the pub and stepped up to the bar. Squire spoke to Juliane Engels, the owner and set the bill at two drinks for each person. Squire paid the agreed price up front then joined one of the many groups assembled about the pub.

Thomas was following Colton as he worked the room like a politician. He spoke of new ideas to enhance their performances in order to advance their position. He was passionate and focused on his delivery. He could have been the leader of the troupe, but he shunned from responsibility.

He was a complex soul. He was open to new things and spouted his poetry with fervor. Yet he was private about himself, who would sometimes disappear for weeks at a time then reappear as if nothing had happened.

The celebration went on until midafternoon. Most had left for rest before tonight's performance. Squire noticed some of them had traded their pints for a meager meal. He could see that some were starving.

Some of the stories and poetry he had acquired for publishing was the work of Trudy Briars. Her poetry had strong potential. Squire sought the opinion of another publisher to see if he too was in agreement. He sat with Trudy for some time. He wanted to see more of her work before he left for Danbury. She was thrilled at his interest and happy to oblige. They agreed to meet later.

Colton approached Squire and said, "I trust you both will join our performance this evening?" "We will be in attendance, I'm sure. I want Thomas to share in the developed arts of London," replied Squire. "Excellent. I look forward to your presence. We'll have a party afterwards and the two of you are invited," said Colton. Squire graciously accepted the invitation.

Thomas and Squire stepped back into the street to find their way back to the Downey Inn. Squire was ready for a nap. Thomas was ready for more.

CHAPTER 47

The Terra Theatre sat near the River Thames. It was a circular building with four entrances. Three were for the patrons and one for the troupe. It was built much like the theatres during the Roman period. It was three stories tall. There was general seating except for the first five rows. Those seats were reserved for dignitaries and benefactors of the theatre.

Squire and Thomas had been seated in the second row from the stage, compliments of Colton. Thomas was excited and could barely contain his enthusiasm. Candlelight and light from oil lamps lit the stage bright. Creating its own auric effect.

Four musicians took the stage and began playing. Their presence was important for every evening performance. It helped to silence conversations before the play began. It also helped to relax and entertain the audience and actors.

The musicians were cued that the play was ready to begin. They concluded their performance and took their bows before the audience. Coins were tossed on stage sounding like raindrops as they hit the floor. A young boy from back stage hurried on to the stage to collect the tokens of appreciation.

He gathered the coins and took his bow before the audience. He turned to exit the stage and pretended to trip spilling the coins back to the stage. Everyone in the audience laughed at his antics. He gathered the coins once more and took an exaggerated bow to the audience. A few more coins were thrown for him and his performance. He gathered those quicker than the ones before since they would belong to him. The mood was set. It was time for the play to begin.

Colton stepped on stage dressed like someone of ancient Greece. He spoke to the audience in a rhythmic tone as if he was reading from a well written script. He moved back and forth as he spoke. He made exaggerated hand movements towards each section of the audience. The last gesture was to the balcony. His words combined with his dance helped to prep the audience for the play.

"And now ladies and gentlemen I give you our production, "A Love Lost to Tears," spoke the ancient from the land of Greece. He took a bow and received generous applause. The curtain closed to set the background for the first scene.

The cast and others scurried behind the curtain as the stage was being set. The actors took their positions, then silence. As the curtain was opening all eyes of the audience were held in anticipation. The actors were frozen resembling manikins. The backdrop with its brightly colored scene widens the eyes of the onlookers. In the time of a single breath, the stage became alive with the characters carrying a story.

A story of love fashioned through passion, and another born from lust unfolding before the audience. The plot delivers with its tragedies of the heart and the heroics of the lovers in loss and gain. The sum of which to give inspiration to the audience in their own matters of the heart.

Thomas was floating on air as he watched the play develop. Words spoken gave the message. Body movements amplified the message. Together they were poetry in full motion.

He looked around the audience to see how it was being received. Some were held captive with the performance. Some were attentive but showed little or no expression. A few were fast asleep while unruly children played their games.

Thomas was inspired with the performance and believed that his destiny was held here in the theatre. He longed to be a part of the spectacle. He was impressed how the power of words could be used in a manner other than simple communication. He could feel his core blossoming like a flower embracing the morning sun.

The sound of a grand applause broke him from the spell. The play had ended. Coins of all sorts went flying through the air and fell to the stage. The audience continued the applause and cheering. Some were wiping away the tears, while others offered hugs to one another. The production was successful because it touched searching hearts and wondering minds.

The entire cast came on stage holding hands and took their bows before the audience. The coins were still landing on the stage. A good sign that the play was worth repeating at another time. Colton broke from the line and gestured for each actor to come forward for their share of the applause.

This practice was used to learn the actor's effect on the audience. If little or no applause came it meant a replacement was needed. A great applause meant a guarantee of employment and a greater share of the nights proceeds.

Abigail Moorhead was a wealthy woman in the higher levels of society. She supported the arts and was a great fan of the theatre. She never missed a performance or the opportunity to promote the actors. She supported some by arranging private showings in her home and the homes of other patrons of the arts. She was given the best seat in the house and her every need was always looked after. She often brought younger men as escorts to the performances. She enjoyed the gossip she could generate from such a display.

Colton summoned Squire and Thomas to come up on stage. "We'll, what did you think? Was it enjoyable to your liking?" asked Colton. "I thought it the best I'd ever witnessed. How you can give so much content in such a small amount of time is a wonder. You presented a most impressive story that had me reflecting on my own life," replied Squire.

"You are most generous with your words sir. Please join us for our celebration at Stacy's Pub," said Colton. "Thank you for the invitation but my aging bones fail me to go on lest it be a warm bed," replied Squire. "How about you Thomas? Are you game for drink and rubbing shoulders with these gifted vagabonds?" asked Colton "Yes, I would like that very much," replied Thomas. "Good answer Thomas," muttered Squire with a smile.

Squire left the stage and turned to look at Thomas before leaving. He could see Thomas was intoxicated with the witness of the evening. He did not know how long he would have Thomas as his apprentice. He did know that one day Thomas would return to London and never return to a life in Danbury. He had found a love greater than family, greater than all the possessions of the world.

Squire also wondered if he should have warned him of the pitfalls that awaited him. He felt it better to allow the lessons in life to speak on their own. Surely all would lead to a clarity of vision that would better serve him later in life.

CHAPTER 48

Stacy's Pub was alive with members of the troupe and some from the audience. Theatre night was good for business at the pub before and after the performance. Conversation and laughter filled the room at every corner. Everyone was enjoying the success of the play. They took in more proceeds than usual. It would mean all would eat and sleep under the cover of a roof rather than the stars.

A portion of the proceeds went to the pub's proprietor for the celebration. Another portion went towards the next production. The main characters all received a percentage, and the remainder was portioned out to the rest of the cast.

Trudy Briars stood on a table at the center of the room. She was reciting one of her poems in a voice filled with passion and desire. She was not addressing the crowd in the pub. She was addressing her rhyme upwards to an audience that rested above ceiling and beyond the stars. She spoke the words as a conqueror who carried a mighty sword. Her eyes fixated on her audience as she raised their hearts for the battle before them.

> "We are never to die in heart or take waste,
> The battle lives on forever with us in haste,
> We go forward in living and bury our dead,
> Are we not the keepers of each other, for in death we do shed,
> The likes of mortal witness of its ups and its downs,
> To walk the narrow paths so that love may be found,
> I beseech those of ear and of free mind,
> To lift up your sword and follow mine,
> To a place held sacred in mind and in heart,
> A place we once called home, a place we did part

Trudy delivered her rhyme from a place within, that received its breath from somewhere else beyond mind. At its conclusion the spell began to leave her presence. She slumped over like a wilting flower about to release its petals to the earth.

Some around her were moved by her performance and helped her down from the table. She received great applause from everyone and took her bows with theatric movement. Those who wore the cloak of jealousy mocked her. The moment belonged to her and the creator within. She was not inspired by the applause. No opinion, be it of favor or not, could come between her and her creative nature. Her audience on high sent a white dove to follow her in all her days to come. Thomas was inspired and took notice of the inspirational poet.

He watched her transform from one reality to the other as easy as one takes a breath. Surely this one was destined for greater things he thought. He wished to approach her but what could he say? Others of the troupe surrounded her in body and conversation. He would wait for another time to share with her.

Colton found Thomas and took him around the room to introduce him to the cast. Most conversations were about the performance. Thomas was astounded by the carefree nature of the patrons and actors. They shared creative ideas and possibilities. One person would start with a theme. Another would add a part, then another until the group had a complete play ready for rehearsal. Nothing was being written down. It was all spontaneous using a spark from here and one from there until the story developed into a production. Then it was dropped as quick as it was created.

The intensity of the energy moved Thomas. He so wanted to join in the conversations, but he knew better. It was their collective awareness and shared desires that created the energy moving through the room. Time and experience was a prerequisite for participation.

Two young ladies approached Thomas. They liked his handsome appearance and an innocence he carried. They noticed how open he was and his apparent awkwardness. "Are you an actor or a patron," asked one of the girls. "No, I'm a writer of song, of poetry and tale," responded Thomas. He was surprised of his response to his new acquaintances. "I'm really a printers apprentice. I apologize for misleading you," said Thomas.

"Oh, that's okay. We fancy ourselves to be actors but really, we are chamber maids to a wealthy family. We like to pretend that work is actually a play we're in. Of course, we are the main characters in the story. It helps to tolerate the toils of the day.

Anyway, where are you from? Oh, I'm Sally. This is my sister Janet. Our parents belong to the troupe." "It's very nice to meet you both. I'm Thomas and I'm from Danbury, three days journey from here," replied Thomas.

"We noticed that you came with Colton. He's real nice and does his best to hold all of this together. He writes most of the work we do when he's not mooching off the ladies and the men," said Sally. "It doesn't matter to him if it's a man or a women, he likes them both. As long as there is a good time, a warm bed, and a few quid in his pocket, he's game," said Sally. Thomas was confused by her words. Sally saw his confusion and said, "What I meant was that he is a lover of both. He beds with them, sleeps with them, makes boom boom, you know? That's how he is. We accept people as they are so long as it is their truth. Pretenders don't last long here."

Thomas recalled Colton putting his arm around him and how happy he was when they met. It was causing him some discomfort. Sally took one look at him and said, "Don't worry Thomas. He likes older men who carry large pockets and influence. He won't be making any patty pat with you. Some of the men in the troupe are lovers of men. That's them over there in the corner of the room. They stay together in public for protection and safety."

"Come and dance with us Thomas. The music is about to begin," said Janet. Both girls took Thomas by the hand and walked to the dance floor. "I don't dance!" protested Thomas. Janet pulled him to her and said, "We'll teach you, don't worry. We can teach you a lot of things tonight if you'll let us. I promise you'll have fun. We love to play games Thomas. Don't you? What kind of games do you play in Danbury? I bet we can teach you some new ones you can take home with you," said Sally in a teasing manner. Both girls giggled as they pulled on Thomas' arms.

The three stood together as the first beat of the drum sounded. It was followed with other instruments and a song was born. They joined hands and began to move in a circle. Thomas was starting to loosen up.

They released hands and the girls danced around him. As each one came around to his face, they allured him with their dance and impish behavior. Some of those seated were watching the display and enjoying it. Others took to the floor to join the dance.

No one here was a stranger. They were family as it was always meant to be. Everyone was accepted without reservation, condition, or expectation. Thomas was enjoying his new friends and the partying that surrounded him.

Contemplation stood at door's threshold. This journey here in witness gave him a sense of familiarity to what was unfamiliar. He knew not the source of the realization but accepted its presence with open mind and heart. He was in touch with his center. These strangers were not strangers, at least not in spirit. He felt open and he felt alive.

The Thomas that left Danbury would not be coming home. That Thomas met his demise on the dance floor this very night. Someone else had arrived holding a new perspective and a strong desire for more. He held his torch not for king nor for family. He held it for the fire and the light it gave from within. Thomas was standing at the ford looking across the river and he was pleased by what he saw.

The music had ceased and so had the dancing. The dancers exchanged pleasures with those beside, behind and before them. This was a community of dreamers, of creators and of family.

Some had nowhere to sleep tonight. They would be the last to leave the pub and its safety. Others had no provisions for the next day's meal. Yet they did not view themselves victims to the past. They saw themselves as victors of this day for they shared life and love with one another. They put their faith in life itself and were grateful for the smallest of blessing. They came to reap the harvest that was placed before them.

CHAPTER 49

The celebration was winding down. Most had left the pub for other destinations. Others were fast asleep at the tables. Children were curled up on the floor asleep huddled together. Thomas was ready to leave as he looked around for Colton. He was nowhere to be found.

"Don't waste your time looking for him. You won't see him until midday, if you're lucky. He's off playing with some tart, no doubt," said Janet. "You will have to come home with us if you want a safe place to sleep. Don't worry. We'll see to it that you get back to your Squire in the morning," said Sally.

The three stepped into the dark and dank street. Thomas followed the sisters as they made their way home. He looked left and right for any sign of danger lurking in the darkness. The sisters sensed his fear so they each went to one side of him and placed their arms through his as they walked.

"Don't worry Thomas. The thieves are asleep, and the robbers are all drunk. The only ones that are still awake are the lovers. They move about their beds slithering like serpents as they drink the potion that comes from the lust of another," spoke Janet as she whispered to his ear.

"Do you carry the lust in your bones for the company of two chamber maids? Could you bring yourself to love us for just one night?" asked Sally. Thomas thought to reply yes meant a safe place to rest. If he replied no, he might spend the night sleeping under a staircase somewhere. "Yes, I have the inclination to sleep with you both," replied Thomas. The sisters rang out in laughter and joy.

The trio safely arrived home. Quietly Sally opened the door so not to wake the parents. The three ascended the stairs like three burglars set on theft. Sally lit a single candle as they entered the room.

The light revealed a bed in the center of the room. There were hand painted pictures of people's faces decorating the walls. Their eyes gave Thomas an eerie feeling. It was as if they were watching him.

The sisters quickly undressed and presented themselves to Thomas. They stepped to him just as they did on the dance floor. Gently they began to rub his body as they seductively removed his clothes. Their lips met the flesh of his body as he surrendered to their advance. They danced back and forth inducing their spell on him.

Thomas reached for Sally, but Janet pushed her away. She stood before Thomas without touch or kiss. The sisters circled him as predators before the prey. He was the hunted, and they were the hunters. A hand appeared from the dark and pulled him to the bed. He fell without resistance and surrendered to their will. The sisters moved about him without a sound or a word. The candle sending out its light to reveal the three in motion with the faces painted on the wall in full observation. They lied in bed most the night without stopping, as they explored new things of love making.

Morning came with the loud crack of thunder. Lightening followed with more thunder. Thomas sat up from the sound of the storm with the sisters asleep by his side. In the doorway stood a man staring at him. "And who might you be?" asked the man. "I'm Thomas sir. Thomas Sonnet of Danbury sir," replied Thomas as a great lump began to form in his throat from fear. "Well Thomas of Danbury, I suggest you get up from there and get dressed. You can join me for some tea before you go on your way," spoke the man. "Yes sir. I will be right there. Thank you, sir," replied Thomas. Thomas jumped up and dressed himself. The sisters were still asleep both wearing a smile while held in slumber.

He was descending the stairs and heard the man speaking to someone. "There he is. Our daughters latest prize no doubt. My name is Charles. This is the girl's mother Ann. We are the parents of those lovely doves you were sleeping between this morning," spoke Charles in a carefree manner. Thomas was feeling embarrassed to stand before the parents. Obviously, they did not take insult. "Sit and have some tea and biscuit. You must be starving," said Ann.

"We watched you dance with the girls last night, so we're not surprised to see you here this morning," said Charles. "Don't mind him, Thomas. He's proud of those two, he is, more so than he should be. Those two need find them a man and settle down for their own good," said Ann. "Be quiet woman! They need to be free and wander about through life. Marriage is like an anchor wrapped around one's neck. It stifles the heart and arrests the soul" declared Charles. "Well, we're married!" quipped Ann. "My exact point!" retorted Charles in sarcastic laughter. A biscuit went flying through the air in Charles direction. It hit his face before he saw it coming. "Put that in your piehole you miserable ogre!" said Ann as she gave to laughter. Charles and Thomas both joined in the laughter with Ann.

Charles looked at Thomas and said, "What you create, your ambitions, your dreams your passions, they are all a part of your inner temple. It's always there and visits in the night with its whispers of guidance. Have you ever awaken in the night with your eyes open staring into the dark at something you don't see but feel? Have you Thomas? That's your spirit calling you home.

There are things we must do in this world that cannot be avoided. All must pay the debts they incurred in full. Once the scales are balanced, your inheritance is restored, and you are born once again. All the things of this world drops away in a flash of light. Then heaven reappears. The tears of all the sorrows and all the suffering come as light to lift you above all things witnessed. Never let go of your youth even as an old man. It will keep you alive while others wither away," spoke Charles.

"I want to thank for your guidance, your hospitality and grace. I especially enjoyed the biscuit throwing. Please give my love to your daughters when they awake. It was a night of much entertainment and pleasure. I was wondering where I might find a carriage for hire?" asked Thomas. "Go out the door and turn left. Keep walking until you see the pub. There's always a carriage waiting there.

Thomas bid his host a farewell and was soon back at the Downey Inn. Squire was seated at a table enjoying a hearty breakfast. Thomas sat down beside him and joined in on the meal. "Did you find favor with the ladies last night?" asked Squire. "I did indeed. And made the acquaintance of their parents. I enjoyed every moment of the experience," spoke Thomas.

"Today we will visit other printing establishments to seek a larger contract. I believe we can produce more in less time so long as we employ one more hand. Rebecca will be joining us this evening for dinner here at the inn along with my sister Kate.

I want you two to patch things up from when you last saw each other. What she did was wrong but given the circumstances I understand things better now. It's important to forgive the past so that the future becomes sound. Would you agree?" asked Squire. "Most certainly sir. I will make my best showing for you and her alike," replied Thomas. "Good now eat up. This will be the last time we eat until dinner," said Squire.

"We are printers, yes indeed. But we also must be salesmen. No one can profit from just a service or product. Profit comes from selling yourself and the service or product. From profit comes investment and from investment comes growth. I plan to teach you all three.

You can apply those principles to anything and get the same results. A sharp mind and a persuasive tongue will see one through all challenges this life has instore. Lend not your ear to doubters or false prognosticators. They tend to suck the fun out of life. Learn from your mistakes and bless your shortcomings. They will be the only real teacher you will ever have," said Squire.

CHAPTER 50

Thomas and Squire left the inn to visit the haberdashery. They wanted to check on the progress of Thomas' suit.

Squire in his own wisdom was pointing out the pitfalls of life that Thomas could expect to face. He stressed that failure in love and in commerce was a part of life's journey. Failures were nature's way of challenging personal beliefs in order to offer a new path. The world and all the things within were held in a constant state of change. Those who were said to be lucky in life and in love were but those who allowed themselves to be carried on the winds of change. Thomas enjoyed receiving advice from Squire. Squire had become his second father and best friend.

They stood before the haberdashery. Squire placed his hand on Thomas' shoulder and said, "When you enter be the salesman not the customer. Beware of their words and their actions. They will try to get you to take less than you ordered. They will try to sell you things you don't need. Here are the coins to pay a generous price for the suit should it be ready a day early. Your challenge will be to get more than agreed on. Better yet, see if you can more for less in coin. Now is the time for you to develop your skills.

They entered the store to see it full of customers clamoring about. They made their way to the rear of the store. There stood Mary bickering with a customer and appearing to win the disagreement. Nichole was waiting on an older woman of renown appearance. She was dressed in lavish clothing and moved in a graceful manner. She appeared more interested in Nichole than the stores wares. She was constantly touching her and at times would be stroking her blonde hair as she spoke.

Nichole spotted Thomas across the room. She smiled at him and started toward him when the woman took her by the arm pulling her backwards. The woman began shaking Nichole and scolding her. Nichole looked at Thomas in distress to beckon a rescue from the woman's clutch. Thomas took one step when Squire took hold of him. "Careful Thomas. It's best not to get involved in the matters of the heart between two people. Let them work it out between them. You did not enter this establishment to procure Nichole' future but rather your own.

That woman who holds her is Lady Belvedere. She's one of the most important people in London's society circles. She possess an appetite for younger men and young pretty women.

You don't want to cross her. She can ruin a man's reputation before he even has one. Besides, I've heard that if she favors a bedmate, she eventually employs them as servants.

It's said that her ancestors were pirates that sacked many ships of their goods and seldom took prisoners. It is wise to sidestep her vision for now. She won't hurt Nichole. Not here in public. See, she's already turned her lose," spoke Squire in a low tone as not to be overheard.

Lady Belvedere approached Mary and appeared upset about something. Mary was trying desperately to calm her. After some exchange in words the two finally agreed on some matter and the Lady Belvedere left the store.

Mary and Nichole stepped to Thomas and Squire. "My, my, my. Wait until you see the proper gentlemen attire, I made you. We worked on it all day and half the night. Your suit is ready a day earlier than we had planned. Why sir, you will be the finest dressed man in all of London. You'll be courted by all the ladies. Why I'd bet you'd even find you a bride by wearing this fine example of tailoring," spoke Mary in a lively tone. Thomas took it all in, remembering what Squire had told him prior to their entry.

Nichole was still wearing her look of distress. Thomas held more interest in Nichole's wellbeing than the reason why he was there. Squire saw it and came to his rescue. "Come now Thomas. Have you come to purchase clothing or look upon the beauty of the fair Nichole?" asked Squire.

Thomas shifted back to the matter at hand. "Yes, you are right. Let's have a look at your handywork Mary. I hope it meets my expectations. At the price requested, I'm sure the thread must be made of gold," said Thomas in his best indifferent tone he could muster. Mary was on to him at the start. "Follow me to the sewing room and you can try on your new clothes. Then you can see for yourself they are the finest threads money can buy," said Mary in total confidence.

A few minutes passed when Thomas stepped out dressed in his suit. Squire was impressed but held his tongue. Mary looked at Squire and said, "Well, what do you think Squire? Is he not the handsomest of the lot?" "What is important is what does the buyer think of his new clothes?" spoke Squire.

"What say you, Thomas?" asked Mary. "I'm not sure of the material. It's course against my skin. I'm not sure this will do," replied Thomas. "Oh, don't let that bother you, Thomas. It's new. It will soften with wear and cleaning. You'll see," said Mary.

"What do you think of it Nichole?" asked Thomas. "I think it be of good cloth and sound stitching. We tried our best to see that no stitching be seen. It is a gentleman's suit for certain," replied Nichole. Thomas had just lost the game of barter. His feelings for Nichole trumped the lesson he sought. Nichole was that beautiful.

"Pay the woman Thomas. Her work is more than deserving of the price agreed upon. Madame, I will tell all of your fine work here at this haberdashery and your fair pricing," said Squire. If Thomas could not barter a better price, then Squire would have her believe that she could have gotten more had she bartered better.

"Mary was that Lady Belvedere I saw you speaking to earlier?" asked Squire. "Why yes it was. She is one of our finest customers. She always agrees with our asking price. She's been to the courts of royalty you know," replied Mary. "Yes, I've heard the same. I thought her much younger than she appears," said Squire. "Yes, well she has her ways of making herself feel younger, if you know what I mean," replied Mary. "I believe I do. Thank you, Mary, and thank you Nichole for your fine work," said Squire. "Come Thomas. It's time to do some business."

The two were leaving the store when Thomas turned to see Nichole. She was having a troublesome argument with Mary. Mary took Nichole by the hands and Nichole tried to pull away, but Mary held her grip.

Nichole started crying and was pleading with her. Mary slapped her across the face twice as hard as she could. Nichole broke away and ran to hide behind a curtain. Mary realized that others in the store had seen what happened and were staring at her. She composed herself and stepped behind the curtain to follow Nichole.

Thomas was furious. He started towards Mary, but Squire stopped him. "What would you do Thomas? Who would you side with? Nichole? Would you rescue her from her peril? If you did, she would have to leave here with you. Then what? What would you tell your wife when you brought her home?

The beauty of a woman can be a blessing and a curse. Nichole has the beauty of an angel, that is for certain. It touched you from the very beginning as it touched the eye of Lady Belvedere. Beauty such as hers tempts the predators also.

At home in Danbury, Mildred's mother met a similar fate. She gave to the community as Mildred does. She had the heart of a saint, but it wasn't enough to protect her from those who sought to harm her. They had their way with her, then killed her to silence their crime. It's the lay of the land Thomas. One must learn to accept sadness with the same heart one has for joy.

There are things more desirable than coin or position in this world. There's control and the power that goes with it. The privileged feed on the poor and the weak. It has been that way from the beginning. Trouble not yourself the things of nature. It's a fools folly," said Squire.

CHAPTER 51

The streets were full of people going about in their business. Soldiers of the Crown were present to help keep the peace between Catholic and Protestant zealots. "This bickering back and forth between the religions is unnerving England and its citizens. So much argument and for what? I tell you, it's more than their souls they are after. I suspect it's more about the size of their pockets that concerns them the most. Their concepts and rules do more to destroy the spirit than to prop it up.

We are merchants. We provide service to all God's creation no matter their religion. Religious movements should do likewise," said Squire.

"I want to visit the establishment of another who is offering contracts for the printing of Bibles. I hear he pays well for those who can deliver on time.

The success in business is to always remain neutral when dealing with the client. Discussion of politics and religion should be avoided unless the client brings it up. Our response need always be neutral. We can acknowledge their position with a grain of salt. But we must never voice our personal position while engaged in the act of commerce," said Squire.

"Here we are. This is the business of proprietor Sir Charles Whittington. He is leading publisher in London and carries a great deal favor with the aristocratic class. He's known for his cunning deals which has made him a wealthy man. He will set the terms for us, and we will accept those terms. He will set a price for our work, but we will reject his offer. Respect between businessmen comes from the exchange each receives through the eyes of commerce. Remember that Thomas and learn. One day it will be you that meets with such men as this one," spoke Squire.

They entered the shop and were amazed by what they saw. There were shelves filled with books on both sides. The center of the room held a decorative stand with a large book opened in the center. The outside of the pages were gilded in gold. The two stepped up to the display and saw that it was a Bible opened to Psalms 119. Squire was admiring the level of craftmanship. Thomas was busy reading the verses and wondering why Psalms 119.

"Gentlemen, may I help you?" spoke a well-dressed mannerly man. "Well, yes. We are seeking Sir Charles Whittington about a business matter," replied Squire. "I see. May I ask where you are from?" asked the man. "We hail from Danbury sir. My name is Andrew Beckett, and this is Thomas Sonnet my apprentice. We have a modest print shop and seek a contract to publish Bibles. We were told that he seeks independent printers to spread the word of the good book," replied Squire.

"Why yes, you are right. You have come to the right place. I am Charles Whittington, and this is my publishing firm. Please step into my office so we may get to know one another and perhaps do some business," replied Charles.

The office was impressive as they entered. A solid oak desk was at the center of the room. Paintings decorated the walls. There were two opposing sofas with a table between them. A wooded bowl filled with delicacies sat at the center of the table. The room had a special feel about it.

"Please have a seat and enjoy the offerings from our kitchen," said Charles. "You have your own kitchen sir? Here, in this building?" inquired Squire. "Oh yes, we do. Each employee receives pastry and tea before the work hour.

At midday they each receive a handsome meal and the time to enjoy it and relax. I find that healthy, happy employees produce better when they are treated fairly," replied Charles. Squire was impressed with his care for the employees.

"How many do you employ Andrew?" asked Charles. "There's just Thomas and I," replied Squire. "We have published a number of Bibles already and made delivery of the same for another publisher here abouts." "That's good to hear. And you have the means by which to bind them?" asked Charles. "Yes. We have everything needed to deliver the work completed," replied Squire. "Excellent! Good to hear," replied Charles.

"The politics of the churches are turning the people against one another. Arguments and violence in the streets and for what! The zealots who profess their brand of Christianity to be of God, justify violence where needed to instill fear amongst the people. They threaten the weak and the poor in heart.

The Bible was written for the people, Gods people. Not for one denomination or the other to use as a backdrop to exact their creed and dogma on the masses. The corrupt hearts of shepherds, corrupt the congregation and its society. We need those Bibles in the hands of everyday people. We need them to read the word as it is written so they can make up their own minds," proclaimed Charles.

Silence fell over the room. Thomas and Squire were moved by his words and the passion he gave each one. "It would be our honor sir if we could do the business at hand in the manner by which you speak," spoke Squire. "That's what I want to hear. If I gave you contract for twenty five Bibles in fifty days, could you, do it? "said Charles. "I think yes," replied Squire. "And if I said fifty Bibles in fifty days, could you, do it? "I could not say for certain sir," replied Squire.

"Here is my proposition to you both. Our contract will read twenty five Bibles in fifty days. However, if you produce more than twenty five, I will gladly pay you extra. If you produce fifty in fifty days, I will pay you for the fifty then double that amount as your bonus. What do you say gentlemen? Have we a deal?" inquired Charles.

"That is a most generous offer sir. We openly accept your terms," replied Squire. "Very well. I will have my solicitor draw up the necessary paperwork. Shall I include Thomas' name on the contract?" asked Charles. "Yes, be so kind as to include his name on such writ. He is my business partner," replied Squire.

"Shall we say forty percent in advance and the balance once delivery is made?" asked Charles. "Fifty percent rings clearer than forty and sixty would have us smiling all the way back to Danbury, Sir Charles," replied Squire. Very well then. Fifty percent will be your advance," replied Sir Charles. The three men shook hands, and their collective intentions were sealed.

Squire and Thomas were back on the streets enjoying the dainties from Sir Charles' office. The two spoke and laughed as they moved along the streets of London. They were happy for their fortune and the possibilities it could bring each.

A black carriage was coming towards them pulled by a black stallion. The driver wore a black suit and a tall black hat. Thomas looked at the passengers. It was Lady Belvedere and Nichole. Nichole had a blank stare on her face like someone being led to the gallows.

Thomas shouted out to her, and she lifted her face to see him. She stood in the carriage and reached out to him. Lady Belvedere slapped her hand down and pulled her back into the seat. She slapped Nichole once, then again as she screamed profanities.

Thomas bolted onto the street after the carriage. The driver cracked the whip at the horse to quicken its pace. As Thomas came alongside the carriage the driver drew back the whip and struck Thomas across the face. Thomas continued his pursuit but couldn't keep up. Lady Belvedere rose up to look at Thomas. She held a dark stare at him until the carriage was out of sight.

He was broken hearted and felt melancholy. He was oblivious to why he felt so connected to her. He wept as he stood in the middle of the street. The lash from the whip cut him across the cheek. The tears burned his wound as he wiped them away. He raised his head to look at Squire for some sort of answer or guidance.

"There's nothing we could have done to change the events that just unfolded before us. Once she grows tired of Nichole she will throw her back to the haberdashery, if there still is a position for her. If not, she will most likely be a lady of the streets. She'll have to sell herself to eat and make quarters," spoke Squire in a sad tone.

Thomas walked with his head low. He could not help but blame himself in some way. He knew Squire was right. He cried as low as he could muster as they walked along the street. His soul was trying once again to release her image from the moment. Squire knew the two were smitten with each other at first sight. He also knew that such an event only happens between souls who hold a common history from another time and place.

Love was never intended to be a realm designed for possession or a commodity for personal gain. It never was to be held within the walls of mind or body. It did not come from this world. It came to this world. It carries no religion, no condition or expectation. It cannot be bought or sold for it has no form to look upon. It is not for mankind because it is of mankind. It comes from a place where Nichole and Thomas' souls once danced the dance amongst the stars.

CHAPTER 52

There are two sides to every story and every discontent.

It was early evening at the Downy Inn. The private room at the inn was occupied with Squire, Thomas, Rebecca, and Kate the sister of Squire Beckett. Squire was pleased to share this time with family. He loved them both and missed them dearly.

Sister Kate left Danbury years ago with her arm tucked inside the arm of a London merchant. His name was Raymond Kilgore. The couple were married and prospered in the import business. Raymond passed away two years ago, and the business was left to her care alone. She changed some things and in a years' time their volume had nearly doubled. She employed more people and expanded their influence on France.

She was happy to have Rebecca live with her. It gave her a new sense of purpose and motivation. She thought of Rebecca as her adult daughter. She was schooling Rebecca about protocol and manners expected of a lady in London's society circles.

Rebecca was prospering under the London sun. Danbury was no longer big enough for her or her aspirations. London was her new garden and she had plenty of seed to sow. She embraced its enormity of culture and promise. There would be no returning to Danbury. London was her home.

Thomas was surprised and pleased to see Rebecca doing so well. She was polite, courteous, and reserved at their reunion. The life in London seemed to have been a good influence on her. He knew Rebecca would never return to Danbury. She was finally enjoying herself. In Danbury she never really seemed happy or content.

He couldn't help but wonder what Danbury would be like when he returned. Would he feel restless and detached for the things he held there? He had a family and a future as a master printer. The things that most people dream of but never find. He was fortunate in life, but would it be enough just to be content with the things handed to him?

The atmosphere amongst them was lively with the sharing of stories and laughter. Catherine, the proprietor's daughter entered the room to serve the guests. She was carrying a pitcher of wine and began filling everyone' goblet. Her eyes were darting about the room with much of the attention directed at Thomas. She wondered about the young woman seated beside him.

"Thomas will you be needing a bath this evening before bed?" asked Catherine. Rebecca' eyes rolled around hearing Catherine' inquiry. "Don't you think you should feed him first before you take off his clothes? Or would you rather bath him here, right now in front of us?" quipped Rebecca. The real Rebecca came to the surface in full display of character.

Catherine was embarrassed. Thomas was shocked. Squire was surprised. Kate looked at Rebecca and said, "Do you expect to advance your position in London when you resort to such antics as this? Such behavior is better spent in Danbury but not here. Not in my presence. You are a Beckett. Act like it. Is there something you would like to say to everyone Rebecca?"

Rebecca bowed her head in silence. "I wish to apologize to everyone present. My display was not that of a lady. I regret my words and hope that they caused no harm." Everyone accepted her apology and continued the conversations with wine vessels filled to the rim.

The meal was served with all the trimmings. The meal and conversation carried on for over two hours. Conversations mainly were about prospects between Squire and Kate. Thomas spoke of life in Danbury and the things that changed. Rebecca was sad to hear about Helen Clayborne' passing.

Each had their own ideas about direction when it came to advancement, yet each were dependent on the other. Four people going in four different directions held together by the heart of life.

Kate knew the inside on supply and price of commodities in London and abroad. Trading with France was good despite the politics with England. Squire quizzed her to learn all he could. He knew once the land was flooded with Bibles the money behind it would cease. He was looking for a new trend to bank on.

Kate was more than open to help her brother in any way. "Why don't you move to London and work for me?" asked Kate. "Thank you, dear sister. A most gracious offer, I'm sure. But I'm not ready to leave Danbury just now. There are things which must happen to the benefit of all concern. No, my roots still need the rains and sun of Danbury. Perhaps later, I'm sure. Thank you for a most generous offer sister," replied Squire.

It was time to say farewell. Hugs and kisses were exchanged with heart. Last minute arrangements and promises were being made that would most likely never be kept. Parting is truly sweet sorrow.

Time and its events coupled with change have their own idea for direction and advancement. It can steer the strongest of souls down an unknown path for better or for worse. Arrangements dissolved, promises forgotten, all carried away on the wind, lost to time, lost to memory.

Squire held Rebecca the longest. Twice she tried to pull away from him. Twice she failed. Rebecca favored her mother in appearance and behavior. It was Squire' way of healing from the loss of his best friend. His eyes were closed tight. He breathed in the fragrance of her hair and pictured his wife the last time he held her in his arms. He knew he had to turn Rebecca lose but the fear of losing the vision of his wife kept him holding her tighter.

"Father, I have to go now," said Rebecca. He released his hold of her and looked at his precious daughter. A tear escaped one eye and slowly rolled down his cheek. Rebecca saw it and felt her mother's love at the same time. She grabbed her father and pulled him to her. She began weeping for her father and her mother.

Somehow, someway the three were connected again as one. It was love held in eternity that entered for a few moments to offer comfort. It was loves way, in loves eternal time. The reason why all mortals dance the dance because the music never stops and neither does the dance.

Thomas and Squire walked the ladies to their carriage and saw them off. The two reentered the inn tired from a long day. "Rest well tonight, Thomas. Tomorrow we'll eat a hearty breakfast. Then we'll load our wagon with the supplies we need. We'll turn the wagon towards Danbury and set out for the journey home," said Squire. The two parted ways. Squire went to his room for a good night's sleep. Thomas went looking for Catherine. He wanted to see her before he left.

He entered the private room they had just left thinking that she might be there. He pulled back the curtain to enter and there she lied on the dining table. Her clothes were on the floor. A man was engaged with her. The same man that Squire warned Thomas about.

Her eyes found Thomas standing there in witness. Her attention switched from the lovers advance to the severe look of disappointment Thomas held. She tried to disengage but the male suitor was not finished with her. She tried to push him off, but he continued his way with her. Thomas turned away and slowly walked out.

Catherine disconnected from the moment while the lover finished his business. She was deeply saddened by what just transpired. She was saddened as she recalled the look on Thomas' face.

She would have left with Thomas to live with him in Danbury never to return to London again. She longed for a simpler life in a quiet town like Danbury. Her misdirected choice wiped away any chance of that happening. She so hoped that there was something she could do to salvage their relationship.

Thomas ascended the stairs one last time at the Downy Inn. His mind shifted from what he had just witnessed to Danbury and those who waiting on him. He undressed and entered the comfort of the bed with the intent to rest well. His bed for the next two nights would be the hard English ground.

He was drifting off feeling the remnants of good wine. Then a knock came at the door that disturbed the silence. He knew it was Catherine. He knew why she was there. He thought it better to leave the image of her on the table as a final remembrance. It would be easier to let go the feelings he had for her.

Finally, the knocking ceased. The only sound was the sound of footsteps walking away from the door. She had received her answer without a word. It would be some time before she'd accept it.

And so, concludes another act on the great stage of life in the arena of love given and love lost. It's shifting sands teaching the value of uncertainty and the practice of patience.

CHAPTER 53

For it to be anything else but love is a fools journey.

It was a new day as Thomas and Squire finished their breakfast. It would be the last good meal for the next three days. There was an air of anxiety with the two. Squire was already missing the company of his daughter and sister. He found himself questioning his reasons for returning to Danbury. He appeased his anxiety by convincing himself he would return soon.

Thomas was also weighing the return home. He missed his family and all the things he held dear. He wondered if things would be the same. He appeased his stress by convincing himself once at home all would fall back into its place. Justin DuBois, the proprietor of the inn approached the two. "I trust that you were satisfied with your stay sir," he asked. "We are very satisfied with the lodging and the service we received on our visit to London. Once again, the Downy Inn offers all the comforts of home," replied Squire. Squire removed an envelope from his pocket and handed it to Justin. "I trust that this will cover our bill," said Squire. Justin looked in the envelope and smiled. "Oh yes sir. This more than covers things. Your generosity is greatly appreciated here," replied Justin.

"It would please me if Catherine received a portion of the gratuity. She made our celebration of the evening past a memorable one," requested Squire. "I most certainly will. She will be pleased by your generosity. I would have her thank you personally, but she has gone off somewhere. She did not sleep in her bed last night and left no word of where she was going. I'm certain she is alright. She has a good head on her shoulders," replied Justin.

An awful feeling overcame Thomas. What if he had answered the knock at the door? He wondered if she was alright. Did he carry some sort of blame or responsibility for her absence? He spoke not a word of what occurred last night.

It was midmorning and the wagon was nearly loaded for the journey home. Printing supplies and binding materials were neatly packed at the front of the wagon. Provisions for camping along the road were the last to load. Gifts were purchased for family and friends. The gifts helped to sooth the discomfort of separation once they returned.

The wagon turned to the west as both men took a last look at London. Squire snapped the reins that began the three day journey for home. There would be plenty of time for reflection. Thomas was filled with promise and strong desire from his experience in London. The thought of returning home to Danbury troubled him a bit. His feet were planted in Danbury. His heart reached for London.

The closer the wagon got to Danbury the more the stories shifted from their adventures in London to what they missed about home. Squire loved the towns people and was proud of his position in the community.

Thomas spoke of his parents and all the love and support they offered. He was certain that his mother had already spoiled Lucille and Mary.

There were soldiers on the road going in both directions. Some were in a hurry. Some wore like colored uniforms while others wore tattered clothing, an obvious sign of mercenaries.

"All this bickering between the rights of the church and state. How do these pretenders know what God wants? Have they sat with him? Have they broken bread with him? I think not. If it be the God of love that directs them then why do they carry sword and shield. I suspect behind the curtain of it all is greed. Greed of wealth and greed of power over the people. An appetite that can never be satisfied even if all the wealth and all the power be theirs," spoke Squire in a condemning voice.

The day wore on and it was time to make camp. Their make shift tent was pitched beside the wagon, and the campfire was built. They shared a meal of dried meat, cheese, bread, and a few anecdotes about where they had been and where they were going.

The sun was setting, and it was time to prepare for sleep. They held quiet conversation back and forth until Squire fell asleep. Thomas was still awake looking upwards at the nights sky without a single thought in mind.

He was held in a state of wonder as he looked upon the vastness of the sky before him. He felt an attachment to the stars and to the darkness that separated them. It wasn't important for him to understand it. It was enough that he knew it was there.

Another sunrise and a sore body eager to awake and remove itself from the hard ground. It wasn't long before the two were on their way west. They saw small camps of soldiers along the way. There were other travelers, some on their way to London and parts beyond. Most were friendly and often stopped to share what was on the road ahead.

Thomas and Squire spoke the least on the second day of their journey. They realized it but could not explain the reason. Perhaps they were waning from the experiences of London and waxing for the hearts of Danbury that awaited them.

Smaller bands of soldiers would pass them by. One band stopped them and inquired them of their business. Only one of them spoke English. The others were conversing in French. It raised Squires suspicions. Why were the French stopping English citizens and by who's authority?

Squire knew better than to challenge them. He would risk injury or perhaps have their cargo impounded to be sold or burned. He knew some mercenaries were criminals at heart and mind. Squire and Thomas were allowed to proceed after gifting them with what food they had left. Thomas and Squire would be arriving in Danbury on the morrow with a full wagon and empty bellies.

Another night under the stars as ones attention winds down. Eyelids become heavy inviting slumber forward to offer the soul peace from another day spent. The dew was heavier than usual. They both awoke the next morning in damp clothes.

"We're hungry and have no food. We're wet and have not the high sun to dry us. We're a day's journey from our beds. I'd say that it's a good start to a beautiful day. What would you say of it Thomas? Be it a good day or not?" asked Squire.

Thomas stood silent; then realized what Squire was doing. He was writing a different script for the day. He was refusing to give credence to the darkness of hardship. Rather he was offering praise to the light of hardship. One who appreciates the most is he who experienced the less.

"Yes Squire! I believe it true. It's a wonderful day. One I'm sure to always remember. Thank you Squire," replied Thomas.

The road home was getting shorter by the hour. No soldiers were seen. No word from other travelers as to their whereabouts. It seemed that things had settled down for now. It gave Squire a sense of relief. He had seen the perils of civil unrest before. Needless death and carnage stirred from a difference in opinions amongst the troublemakers and their legions of ignorance.

The first sight of Danbury was in view. It was the longest quarter mile of their journey. "I say we go the inn first and fill one leg with hot food and the other leg with strong ale. What say you, Thomas?" asked Squire. "Sounds better than eating our horse," replied Thomas.

As they neared the inn, they could see something had the towns people upset. Men were arguing with one another. There were no children about playing as usual. The women stood close to their homes. They were giving the likes of Thomas and Squire a hard stare over their brows.

Reverend Richard came running up to the wagon and stopped them. He was wearing a troubled look on his face. "They were here! They came looking for you and you Thomas!" shouted the Reverend. "Who came? Speak up man, who came?" asked Squire. "The soldiers. The soldiers that are loyal to the Church of Rome. They were here about the Bibles you printed. They entered your shop and took your printing stock. They tore up your building and posted a notice on your door. They asked where you were. I told them that you were in London but said nothing about your planned return," replied Reverend.

Squire sat with a blank stare on his face. Thomas sat staring at Squire wondering what he would do. The Reverend and some of the towns people were also waiting to see how Squire would react to such tyrannous acts. Squire lifted the reins and snapped them to cue the horse to proceed. He was going towards the print shop.

"Let's see the work of puppets whose strings reach all the way to Rome," said Squire in a low tone. The horse stopped in front of the shop. There on the door was nailed a notice. He and Thomas dismounted the wagon and took hold the writ. The two quietly read it as the small crowd looked on. Squire released the writ and it fell to the ground. He stepped away and looked upward to the skies.

"I am a merchant of honest stock and goodwill. I give praise to the only one who gave me breath and sight. I rule from my heart, and I give no malice to man or beast. I am not a ward of the church nor am I a servant to absolutism. I am a free man by birth, and it shall be the same at deaths doorstep. Let these pagans return to deal with my independence. I will not stand for such domination," declared the lions heart within him.

"Thomas, let us enter our home and place of business and restore it so that we may publish enough Bibles to reach from the town of Danbury to the steps of Rome! If enough paper be in supply, then it shall be so. Let this pontiff follow the trail that leads back to my steps. Let him stand here before me and look me in the eye. I await the day!" shouted Squire.

The townspeople had feared the words of the soldiers. After hearing Squire' declaration they were more afraid of his. What trouble would he bring down on their way of life. Their fears and worries were greater than the actual threat. These soldiers relied on the measure of fear they could instill within. If correctly applied a white flag would be raised without use of sword or arrow.

The Reverend stood before Squire as a boy seeking help. "They threatened me should I ever speak out against Rome. They said the day would come when they would return to burn down our church. It has my wife upset. She cries in the night for fear they might come as thieves. We have no one to protect us from them. What are we to do?" plead the Reverend. Squire looking at his shop, turned and looked at those who stood by. He looked on the Reverend as he held a cowardice stance.

"We'll come together. We'll come together and fight the bastards. We'll send them back to Rome tarred and feathered on a rail. When we finish with them, their kind will go around us for fear of a tar bath. We'll come together and stand as one.

If you Reverend are assaulted by one, the same be as if they assaulted us all. Soon we can take counsel together at the inn and lay out a plan. For now, I have Bibles to print and deliver to London. I want their anger to be red hot when they return. An assassin that comes in emotion is much easier to defeat than one set in mind," spoke the warrior inside Squire. No one present had ever heard him speak in such a manner before today.

CHAPTER 54

A pauper remains a pauper for lack of will and intent.

The sun raised its head this morning sending rays of light across the fields and treetops. As it began to burn away the mornings dew small clouds formed in patches across the landscape. The birds welcomed the light and sang their songs from the tops of trees to announce another day to embrace.

It was quiet in the town of Danbury this morning. The chimneys were vacant of smoke. Long shadows were beginning to form as the suns light rose well above the horizon.

An eerie silence crept over the town. The kind that comes when something had changed but you're not sure what. Perhaps it was the return of Squire and Thomas. Perhaps the soldiers threats and their promise of returning. No one could say for certain.

Thomas and Squire had spent the rest of yesterday and some of the night unloading the wagon and restoring order to the shop. Thomas woke up tired from the journey and the news they received.

A knock came at the door. He walked to the door and opened it. There stood his mother and Mary holding Lucille. Diane was the first to step into the shop. She grabbed her son and held him tight. Seeing him silenced her worry. She held his face and kissed it as she told him how much he was missed. Her jabber gave no pause or end. "Here Diane. Hold the baby so I can kiss your baby and tell him how much I missed him," said Mary in a teasing manner. Diane realized herself and laughed. "I'm so sorry Mary. I forgot myself. Let me hold Lucille," replied Diane.

Mary took Thomas' hand and kissed it. Then she took him by the neck and pressed her lips to his. She held the kiss long. Long enough for Diane to feel the wait. Lucille was not going to be left out. She was squirming and rocking in Diane' arms. Once Mary had released the embrace, Lucille started making noises and reaching for Thomas.

Thomas took his child and held her to view. Her deep blue eyes matched his as did the smiles they exchanged. The little one looked at him and made a face that caused Thomas to laugh. Lucille laughed back at Thomas. Then the ladies began to laugh and cooing over the scene.

"Let's go upstairs and join Squire. I think he might still be sleeping. The journey was a long one," said Thomas. He led the way carrying a basket Diane brought from home. Diane placed a water kettle beside the fire for tea. Squire was still sleeping so everyone was quiet in words and movement.

Thomas began sharing some of his experiences in London. He spoke of the vastness and numerous opportunities it held. He was excited as he told them about the theatre and its glamour. He was keen in describing the actors and their families. Their love was for life and its expression through words felt from the heart was foremost before possession or wealth.

Diane and Mary could see the depth of his admiration and passion for such a life, and it gave them worry. Diane quickly changed the subject.

"Thomas, there are some things we need tell you. While the two of you were away soldiers came through town. They asked about Squire and his dealings. They wanted to speak to him in a bad way. These were not soldiers of the Crown. They behaved more like criminals. There's something going on, but we don't know what it is," spoke Diane in worried fashion.

"Also, there was a man who came to visit Squire the day after you left. He said his name was Miles Davenport. He spent a night at the inn. When the soldiers came looking for Squire, he left in the middle of the night. Do you know this man or heard word of him?" asked Diane. "Of course not mother. I've never heard of such a man," replied Thomas. "It's told he left word with John Clayborne at the inn. He promised to return one day soon. We and others are concerned about the goings on of you and Squire and this stranger who came looking," spoke Diane in her worried tone. "I cannot say what their business was mother. I hear Squire waking up. He'll be out soon. Maybe he can offer light to the matter," replied Thomas.

"What's this? Have I slept through breakfast and tea not to mention the company of three lovely maids?" asked a sleepy Squire. "Come and sit Squire. Please take my chair while I make you tea," said Diane. "Thank you, Diane. You are blessing to us who journeyed long," replied Squire.

"Now what is all this worry I heard about as I awoke? Soldiers? A Miles Davenport? "Squire, do you know of this Davenport fellow they speak of?" asked Thomas. I know the name William Davenport. He was a translator of the good book. His work was in direct conflict with Catholic doctrine. He had to flee England and take to the mainland for fear of his life. They found him eventually after he was betrayed. He was burned at the stake once they caught up with him. I ask you, is that the work of the living God to kill one who dare to publish His word of love and peace word for word? I think not! One must ask themselves, who or what is this god they profess to serve?

It was the advances in printing that made his work valuable to some and a threat to others. He had the heart of a rebel and a scholars mind. Much like young Thomas here. People go on about how lies and deception can bring death to the bearer of such practice. But I say to you, more have been killed for revealing the truth," spoke Squire in a solemn tone.

"If he was killed, who is this Davenport that comes to our home," asked Thomas. "It must be a grandson or nephew. I'm not sure. One thing I'm sure of is that our publishing of Bibles has much to do with Davenport and the soldiers. One comes to enlighten the hearts of seekers. The other comes to repress knowledge and the truth offered to all.

I have spoken it in all my years. If one must know the living God one must stand away from the church and its ways, be they Protestant or Catholic," declared Squire.

"This man called Davenport, they said he carried himself as one of renowned stock, yet he spoke as a common man to those who took words with him," said Mary. "Did he leave note as to his reason for the journey here?" asked Squire. "I couldn't say, but I heard he spent time with John Clayborne at the inn," replied Mary. "Enough of that. Please, tell me all the gossip that I missed out on and don't leave anything out. I must be up to date on the latest or else I'll fall behind and spend my days lost," joked Squire.

Soon the conversations were exhausted along with food and tea. The women were preparing themselves to leave. "Thomas, you go and visit with your family today and return to me on the morrow. Enjoy their company and fill the duties of a husband and father. I will begin preparing for the work at hand. There is an urgency to our work I feel that must be completed no matter the consequences. There is a cloud hovering above us. I know not if it be for protection or if it be for doom," spoke Squire in a prophetic tone.

Thomas gathered his belonging and the gifts he brought for everyone. He hurried out the door with the ladies while making faces at Lucille. They loaded the wagon and set out on their way. It felt good to be together with family. Thomas could not think of anything else. He longed to see his father and the farm. He wanted to play with Lucille and take her to his special place in the forest.

The Sonnet home came into view. The closer the wagon got, the greater the anticipation. Edward was waiting as the wagon entered the yard. Thomas jumped from the wagon and hugged his father. Edward held him tight while lifting his feet off the ground. "I missed you son. We all missed you. Come inside. I know you have much to share with us. Diane did you feed him before you left town?" asked Edward. Diane gave him a look she gives when she refuses to encourage his stupidity. Seeing her look, he dropped the question.

"I'll go the Roses and let them know you're home. They're anxious to see you also. I'll be right back. Don't start with any of your stories Thomas until I get back. Otherwise, you'll have to tell them again," said Edward as he ran off.

The smell of freshly plowed ground was in the air. A reminder of fresh vegetables to come to adorn ones table and feed well into the winter. Livestock feeding on green grass to give milk and meat when needed. All the things to sustain life and the celebration of it surrounded their world of life.

Diane had everyone settled and was preparing tea. Thomas and Mary were holding hands while seated at the table. Lucille took turns with each parent as they conversed. The front door opened and in walked Edward carrying one of the twins and Jonathan carrying the other. Lydia followed carrying deserts she had prepared for the occasion. She was dressed in her best attire. She smelled of rose water with a flower tucked into her hair. She appeared as grand as the women of London.

She walked to Thomas and gave him a hug and a kiss. "Welcome back Thomas. Your presence was missed by all," spoke Lydia. She took Judith from Edward and took a seat at the table. Diane took Liam from Jonathan and sat down joining Mary and Lucille.

The men must have asked Thomas a hundred questions about his adventures. Thomas could barely finish one answer when he was asked another question. He enjoyed the attention and sharing with everyone. Thomas even blended a little exaggeration in with his story telling. A common practice among men. Why not? It wasn't a lie, just a little spice added to the mix.

Mary showed the least interest in hearing about London. Her place was here in Danbury. Meager as it may be in comparison to London, it mattered a great deal to Mary. She would fulfill all her desires here in the place where she was born and raised. Her dream was to elevate herself from the country life and hold position and reputation within the confines of Danbury. No more or no less.

The Roses were preparing themselves to return home. Thomas' adventures of London had finally run dry. Lydia stepped to Thomas and whispered something in his ear. She kissed him on the cheek and turned to leave. Mary took her place beside Thomas as she held Lucille. She said goodbye to her parents and siblings and watched them walk towards home.

It had been a long day for all. Diane and Edward were cleaning up from the meal they shared with the Roses. Thomas and Mary retired to the bedroom. Lucille was already asleep, so she was placed in her crib.

Mary lit a candle and placed it on the beds table. She wanted a second child, and she knew she was ripe for Thomas' seed. She let her hair down and ran her fingers through it give it a fuller look. Her clothes fell to the ground, and she stood before him. He undressed as she looked on, awaiting to advance him.

Slowly she stepped to him and stood a foot apart. Their eyes never blinked, neither spoke a single word. She took a half step until their lips were less than an inch apart. Their breaths moving back and forth across the others face. He raised his arms to hold her. She objected to his advance and pushed them back to his side. Mary would tease and taunt his advances to build the energy of desire. They stood face to face, lips close with an occasional brushing. She turned her head to one side and placed her lips on his. He could feel her harden nipples touch his chest. He became like an animal and pulled her to him. He began kissing her frantically without pause. He was careful not to make a sound that would wake the child.

He reached down and took her by the thighs and lifted her. She wrapped her legs around him, and he entered her. The heavy breathing had reduced to an occasional breath. Eyes still held in contact widening as each felt the orgasmic energy building around them. Then, ecstasy.

Her body trembled in his hold as she continued to enjoy the rush of pleasure. Her body went limp, and her feet returned to the floor. She looked at him with seductive eyes, her hair falling forward as she began to kiss him. Her hands ran through his hair back and forth. Her head rolled back with eyes closed as she was still engaged in the remnants of ecstasy.

They kissed each other softly as they turned towards their bed to enter it together. The light from the candle was beginning to flicker. A sign that it was about to lose its flame.

In another place not so far away, another candle was flickering its light. Close by lied one who also longed for Thomas touch. Eyes stared off into the darkness beyond the flame' reach as memory recalled a time from the past when a spontaneous rendezvous rendered the fruits of passion.

CHAPTER 55

To all things love is given.

The morning dew was thick as it covered the earth. The droplets appeared as diamonds as the sun's rays danced through them. Man and beast began to stir about, each in their own manner.

Thomas was curled around Mary. Her hair smelled like lavender. Lucille was beginning to stir from sleep. Mary woke hearing her call out. Thomas kissed Mary as she started to get up to attend to Lucille. Then fell back to bed to kiss Thomas before starting her day. Each time she tried to get up he'd pull her back to bed and kiss her again. They laughed at their little game which sent Lucille to one of her fits. She was not about to be left out the fun. Mary rose from the bed lifted her into her arms and rocked her back and forth. Thomas lied there and watched the two play.

Diane was already up preparing a meal for everyone, especially Thomas. She wanted him to have a full breakfast before he left. Her heart was still heavy from missing him. In Diane's book of life, feeding others was her way of expressing love. If she prepared a heavy plate for someone then she either loved them a great deal or missed them terribly.

She called everyone to meal. The family came together at the table. Bowls and plates of food were passed around so all could share a portion. Food was still cooking beside the fireplace. Diane would jump up to stir a pot or check on the progress of baking bread. This is what she did. She brought people together before food and drink from the heart. Her eyes checked each plate several times making sure they held enough to keep hunger at bay.

Thomas stood to leave but not until he had pushed some biscuits into his pockets. His mother handed him a fresh loaf of bread for Squire. "Make sure Squire receives this as soon as you arrive," said Diane. "I will mother. I know he will enjoy it before any work begins," replied Thomas.

Jonathan Rose was going to town on this morning for supplies. He had offered to take Thomas to town, and Thomas gladly accepted. Thomas began his trek towards the Rose' home. He enjoyed the scents and sounds of early morning. The thought of new things, experiences, and opportunities were tucked away in every morning. They were always available for anyone who were open to receive them.

Thomas approached the house and could see Jonathan in the barn caring for the livestock. "Good morning, Jonathan!" shouted Thomas. Jonathan turned his head to look on him and waved. Thomas stepped up to the door of the house and started to knock. The door flew open and there stood Lydia. The shoulders of her dress were pulled down exposing her cleavage. Her presentation held his attention. "Come in Thomas. I've been waiting on you. Jonathan will be here shortly to take you to town. Is there anything I can do for you before you begin your journey?" asked Lydia. She opened herself to him and he felt it. It was in her eyes as deep as the oceans floor.

There she stood, with her beautiful dark hair and eyes, smiling with a yielding expression. She stepped closer to him, and his heart began to race. Both were sharing a voice within that was calling out beyond human touch, beyond the bounds of physical exchange.

Their heads slightly tilted back as if held in trance. Breathing had slowed and was nearly absent. Flashes were appearing behind their eyes then disappearing. They were of the times, some ancient, some recent. Faces of strangers coming in and out of light. A flurry of flashes racing before them and then abruptly stop. The energy that enveloped them dropped away. There they stood looking at each other not knowing what had just happened.

Lydia appeared overwhelmed by it all and had to sit down. She placed her hand over her mouth to prevent crying. Her eyes filled with tears but not a single one was released. She looked at Thomas unable to describe what she had felt, what she had realized. He stepped towards her and began stroking her hair. She reached for his hand and lifted it to her face. She kissed each finger and thumb then placed his hand to her breast. She looked up to him with longing eyes, still holding the tears. She opened her mouth to speak but nothing came out. She shook her head left to right then brought his hand to her forehead.

Jonathan was heard approaching the house. Thomas stood away and sat at the table. Lydia wiped at her face and pulled the shoulders of her dress up. Jonathan entered the house in a celebratory mood. "Good morning young man. Are you ready to go to town? I want you to know how proud we are of you," said Jonathan.

"Thank you, sir. That means a great deal to me. I'm ready to leave when you are," replied Thomas. "Lydia, did you think of anything else you needed from town," inquired Jonathan. "No, I believe I have all I need. Thank you for asking," replied Lydia.

The two men left the house with Jonathan in the lead. As Thomas stepped through the doorway, he turned to look on Lydia one more time. She was sitting there slumped in her chair. Her dark eyes told the story and condition of her heart. He nodded at her and started to leave. She reached outward towards him beckoning him not to leave, knowing well he had to. He closed the door behind him, and a great sorrow overcame him. He mounted the wagon sitting beside Jonathan. Neither man spoke a word until they were well into their journey.

"Did you enjoy the town of London Thomas?" asked Jonathan. "Yes, yes I did. I want to go back and see more of it. The people there are different and hold things dear that we have never held to my recollection," responded Thomas.

"I heard that one can prosper there if he be of sharp wit and strong in back. Me, I prefer a slower way of life. One that is simple and giving each day. I lost two sons and thought I'd never heal from it. I was bitter at times and drank too much to ease the pain. Then Judith and Liam came. Now the pain is no more nor the heavy drinking. I have new life in my feet now. They have given me a reason to live and love. You must feel the same with Lucille. I like to call her Lucy. If you look at her and say, "Lucy!" she will laugh at you. Try it sometime," said Jonathan.

Jonathan and Thomas were bonding the way men bond together. Their conversations for the rest of the trip were light and sometimes humorous. They were rounding the last bend before Danbury and there stood Mildred waiting on them. Once they were by her side, Jonathan stopped the wagon. "A good and pleasant morning to you both," said Mildred. "May we offer you a ride to town Mildred?" asked Jonathan. "No, I think not. I need to speak to Thomas about some pressing matters. Thomas, would you come down from the wagon and walk with me a spell?" asked Mildred. "Why yes Mildred. I would enjoy a walk and conversation with you. Would you excuse me, Jonathan?" asked Thomas. "Yes, of course. I have enjoyed our travel together. Please give my regards to Squire," said Jonathan.

Thomas leapt from the wagon and landed beside Mildred while still holding the loaf of bread meant for Squire. He was excited to see Mildred. She always made him feel special. The two exchanged pleasantries as they strolled side by side.

"I saw you in London while I slept among the trees. As you walked in the day, there was another one following you. I know not if he was spirit or man. He watched you from afar and up close. I could not see his heart to see if he was good or evil. It was being hidden from me by another power. He knew I could see him, but he was indifferent to my presence. I believe he might be an arranger," said Mildred. "What is an arranger?" asked Thomas. "They are spirit guides who clear the path for those they have charge of. They too walked this earth as we do. They were able to succeed from the bonds of birth, life, death, and rebirth.

All that we do, we do for a common cause without ever knowing it. We are but actors on a common stage reading from a script we wrote to weave the tapestries of destiny in our hours of sleep and slumber. And when the grand curtain rises, that being our sun, we take to the stage and dance together under blue skies and stormy clouds.

Soon a man will pay you and Squire a visit. He carries a treasure from the land of kings. His message will prepare you for what is to come. Pay close attention to what he says. There are ways to hide truth to protect it from deceivers and those who practice treachery. The written word, the printed word will stand the test of time."

"You are one of the chosen. You and others like you are to bring light to those who long to see. Thomas, you have journeyed many times on this earth for the same reasons. You have seen some of these things already. I can see a new light in your eyes that wasn't there when last I saw you," said Mildred.

"Yes, yes this very morning I was with......" Thomas paused. "You were going to say Lydia," replied Mildred. Thomas' head dropped and he acknowledge her. "I want to tell you something that you might have trouble understanding. Don't invest yourself too much into the ways of king or queen, of pope or vicar. And most of all the opinion of others. All these things are designed to shackle the human spirit in its growth. They repress the true meaning of love and turn it into a mockery.

You must take belief in yourself if you are to succeed at the level you desire. The spirit of life gives openly to those who have ridden their selfish pride and their need to possess the things that render themselves to dust. Be without anchor and carry a great sail as you travel the seas of life and death. Allow the passion within you to be your chart. All things come to those prosper in mind and spirit."

"Lydia will be by your side until her mortal death. Then she will be in your heart as you carry on till death finds you sleeping one night in your bed. She will be the one you go to when no one else can deliver. Her absence and the pain that comes with it will be the motivation for the things to come your way. "The same pain lives within us all, mind you. We long for love and its fruitful rewards. We search the world over, but it can never be, so long as we look outside our own being. Heartache attracts heartbreak. Expectations attract disappointment. Anger rejects love. There is no other way to learn these things except to embrace the moment with the same measure of zeal be it kind or harsh. Then and only then will you find heaven' embrace.

Experience is the teacher. Time, the task master. Each life is a continuation of the last. There is no escaping it through death. You can't run away from it because it lives within us. When will we, the souls of the great spirit, awaken to the truth? We are those who can give answer to such a question. We hold the power and the will when we stand as one.

There stands Squire with his hands planted on his hip. He must be wondering where you've been since Jonathan passed some time ago. Go to him and remember, the gifts of kings await their time in the sun. Your soul walks amongst the stars," said Mildred as she waved at Squire. Mildred turned to the forest and was gone from sight.

"Thomas, I hope that parcel under your arm is intended for me and my consumption," growled Squire in a joking manner. "Yes sir. Mother knows the power of her influence over you comes from fresh baked bread," laughed Thomas. "It be so young man," replied Squire. Squire unwrapped the bread and held it to his nose. He inhaled as deep as he good taking in its aroma. His eyes were closed as he exhaled. He held the loaf as if it were a beautiful woman. Thomas was waiting to see if he was going to speak sweet words to it. "I'm going to dress this gift with jam and honey. Please service the presses and prepare them for battle. We'll see how much ignorance we can wipe away in a day's time," said Squire.

Thomas went inside the shop and prepared things for printing. They had only a few weeks to complete their agreement with Sir Charles Whittington. That would mean another trip to London and another brush with those of the theatre. He was anxious to learn what happened to Nichole and Catherine.

He loved Danbury and everyone who lived there. All the things of love and security were held here for him. He was satisfied and he was unsatisfied. The unknown called to the pilgrim within him. His feet were restless, his heart waxing for adventure. His focus was on the printing of bibles. This was his ticket to faraway places and new discoveries. He never felt so alive as he did now.

Thomas could hear Squire coming down the stairs. "All the bread must be gone," he thought. "Let us begin Thomas. We have paper and we have ink. We have leather for binding and thread to hold it. We have heart and we have mind. What we do will bring light to places that once held darkness. We serve to foster the common man above the ignorance that plagues this world.

It will never be the power of Rome that tells a man, woman, or child how to live their life. Nay! Nay, I say! It shall be the goodness held within the book that directs the seekers on their journey. This doctrine they spill out for us to drink is nonsense! Do you know why it's nonsense? Because they try to force it on people.

They spout out that we are damned to the gates of hell if we do not bow to them. God never forced his will on us, never. He gave us mind to think and error by which to learn. He gave us the heart of a lion so we may roar over all tyranny and injustice.

Thomas, I want you to remember this. Every Bible we print will be held in the hands of someone. The contents will shed a light of understanding to the reader. The understanding they will receive will in some way lift them up and encourage them to reach for more. We are not publishing these books for Sir Charles Whittington. No son we are not.

We are publishing them for the hands that await the arrival of such a text. So, let's make every one of them special by putting all we have into their creation. They will outlive all the kings and all the queens that England will ever see. We'll leave this world better than it was before our arrival. Today we are the kings of Danbury.

CHAPTER 56

The will of the Father rests with every individual.

The afternoon was winding down. The day's work was piled neatly beside the work bench. Thomas was cleaning the ink from the typeface. Squire sat down and began surveying the shop with his eyes held in deep thought. Thomas began sweeping the floor as he always did at closing.

"All done Squire," said Thomas. Squire rose from his chair and said, "I think a pint of ale would be a good elixir for all the ails of the body and soul. Come let us pay John and his new wife a visit. They might even have some pork roast to suit our liking. What do you say Thomas?" "I'm famished Squire," replied Thomas.

Both exited the shop and started walking towards the inn. Squire stopped and turned to look at the shop. He looked it over top to bottom without a single comment. Thomas wasn't sure why and thought it best to wait until dinner to make an inquiry. Squire took one long breath and released it. He turned towards the inn and the two walked in silence until they arrived.

Squire reached for the door and opened it. He stood to the side to allow Thomas to enter first. Just as Thomas stepped through the door Squire spoke to him in a gentle voice and said, "I've opened this door for you. Before the sun sets, I will open another door for you. Should you decide to step through it you will find no walls or roof. It's vastness is limited only by your expectations, be they small or be they large." Thomas looked at him with stark confusion.

John and Susan Clayborne were seated at the main table. Susan was the first to stand. "And what stories do you have for us about London. Is it as beautiful as I've been told?" asked Susan. "First things first Lady Clayborne. I would share with you every last detail of London. But I'm sorry to say I cannot. My throat is parched and can only be relieved by consuming a pint of your finest ale for me and one for Thomas," said Squire. Susan laughed at him, and John followed. Susan drew three pints and delivered the same to the table.

"John, I'm told that soldiers came and lodged here while we were away. That a stranger also came looking for me," said Squire. John looked at him and said, "First let's drink a pint while you and Thomas tell us all about your journey to London." "Yes, of course. Where are my manners?" replied Squire.

The stories from Squire and Thomas held their audience captive. Susan wanted to hear about women fashions. John was interested in businesses and London's expansion efforts. So long as the ale flowed so did the stories with a few tall tales mixed in. Susan left the conversation to prepare the evening meal for everyone.

"I have a proper announcement to make on this occasion," spoke Squire. He clasped his mug with both hands and sat in a moments silence. He turned to Thomas and said, "You have the presence about you that I would want in a son. You have proven your character to be solid and true. Not once have you ever lodged a complaint against anyone or anything. You have the gift of a messenger and a patriot to what is good in this world. Your rationale is beyond your years. All of this I see in you leads me to what I'm about to say.

It is not without study or thought that I, Squire Andrew Beckett, make this offer. Thomas, I am making you a full partner in my business. One half of everything I own is yours moving from this day forward. The business, the shop and the residence is half yours. You will share in half the profits of all our ventures. I ask you. Will you accept my offer young man?"

Thomas sat in shock. He looked at Squire then at John and back to Squire. He was excited and fearful at the same time. "Why, yes sir. I accept your proposition. It would be my honor, I'm sure," replied Thomas. He smiled then he laughed as the offer was sinking into his reality.

"Good, then it's settled. I will have the papers drawn up to make everything legal. Soon Mary and your precious daughter can reside in the living quarters. I will take residence here at the inn for the time being," said Squire. "I'm lost for the right words Squire. I never dreamed of such a gift," said Thomas. "The heavens guide your path. I can see that in you. This is but a steppingstone for you as you stand before the grand stairway. Consider this gift one of many to come as you search your destiny," replied Squire.

"Susan! Susan, come out here and meet Danbury's newest business owner," yelled John. Susan came from the kitchen and looked around searching for someone that might have entered. She saw no one then looked at John. "It's Thomas dear. Squire made him his full partner."

Susan looked at Thomas and put her arm around him and said, "I'm happy for you and your family. Your mother will be thrilled to hear such news. When you were younger, we knew there was something special about you. I will set a feast before you tonight and we shall celebrate Danbury's new shop owner, Thomas Sonnet."

John and Squire applauded Susan's speech. Thomas was pleased to be honored in such a way. As the men spoke Thomas drifted away in mind. The reality of it all was overwhelming. He looked over to the bar and there stood the spirit of Helen Clayborne.

She looked at Thomas and gave him a warm smile. She lifted a mug high to toast his good fortune. She took a long drink and sat the mug down. Then she turned and walked away. His heart ached for her and the care she gave.

He turned his attention back to the men's conversation. Susan entered with a platter filled with pork, potatoes, and enough bread for twice as many people. She placed it on the table and said, "Enjoy your meal while I prepare fruit tarts for the sweet tooth in you. Now eat before it goes cold."

The men held light conversation during their meal. Susan had delivered the tarts and all, but one were eaten. She drew each another round of ale. She knew it was time to talk about the soldiers and the stranger.

John took a long drink of the ale before speaking. "The soldiers came looking for you. They were not the soldiers of the crown. They were men paid by a private benefactor. It was about the religious and political interests of those who would place a yoke to the shoulders of mankind and have them behave as oxen.

They were sent to stop the printing of bibles. It appears that educated free thinking souls are a threat to politics and religious dogma. They left here going north to repress similar efforts as yours. The printers in London are protected by the crowns soldiers. We have no such protection here in Danbury. They pledged to return but did not say when. Most of the towns people will support you until they draw swords. Then they will turn tail and run away," said John with a worried look.

"I was born a free man to free parents. I'll be a free man when I die. No king or pope may stand over me as if I was a puppet. No sir. I will not have it. I'm a businessman of honor and good will. I'll publish the word of God, I will. The soldiers be damned!" shouted Squire.

The room fell silent. John took another long drink and said, "There is another way Squire if you'd so be inclined to hear." "And what might that be my friend?" inquired Squire. "They are men of coin, not of state or religion. You could pay them to turn a blind eye to your work. That would give you all the time you needed to complete your next printing. What say you Squire Beckett? Have you a few shillings for men who dance to the sound of jingling coins?"

Squire sat there and mulled over Johns proposal. "I see your point old friend. But how much would it take. I can't pay a ransom," asked Squire. "Two of them were the leaders. The others, five for certain, followed what the two said. Bargain with the leaders for a fair price and let them worry about the other five. You could even offer them room and board while they were here. One nights lodging with ale and some of Susan' cooking should satisfy them, I'm sure. I would charge you my cost for their lodging."

"Then let's do it. I like the arrangement. Thomas can help me through this. Why shouldn't he? He has a stake in this as well. What say you, Thomas? Have we the backbone to face such an adversary?" asked Squire. "Of course, Squire. Of course," spoke Thomas. His courage was present in recalling Mildred's earlier words about being protected.

"Then it's settled. Let's move on to the next order of business. What of this stranger named Miles Davenport? Is he kin to William Davenport?" asked Squire. "Yes, I was about to get to that. Let me fetch the note he left for you. I have it upstairs. He gave me a full pound for my trouble. He was a mysterious man. The few words he offered carried a great deal of weight. He is a man on a mission.

"So, what do you think Thomas? Is it wise to bribe another if it profit the soul?" asked Squire. "I think it best Squire. If it keep sword and lance at bay so no harm comes, then it is a good practice. Besides there is more to this than what we know or realize," replied Thomas. "What's this you say? From where did you receive such a thing? Oh, I know. You were speaking to Mildred this very day. Say no more. Her word has been good here since the day she was born," said Squire.

"The sun shall not set on us until we have finished our work. We are protected by powers we cannot see nor hear," spoke Thomas. Squire was amused by Thomas' prophetic tone.

"Here it is Squire. I trust its contents will be appealing to you. Now we must close for the night unless you want to sleep here," said John. No John, thank you for your kindness and hospitality. We'll be back tomorrow," replied Squire.

"Thomas, you will be helping me up and walking with me. I've had too much ale and too much pork to trust my legs to get me home safely. Thank you again John," said Squire.

Thomas was holding on to Squire as the two ventured through the dark. Cries and screams were heard from the woodlands that were distressing to hear. Squire stopped and listened. He put his arm around Thomas and hugged him.

"Dear Thomas, I pray to the powers that give us breath and free will. I pray for mercy for the broken souls that wander the earth without reason or direction. I pray for understanding of why these things must be. Yet I have yet to receive an answer to give me peace of mind. Why do some walk in darkness and some in light? What is the purpose of poverty and starvation? Who shall come to lead us to the place where we might seek our answers? I accept the things that are set before me, but I do not possess them," spoke Squire.

"I know the one that cries out in anguish. I've heard her many times before. Why woman? Why do you tarry so with one who offers no love, only grief? Do you walk by his side to exact a punishment on yourself? Is that what you think you deserve? I forgave you long ago," said Squire as he addressed the darkness of night.

He walked towards the shop on his own accord. Thomas followed close behind. He knew a great sorrow had overcome Squire. The two entered the shop and Thomas lit a lantern while Squire fell into his chair nearly turning it over.

"Bring the light closer Thomas I want to read this letter before bedding down," said Squire. He opened the envelope and began reading. All Thomas could do was watch Squires face as he read it. He watched Squire' eyes go back and forth like he was reading the same line more than once.

Squire's arm that held the letter dropped to his side as he stared off with a blank face. He lifted the letter back to his face and read it again. "Oh, my heavens," he said and once again the arm fell beside him. "It was as if he'd seen a ghost," thought Thomas. I'm as sober as the Reverend now. I best sleep on this and see it different on the morrow. We shall read it together on the morrow, Thomas. You and me," said Squire.

"Please tell me sir. I will not be able to sleep unless you share a portion for my curiosity," said Thomas. "Very well. It is not bad news of any sort. It is news from the ancients in a land far away. A place where once stood the kings of the world. A land filled with secrets and mysteries. A place where truth was received and practiced until corrupt hearts sought to abuse it by overpowering the will and minds of their world.

It states here that those same truths and wisdom were hidden within the Bible in a code. The code protects those truths. There is more but it will have to wait until he arrives again, soon according to this," replied Squire. Let us rest and renew our selves. Tomorrow is a new day, and we shall treat it as such. Good night, Thomas," said Squire.

CHAPTER 57

There are more ways to wake up besides the opening of eyes to consciousness.

Thomas lied in his bed feeling the effects of fatigue and strong ale but could not sleep. The day's events were still strong in his mind. He felt restless but didn't know why. His eyes opened as he stared off in the darkness unable to grasp the magnitude of such a day.

"There, there was the screaming again coming from the woodlands," he thought. He wondered who she was. Squire was upset to hear her cries. The tormented woman never once called out for someone to help her, why? He knew the woodlanders lived by their own laws and their own ways. They kept to themselves and did not entertain anyone who tried to interfere with their way of life.

Then more screaming. He heard a man cursing and screaming at the woman while she begged him to stop. The crying mixed with screams sent chills across him. Then silence. A few moments of silence passed. The next sound was the gentle chirping of crickets.

Thomas lied there waiting to hear anything, but nothing came except the eeriness of silence. Thomas' eyes were weighing heavy, and he drifted off to sleep. He felt light, like he was floating upward toward the sky. As he looked down the light of a silvery moon cast its rays about the countryside. There in the field below was the body of a woman lying face down in the wet grass. There was no life left in the body. He looked about but saw no one.

Then he heard a woman's voice say, "I'm Carol. Are you the one who has come for me to carry me home? They told me that an angel would come for me. Are you an angel? I always thought angels had wings. You don't have any wings." "No, I'm not an angel," replied Thomas. "Then who are you," she asked. I'm Thomas, apprentice to Squire

Beckett the printer," replied Thomas. "Squire is my father. I'm Carol Beckett, oldest daughter to Squire Beckett."

Thomas looked at her in her ghostly form and said, "He never told me he had another daughter." "No, I wouldn't think he would. We had a terrible falling out in my youth. I fell in love with an older man of questionable character. He was married and had two children. Father forbade me from seeing him. It was a huge scandal for the likes of Danbury. His wife fought desperately to keep him. We were shunned by everyone who knew us. There was even talk of imprisoning him. So, one night we just ran away. We left family and friends behind for what we thought was love.

We had fun in the beginning until the money was all gone. Then tragedy entered our lives. I was with child begging for food. He stole what he could sell and spent the money on strong drink. He blamed me for our trouble and began to beat me whenever he drank. We moved back here to live the best we could. The beatings continued and eventually they seemed normal. He can't beat my body anymore and make me cry. I'm free. Free of that body and free from the hardness of life I witnessed. Love can blind as well as give sight.

I've watched you from the trees. I see how much my father adores you. He always wanted a son to carry on his work. I guess he got that in you Thomas. You are good for him and your presence in his life gives his heart a way to heal," spoke Carol in spirit.

"I see one coming to me. That must be my angel! I have to go with them. It was a pleasure sharing with you," said Carol in a loving voice. Thomas watch her ascending as she turned toward the figure meeting her.

He watched her reach out to receive someone. Her eyes opened wide, and a smile came to life. She cried out, "Mother! Oh, mother you came for me! I'm so sorry mother for the pain I caused you and father! Hold me mother. Hold me and never let me go! I need your love, mother. I am so sorry, so sorry." Carol was weeping uncontrollably. All the pains and all the regrets she endured in life were falling away in the form of tears as they fell back to earth.

She wept until she could weep no more. The tears she released took away all the sorrows and pains. All that was left was love. Her mother reached for her and held her tight. Their love they shared owned the moment. They spoke to each other, but Thomas could not hear their words. He watched as a beautiful silver light surrounded the two. Slowly their form began to fade from his vision.

Thomas became aware of his body and the bed he was lying on. His eyes opened as he processed what he had just witnessed. His time with Carol was as real as anything he experienced in the material world. Thomas would walk between the two worlds for the rest of his life.

The cooler air crept its way through the open window consuming the left over heat from the day before. The light of the silver moon also found the window and its light shown down on his face.

He felt himself being lifted upward again and he began to laugh as a child. "Helen! I saw you walking amongst the mourners at your wake. I saw you at the inn this very night wishing me well!" said Thomas. "Yes, you did young man. And I made breakfast for you the morning when I passed. I refused to leave that world until I could make you a proper breakfast," said Helen.

"We're all here Thomas. All of us. We walk amongst you, but you cannot see us. We're always here going about our lives like we did there. We can't interfere with you. We can only witness parts of what you are doing. It's the same life here, but it's not the same thing. I can't explain it in words. You have to feel it.

I've come forward on behalf of the rest to speak to you dear child. Oh, Thomas my son, you carry the golden laurel about you. Those mortal eyes of yours cannot see it but it's there. As long as it rests upon you no harm shall come upon you. But with all its powers, it can't keep the harm you create from hurting you. You have free will and no power of light or darkness can interfere.

You are a messenger and a messenger you will always be in this life and the next. Love has many faces, Thomas. All of us, no matter our position, must look upon each other with kindness if we are ever to realize the way of life everlasting. The wind carries each one of us to awareness at its assigned time.

Ask yourself each day, what do I love at this moment? Is it the heart of another? Is it held in an earthly possession? A house, the fastest horse, the brightest of clothing? Know that whatever it may be, it be ruled by time. A child may fall to death, the house may burn, the horse grows old, and the clothes do tatter. All things held in time belong to time. Ashes to ashes, dust to dust.

Love is the only thing that matters. Love called us and we answered. Here we will stay until all we have has been given without promise or expectation. It's called unconditional love.

I love you Thomas, we all do. Love is different here. Carry forth the story in your heart and hold it as a newborn child. We count ourselves blessed for knowing you and others like you.

Squire will need you once he learns of Carol's death. Her passing will effect many lives. Buried secrets and desires will bring their faces to the light for healing and understanding because of her passing.

Squire will want vengeance for her death. You are to discourage him from such a thing. The woodlanders exact their own justice in their own way. Stay clear of the woodlands for a weeks' time. There will be unrest amongst those who seek vengeance.

It's time for me to leave you. They're calling me back. Goodbye Thomas. I love you dear," spoke Helen.

CHAPTER 58

When two come together in love, a celebration is born.

A loud pounding came at the shops door. Thomas' eyes popped open. He heard the sound of Squires feet crashing on every step as he descended the staircase. He could hear the sound of muffled voices. Then the sound of Squire crying out, then a loud thud.

Thomas jumped from the bed and hurried to dress. He ran down the stairs to see Squire lying on the floor holding his chest and wailing like a child. Tears were rolling down his red plump cheeks. His eyes were troubled, his mind incapable of thought. He looked up at Thomas with a bewildering look. He was unable to speak. He made hand gestures instead of words. A very old wound from the past, buried deep within, had returned to the surface for its redemption.

Thomas was quick to recall his time with Carol last night. Thomas looked towards the field where he had seen her body lie. There stood a small band of people around something in the tall grass. "That has to be Carol," he thought. He felt a tug at his pant leg. He looked down to see Squire looking up at him like he was a lost little boy. "Help me to get him up, won't you?" said Thomas to the men standing just outside the door. Carefully they lifted him up and placed him in his chair. Thomas ran upstairs to get a towel so Squire could wipe away the effects of his grieving.

One of the men asked, "What sir? What would you have us do with the body?" Squire still could not speak. He tried, he desperately tried to speak but not a single word came forth. He turned to look at Thomas with a look that said, "I can't. You must."

Thomas turned to the men and said, "One of you go to the Stagg Inn and fetch Susan. Tell her what has happened so she may bring comfort to Squire. I need one of you to go to the carpentry shop where my father is employed on this day. Ask him to come and help me with what must be done. The two men hurried on their way as Thomas had asked.

Squire sat crying as Thomas looked out across the field at the lifeless body. Squire took Thomas' hand and gave it a tug. He was soliciting the need for a hug. Thomas shifted to his knees to be at Squires level and the two embraced. Squire held Thomas tight while still weeping.

Susan and her stepson Stacy stepped through the doorway. "What's going on here? Look at you Squire. Let us sit at table and take account of ourselves." said Susan. Squire rose from his chair and the two embraced. Squire rocked back and forth as he held her. "Come Squire. Let's go upstairs, you and me. We'll have some tea and honey butter to sooth the heart and refresh the mind. Come now. Let Thomas and the others take care of her body while you and I take account of her kind soul. She loved you. You know that don't you?" asked Susan as she guided him to the stairs.

Thomas stepped outside and walked to where her body lied. "Why do you stand here over her body?" asked Thomas. "To protect the body sir. We wish to keep the animals away from her body," spoke a man wearing a green hat. "She was one of us and we take care of our own. We do not judge each other by what we have gained. We judge each other by what we share. She shared all she had to whomever extended a hand her way.

She was the angel amongst us. She was a story teller and a reader of books. No matter what that bastard did to her she never complained. We'll deal with him later once he's found. For now, we look after Carol. What of her body young Thomas? We know you can speak for Squire," spoke the man wearing the green hat.

Thomas looked at the man and could see he was educated and well-mannered. "If one of you could fetch the barrow from behind the shop and bring it here. We'll load the body and put it in a safe place away from the forest animals. Without the smallest of hesitation, the man in the green hat took off to get the barrow. Thomas was certain that he carried Carol in his heart by the way he spoke of her.

The sound of approaching horse and wagon was nearing. It was Edward, Thomas' father. His eyes caught sight of Carol lying face down in the grass. He leapt from the wagon without stopping the horse or setting the brake. The horse continued until some of the men caught up with it and turned it back. Edward fell to his knees beside her body. He clasped his hands together and cried out, "Why?!" He began weeping, then stroking her hair. He moved from his knees to a sitting position on the grass. His eyes closed as he wept for her. Thomas watched his father and was surprised to see him grieve so passionately.

He had his reasons. Everyone has their reasons. The events and the secrets of the past are held within. They await the day when clarity renders the understanding needed for closure. A time for release and a time of acceptance.

Edward stood, staring down at her body. "Who did this? Her neck has been broken," said Edward in a vengeful tone. One of the men made a gesture towards the man in the green hat pushing the barrow towards them. "Him! Was it him?! yelled Edward. "No sir, but he knows who it was," spoke a bystander. Edward looked at the one in the green hat and asked, "Do you know who did this?" "I do. And we will take care of him once we have seen to Carols needs," replied the one in the green hat. It was obvious to Thomas both men held something in their hearts for Carol.

"Father, do you have a coffin ready that can receive her body?" asked Thomas. Edward looked at Thomas for the first time. He realized his son had witnessed his emotional display. "Yes, son I do but this flower's bones will not rest in it. I will craft a coffin for her befitting a queen from these hands that once held her in love," spoke Edward with a heavy heart.

The man with the green hat placed his hand on Edwards shoulder and said, "May I in some way or manner be a service to you in this?" Edward looked at him and could see his pain for Carol. "Yes, of course you can. Let's lift her body into the wagon so we can carry her to the shop," said Edward. The men approached her body with reverence. They turned her over to reveal her face. Both men began to quietly weep. Each attempted to lift her in their arms to carry her. They stopped competing over who would hold her. So, together they gathered her limp body and placed it gently in the wagon. Edward gestured for the man to join him in the seat of the wagon, but he refused. He wanted to walk behind the wagon as it journeyed through town just to have more time to look upon her.

Carol' death would bring a few stories and a few secrets to the surface. It was time for what was held in the shadows of the mind to have their time in the sun. It was a time of reckoning.

CHAPTER 59

It was once said that a pilgrims quest was for the journey and the journey alone.

Thomas was approaching the print shop when he saw Lydia standing outside waiting on him. She came with Jonathan this morning on a supply venture. Their eyes met and smiles were exchanged. They embraced each other careful not to arouse any suspicion.

Song birds began to collect on the roof of the print shop. A few began singing. More song birds gathered on the roof until the roof could hold no more. The towns people and the woodlanders began to gather to watch so many birds in congregation.

The birds lifted upwards to the air to create a whirlwind that spiraled up as high as the eye could see. It grew in size as more birds joined in. The highest ones descended towards the ground as the others followed. Then upwards again to a great height and down again, singing their songs as they flew.

Laughter and excitement filled all those who witnessed the display. Children jumped upward flapping their arms trying to join the birds. The adults watched with intent and wonder. The birds were forming into the shape of a ladder or staircase. It appeared to stretch all the way to heaven.

Some began to cry for the display gave them hope of something better to come. All who stood in witness stood together as one. As quick as they assembled the birds disappeared. The witnesses were still holding their smiles as they went about their business. The display made life a little easier to accept.

"Thomas, have the good sense to invite Lydia into our home. Or should I say your home," spoke Squire from the doorway of the shop. "We must be about our business and I'm sure Lydia can lend us a hand.

The couple entered the shop and Lydia was quick to offer her condolences for Squire' loss. His face was swollen from all the crying.

Susan Clayborne was excusing herself to everyone so she could return to the inn. She was needed because the inn was full of guests.

Squire turned to Lydia with bloodshot eyes and said, "I have news I wish to share with you especially since it involves your daughter. I have given half of the business to Thomas. Furthermore, I have decided to move out of the residence so Thomas, Mary and Lucille can be together as family. I plan to take residence at the inn for the time being."

Lydia looked at Thomas with a blank stare. Thomas thought she'd be pleased with the news but that wasn't the case. She appeared troubled about the arrangement. She turned to Squire and said, "You are most generous sir. Mary and Thomas are blessed to have you in their lives. I know Mary will be pleased but Diane will morn. She calls Mary daughter and Lucille her little sunshine. Tell me when will this arrangement begin."

"Why not today? I'll send one of the Clayborne boys to fetch my things later. Consider it yours as of today, Thomas," said Squire. "I will return home soon to give everyone the good news," said Lydia in a dreary tone. "Jonathan will be looking for me so I will join him. Thank you again Squire." Lydia turned towards the door and left without giving Thomas a look.

"We'd best be tending to Carol's body now and the wake to come. Thomas, tell me what arrangements have been made thus far," inquired Squire. "Her body is near the carpentry shop where father works. He and another are taking care of her wellbeing. One stands guard while one prepares the final resting place for her body," responded Thomas. "You have done well and have given me some peace of mind. Let us venture there and see what progress has been made," said Squire.

As Squire and Thomas walked through town there were those who came forward to express their sorrow for Carol's passing. Many knew her since she taught the children how to read and write. Some of the adults present were once students of hers. Her love and care for the children will be dearly missed.

The two arrived at the carpentry shop and stood close at the wagon. Her body had been covered with white cloth. The man with the green hat was kneeling on the ground. His eyes were shut tight. His lips were moving as if he were speaking but not a word was heard.

"Who is he Squire?" asked Thomas. Squire stood watching the man in deep prayer. It was obvious that Squire knew him. "He once came for Carol's hand in marriage. I turned him away. He had no good means of support or family about to support him," said Squire. "But look at him Squire. He's still in love with her and weeps for her still," said Thomas. "I know. I never once said I was void of foolishness. The man was a dreamer. A weaver of story and rhyme. He believed all things were of love and that love could overcome all.

I still have some of the poems he wrote for Carol. She loved his poems and the way he spoke to her. When she ran off with that cur, he followed them to London just to be near her. His name is Henry Jamison. He came here from London looking for the meaning of life. He must have followed her back here. He still wears that green hat she gave him when they first met," spoke Squire in a regrettable tone.

"And my father Squire? What about my father? He too wept for her. I never saw my father weep until today. Did my father love her also? Even now he prepares a coffin for her body. He said it had to be made with his hands and no one else's. Why does my father care for her so?" asked Thomas.

"It is not for me to say Thomas. You will have to ask him why, so he can tell you in his own way. That privilege belongs to him and him alone," responded Squire.

"Carol's nature was appealing to many of the men folk in Danbury. She was the opposite of Rebecca. Carol loved life and everything in it. She didn't care about possession, money, or reputation. She loved animals, especially horses. She worked in the livery often without pay just to be with them. She would take food from the garden and give it to the horse. Her mother would scold her, but she just laughed at her and kept on pleasing the horses," spoke a smiling father about his daughter.

"Come let's see your fathers handiwork," spoke Squire. They entered the shop to see Edward planning a board. He was crying while he worked as if she were of his bones. Edward didn't see the pair as they looked on. He would wipe away the tears with his apron then return back to work. At times he was troubled as he assembled her coffin. He was focused on every detail to make it perfect for her.

"Come Thomas, let us leave this man as he grieves his own way. One day you will understand," whispered Squire. Quietly they left and began to walk to the inn to make arrangements for Carol's wake.

Along the way they were met by the Reverend Richard. "Good day to you vicar," said Squire. "Good day Squire. I'm afraid I have some distressing news for you. The town folk have elected me to inform you that Carol cannot be buried in the town cemetery. Mainly because she disgraced herself and your family. Furthermore she was of the woodlanders. We don't want them buried beside those we loved," spoke the Reverend Richard.

Squire stood speechless as his face turned red. "Sir I will have you know that she brought no shame to our family, only sadness. Sadness is a part of life and bears no semblance to sin," spoke Squire in a frigid tone. "Yes, yes, it is as you say but it still remains, she was of the woodlanders," retorted the Reverend.

"Thank you so much for the demonstration. Your pious brand of religion is a hypocrites folly. And you sir, you are its messenger, are you not sir? It's but a hardness of heart that your religion doles to the flock. You claim to be the word of the one called Jesus. Yet are not the woodlanders the least of us? Did not the Rabbi say that to serve the least of them was the same as serving him? Your hypocrisy sir and the hypocrites you serve could learn what it means to be a true Christian."

"And for what it is worth, I am aware of your adulterous dealings with my daughter Rebecca. Do you know she is with child? Do you sir? Be it yours? I wonder sir. I had to send her to my sisters care to protect whatever reputation she had left in this town. So, before you or someone else decides who is worthy to enter the cemetery and who is not, I think it be wise to decide who gets into heaven and who is not. Good day sir," spoke Squire.

Reverend Richard was as white as the cloth that covered Carol's body. He felt light headed and had to drop to the ground. At first, he started shaking, then he began to weep. Those in witness heard Squire's words and stood away from the Reverend as they looked on.

Squire along with Thomas entered the inn to see John and Susan. John was serving some of the lumbermen from the camp. Susan was busy in the kitchen. Business was very good. John brought Squire and Thomas a pint each as they sat at a table.

"You did everything for Carol that you could. She never complained one time about her life or the decisions she made. She had a heart of gold like her mother," said John to Squire. "Thank you for that John. I thought myself a good parent while the girls grew. Looking back, I'm not so sure," said Squire. "What's important to remember is this. As long as your heart was in the right place when it was to you to guide them, there should be no quarrel with yourself. Not yesterday, today nor on the morrow. We do not have Gods vision so we can never be at fault," spoke John in sincerity.

"I think I may have to pay you for your words John. I have a better sense of self now. Thank you, my friend. I'll be lodging here for a while. Thomas' family will be moving in so he may have a better sense of family life," spoke Squire. "I'll have your usual room ready for you," said John.

The two finished their pints and left the inn for the print shop. Both were heavy in thought and wonder. They were like father and son.

A small crowd stood outside the print shop to offer condolences to Squire. Mary, Jonathan, Lydia and Lucille were arriving at the shop in a wagon carrying all Mary' possessions. Mary saw Thomas and Squire and began waving at them in excitement. It was obvious she heard the news and was in a hurry to see things for herself. She would not waste any time about moving in and turning the shop into the home she always dreamed of.

Thomas stepped to her as she held Lucille and gave both a kiss. Lucille reached for Thomas to be held. He took her and gave her another kiss. They stepped inside while Squire spent time with friends as they offered him comfort in words and blessings. Squire was enjoyed the kindness he was receiving. His heart was feeling the love and care from friends. It helped to relieve the pain he had carried for so many years. The reckoning had arrived.

Mary flew through the print shop and the living quarters. She was imagining how she would decorate the home to make it hers. She was in her glory. It was the grandest of gifts she could ever receive. Her desires were manifesting around her just as she had imagined. Living in town, socializing, and belonging to something greater than country life. She was smiling with joy and wonder. This was Mary's day. It belonged to her.

CHAPTER 60

All things come to those who wait.

The sun rose once again to offer a new day for those who sought the same. Today was Carol's day in Danbury. Today was for those who wished to honor her and pay their respect. Today was a day to offer goodbyes, not only for Carol but for broken dreams and unkept promises. It was a day for reckoning, a day for healing and letting go.

Squire was waking from a long nights rest. He hadn't realized where he was when he first woke at the inn. He knew it wasn't his bedroom. Then he remembered where he was.

Today he'd embrace the feelings that laid dormant for so long in his heart. He was ready. The ghosts of the past were ready to come forward to be embraced so that they too could leave the haunts of darkness.

The woodlanders were preparing for the wake. She was one of them. She was a saint among them. She was respected for her kindness and her willingness to help others, especially the children. All the camps of woodlanders would gathered under the sun as one to honor her life and all she gave.

The sun moved across the sky until midday had arrived. The field before the print shop would serve as the site for Carol's wake. There were makeshift tables scattered with seats fashioned from crates and logs. The table for the banquet was covered in a bright green cloth. Stones were placed on each end to keep the wind from blowing it away. Susan and the boys were setting up the food in buffet style to serve everyone.

The townspeople were few in attendance. The woodlanders were many in number. They came from every direction. Some in small bands, some alone. Some brought gifts for Carol that would follow her to the grave. Some of the gifts were ones she had given to others in their time of need. What she had given would be returned to her with the same amount of love she gave.

One child carried a book Carol had given to her. She learned how to read from the same book. Some said, because of Carol, that the woodlanders were better educated than the townspeople.

Those in the crowd were mingling together to share their stories about Carol. Thomas walked among them listening to as many as he could. He didn't know her, but from listening to the testimonies he wished he had. One by one they stepped to Squire to share a quick story or offer sympathy, adult and children alike.

Thomas noticed one young man that stood alone listening to the stories about Carol. He spoke to no one yet was careful to listen to every story until the last word was spoken. When one story had ended, he turned to hear the next. He was like one gathering fruits in a basket for later pleasure. He was dressed in shabby clothing and had no shoes. He carried the look of someone lost without direction. Thomas could see there was something about him that made his presence special among the crowd.

Susan rang her bell to let everyone know that the food was ready to be served. They gathered and formed a line. One by one they were served. When the plates were all gone Susan resorted to using the shops paper to hold the offerings. The stories still flowed as did the ale and teas. It was a celebration under the sun like no other seen before in these parts.

The Rosenheim family were arriving carrying their instruments. Patti was in the lead as the rest followed. The family were descendants of the Druids. Each one paid their respects and shared in the bounty of food. The Rosenheim men took a few pints of ale as they mixed with the woodlanders. Patti called out to her father and brothers. It was time to serenade the guests and Squire. Their music was lively, and some took to dancing. In this part of the world a wake was a time for celebration and sharing. All who gathered were celebrating the life of Carol. Patti played her flute as she mixed with the crowd and danced with the children.

Squire, seeing the spectacle before him, was feeling melancholy and joyous at once. All this, the people, the celebrating and all the stories that crossed his ears of his beloved Carol made him aware of his daughters true beauty. "Damn be the opinions of others. Damn be one who partakes in their ways," thought Squire. He dropped to his knees, clasped his hands together and looked upwards. He let out a yell for God to hear and all who had gathered. He wept and he cursed the darkness within. All the blame, all the heartache held in deep regret was ready for embrace, ready to be released.

The music ceased. The crowd began to circle Squire. They watched as the ghosts of yesterday were taking flight from his soul. He sobbed as his shoulders slumped with his head hung low.

A voice from the crowd said, "She gave us hope when we had none." Another voice sounded saying, "She delivered my children to me." "She loved me when no one else would," rang out another. "She was my mother," came a voice in the back of the crowd.

Squire heard it and ceased his sobbing. "What? What was that you said?" beckoned Squire. The air was silent. The crowd began to part from the direction of the voice. "I said she was my mother. Those who stand here can bear witness of me," said the voice. A figure appeared to Squire but he could not see him well. He wiped away the dears with his shirttail. And looked upon the lad once more. "Have you a name son?" asked Squire. "Yes sir. My name is Ian." "Then you would be my grandson? Is that so?" asked Squire. "It be true sir. I am of your flesh and your bones. I am the son of Carol and Jacob. I am a woodlander and hold my mother's legacy to heart," replied Ian.

Squire struggled to stand so some of the men helped him to his feet. Squire brushed off his clothes and extended his arms to Ian. "Come to me flesh of my flesh, bones of my bones. Come to me so I may hold you as one of mine. Come son. I await you," spoke Squire as he continued to weep. Ian slowly started walking to Squire. When he was but a few feet away he ran to Squires waiting arms. Squire held him tight as if never to let him go. Squire eased up on him and kissed his cheek. Everyone began to cheer and clap their hands to the witness.

"What God is this that takes one from me so I may hold another with equal love? It is the wiseman that can understand the heart of the true God. Music! Please, back with the music and dance. Let us celebrate the day as it was meant to be. For once I wept in sorrow for the loss of a daughter. Now I weep graciously for the gain of a grandson!" cried out Squire. He and Ian sat under the shade of a tree sharing in words and laughter.

The wagon carrying Carol's body was approaching. Edward held the reins as the horse drew near. Everyone became silent with heads turned to the wagon. The man with the green hat walked behind as a pallbearer. The wagon came to rest before Squire and Ian. Edward dismounted the wagon and offered his respects to Squire. He then stepped to one side for them to view the coffin holding her body. The coffin was made of oak plank. A Celtic cross was carved across the top. A Bible was tied to the coffin so that it hovered above her heart.

Squire and Ian stood side by side in silence. Once they stepped away those who knew her paraded passed the coffin. Those who brought gifts for her placed them on the wagon beside the coffin. Those of Catholic mind made the sign of the cross as they passed. Children placed wild flowers and colorful stones as gifts for the one that fed them knowledge and love.

A young girl stood alone at the wagon holding a book. She held it to her heart as she looked on at the coffin. She brought the book to her lips and kissed it. Then she placed it on the coffin beside the Bible. She cried a little then walked away.

This daughter, this wife and mother lives on so long as what she gave to others inspired them to do likewise. The earth that was once her home gave her up to a finer place where she continues to give of herself to those in need.

Patti Rosenheim climbed up on the wagon seat with flute in hand. She looked across the gatherers for their attention. "Here lies the body of Carol. Her spirit touched us all in one way or another. We gather together today because of her death. We gather together today because of her life.

She is our sister, our daughter, our mother, and our friend. She chose to shelter with the woodlanders rather than knock on Squire's door when she returned to us. She lived where her brand of love and care was most needed. I heard one of you talk how she held her body against yours to keep you from freezing in the nights chill. Another spoke of how she went hungry because she had fed you, her food.

The stories of her charity are many, too many to count. I know she is in heaven surrounded by gold and silver. She's probably trying to find a way to send all of it our way so we would never go hungry again." The gallery of souls began to laugh at her humor. Once the laughter subsided Patti looked across the faces and said, "Let us bow our heads and send her what we hold for her in our hearts so she may be heralded among the angels that watch over us."

A moment of silence overcame the whole countryside. The birds held their song and the rushing water of a nearby stream was all that could be heard. Patti raised her flute to her lips. She drew a deep breath and sounded one continuous single note that caused most to raise their head. Then she broke to two notes, then three, then four. One note for her birth, two for her life, three for the life she lived and the fourth for her farewell.

The Rosenheim family played an old Celtic song about lost loves and the promise of new loves to come. Some held each other and slow danced to the music. Others started to return to their place amongst the trees. The crowd was wanning, as the sun moved towards midafternoon.

Henry Jamison, the man with the green hat, stepped to Squire with hat in hand and head bowed. "May I speak with you sir about a sensitive matter?" asked Henry. "Of course, you may. Ian, please excuse us while we speak," replied Squire. "No sir. I beg of you. What I have to say concerns young Ian also," replied Henry.

"Carol, your daughter was one of us. She was happy with us. Her place with us was one of respect and adoration. I petition you sir to allow us to bury her our way, in a place where our dead lie in rest. So she can continue to be with those she loved and cared for," spoke Henry in humble manner.

Squire lowered his head to think about the proposal. Ian looked up at Squire. Squire saw in Ian's eyes the answer. "I'll leave that decision to Ian. What say you child of Carol?" asked Squire. "I think it proper that she be buried according to our ways," spoke Ian. "Then it shall be as you say Ian." Squire addressed Henry, "When would you be giving her body back to the earth?" "Tomorrow sir. It will return back tomorrow," replied Henry. "You have our blessings, Henry. Good day to you and thank you for everything," said Squire.

Edward boarded his wagon a second time. He followed two men to another field where a fire was burning, and others waited. The coffin was carefully unloaded and placed on green grass. Those in attendance would sit with the body through the night to protect it until its burial tomor-row. This was the way of the woodlanders. They were poor of possessions but rich in custom and respect.

The sun was about to set on Danbury. A day of witness filled with joy and sorrow, song and dance still resonated with all who partook.

Destiny laid down its pen for today's story. It was put to rest. The sun would rise on the morrow, and destiny's pen would be lifted once again for the lives of those who stood under the sun.

CHAPTER 61

Gullible is he who claims to know the heart of God or from where the wind blows.

Yesterday the book of life turned another page. Today's page appears blank, white as snow. The souls which gather together who author this book of life shall be the same who stand witness to the contents held within on their day of reckoning. There will be entries of sadness and gloom, happiness, and joy. All things human, all things under the sun have their place within. It never was a question of right or wrong. It never was. It was a matter of right and wrong. It was a matter of balance.

Thomas clung to the wisdom of Solomon. It gave him peace when he lacked the understanding to the "whys" of life. The tenets of Ecclesiastes said it best, "There is a season and a time for every purpose under heaven." He could not explain the reasons for the events of recent memory. But he could find the peace to accept the witness.

Thomas felt a tugging on his lip. He opened his eyes and saw Lucille perched on his chest. Thomas couldn't help but laugh at her. He held her and rocked her back and forth until she was giggling.

The sound of clanging pots and dishes meant that Mary was up and already at turning the home into theirs. She was shining on this glorious day. She had her husband, her family, and a home of her own. All that she desired was at her feet. It was her heaven on earth. She felt complete and grateful.

The front door opened from downstairs, and someone yelled out, "Is anyone up yet?" "Yes mother. I'm up!" shouted Mary. The sound of feet ascending the staircase stirred Thomas to rise but Lucille had other plans. "Thomas are you still in bed?" shouted Diane. "Yes, mother I am. I'm being held hostage and unable to rise," replied Thomas. Diane entered the room and saw Lucille perched on Thomas. "Lucy, come to grandma sweetie," said Diane as she extended her arms to receive her."

The women began preparing the meals for the day. Jonathan and Edward were checking the building over to see what repairs were needed. This was a family affair. All were invested for the higher good and comfort of all present.

Squire awoke to a grandson on this special day. Ian had a grandfather and someone to love him and care for his wellness.

Squire slept sound as the few ghosts left from his past left in the night having had their embrace of acceptance.

Ian did not sleep sound. He wasn't used to sleeping on a bed or by himself. The woodlanders slept in groups usually on the ground for protection and warmth. So, he slept on the floor where he felt comfortable.

Squire knocked on his door and said, "Ian, are you up lad?" "Yes Squire. I'm awake," replied Ian. Squire opened the door to see him still on the floor. Ian stood up and began brushing himself off, as he would from sleeping on the ground. Squire smiled at his grandson and his heart grew as he looked at such an innocence.

Ian was still grieving within for his mother's touch. She was his life, his light on earth. He felt sorry for what his father had done.

Beatings were normal in this family. Anytime his father drank a beating wasn't far away. All too often he stood between his parents so that the blows intended for his mother would land on him. His father would disappear for days after the really bad beatings.

"Come son. Let us sit and enjoy a meal while we learn about each other so that we may bond in heart as well as in blood," said Squire in loving manner.

The two walked down the stairs together. The air was filled with the aromas of food. Ian perked up and looked around at others eating as they spoke to one another. The two chose a table and sat down to wait for the service. It was all so new to Ian. He wondered why everyone was eating while they sat there hungry without food.

Three men were getting up from their table to leave. They had left food on their plates. Ian watched them as they made their way to the door. His plan was to eat the food from the plates once they were out of sight. His body tensed. He stooped to make his figure smaller. His feet turned towards their table and were ready to spring. Then a loud noise at his table startled him. Susan had placed a platter full of food before them. He looked at the food then at Susan. "When you finish that, I'll get you more," said Susan as she walked away.

He couldn't believe his eyes. He reached for a sausage and ate it in two bites. His mouth was full as he reached for another. Squire could not help but chuckle at him. As soon as the last bit of the first one was swallowed, he opened his mouth to receive another. "Slow down Ian. You don't have to eat the whole platter at once," said Squire. Ian acted like he didn't hear what Squire just said. "No matter," thought Squire.

Ian was showing signs of stress. His belly and pockets were full but there was a hole in his heart where his mother once lived. His mind was off somewhere else as sad eyes came to bear. Eyes became watery, a tear ran down his face, then he wept.

"Here, here, what's this?" said Susan as she approached Ian. "Come to me son. Stand and let me hold you," insisted Susan. Before he could finish standing, he reached for Susan and held her close. His crying turned to sobbing as he buried his face in her apron. She held him as she ran her fingers through his hair.

"No one will ever you beat you again as long as I take a breath child. You will never go hungry again so long as I take a breath child. God as my witness from this day forward you will grow in the light of love so long as we all draw breath. She rocked him back and forth calming the hurt he carried within. His tears ceased and he became relaxed feeling safe in her arms.

He felt his mother. She was holding him now through Susan. He could smell her hair and feel the warmth of her heart. Mother and son, reunited in this moment of a new day and a new way. Letting go of the past to embrace the future is always heartbreaking. In order to gain one must learn to lose.

"There is a season and a time for everything under heaven. A time to seek, and a time to lose. A time to keep and a time to cast away." Ecclesiastes 3: 6.

CHAPTER 62

The still of the night was made for the still of the soul.

Susan had prepared a hot bath for Ian. There were clean clothes waiting for him that her sons had outgrown. He'd never seen a bathtub before. He just stared at it not knowing what to do.

"Come on Ian. Take off those clothes of yours and get in. Don't you worry that I'll see you naked. I raised three sons on my own. Now either take them off and get in the tub or I'll take them off for you and wash you myself!" spoke Susan.

Ian was quick to render his clothes to the floor and jumped in the tub splashing water all over the floor. "You'll find soap and cloth in the water. Make sure you scrub really good, or you'll be having a second bath" as she left him alone.

In short time Ian and Squire were taking a stroll through town. Ian was trying to get use to the clothes Susan gave him. The shoes he was given were a little big, but he wasn't about to complain. Some of townspeople greeted Squire and asked about Ian. Each time Squire spoke of Ian it gave Ian the feeling that he belonged somewhere and that he mattered.

As they walked along, Squire explained the history of Danbury to Ian, but Ian's attention was elsewhere. He was searching the tree line where he used to live. He wondered if he had been missed or if anyone took notice of his absence.

"Come Ian. Let us visit the print shop while the air is still cool. You just might have a future there. Tell me son, can you read?" asked Squire. "Yes sir. I can read and write. I have books that I treasure and keep safe for mother," replied Ian. "That's good son. We could use you in the print shop. You could work for us, and earn a coin or two for your pocket," said Squire. "What would I do with coins Squire?" asked Ian. Squire let out a roaring laugh. "You make a good point grandson. A very good point," said Squire. Ian had no idea what was so funny.

Diane and Lydia finished preparing food for everyone. There was much to do and no time for idle seating. The women were going back and forth on how to decorate the new home.

The men were quarrelling over which job took priority and how to go about the repairs. All the complaining and disagreement going on was the recipe for the bonding for others to come under one flag, one cause united. Whatever came across the threshold for one, would cross the threshold of all. It's the compromise that builds unity. Along with the occasional biting of ones tongue whenever necessary.

A knock came at the door. Thomas knew it was Squire and he must have Ian with him. He ran down the stairs and the men followed. The women held themselves in conversation never giving any mind to the men or the knock at the door.

Thomas threw open the door. "Come inside please. Come in and join the party," said Thomas in excitement. "Hello to everyone. It's good to see family about caring for each other," said Squire. "There is food upstairs. Come and eat," said Thomas. "Thank you no, Thomas. Susan fed us well," replied Squire.

Jonathan and Edward joined in and thanked Squire for the opportunity he afforded their children. Each shook his hand and the hand of Ian. Edward took a hard stare at Ian. It made Ian feel uneasy. "You have your mothers eyes and her gentleness about you," said Edward. There was a brief moment of silence. The conversation returned as each shared a story or two. Thomas and Squire thought Edward was seeking to fill some sort of loss of Carol through Ian.

Squire took Thomas to one side out of earshot from the others. He reached inside his pocket and removed the letter from Miles Davenport. "It's time we sat down together so I can read you the contents. It is very important, and we must decide if we are willing to go the distance. It will not be easy to say the least, and it could be dangerous. Are you ready?" inquired Squire. "Yes. Let's hear what he is offering," replied Thomas.

Squire opened the letter and began to read it aloud.

"Dear Sir, It is with respect for you that I tender this letter in lieu of speaking to you in person as I had originally planned. Please know that I will return at a later date to explain my position in full. Although this letter is to give insight to my visit, I'm afraid that the depth cannot be properly expressed in words. So, with that said, I will begin.

Through the ages of time it has always been that one day the populous of this land would be restored to its original state. The state I speak of is before the so called original sin. It was always know that mankind would eventually return to the state of bliss. How it was done and when it would be done would be left to mankind to decide for themselves because of the gift of freewill. The journey from one end of the rainbow to the other would take a great amount of time. It would take many lifetimes of witness before enough of the populous was ready to receive truth.

A map or code was created to show the way home when things were ripe for it to surface. To protect its truth and light the code it had to be hidden, tucked away under the noses of everyone. It was necessary to keep it from those who would use it to harm rather than to heal. There are a number of sacred texts that carry the message in one form or another. The Bible is one of them.

As you are most aware, there is a rebellion about the land between the religions. One demands change while the other insists on keeping all things the same. The reformation is allowing the spread of English Bibles to the populous. Those of reason and concern feel the time is right to continue the spread of the message. There are a number of Bible burnings going on throughout the European countries. It's feared that it could stretch well into England which brings me to why I came to you.

Others like me believe it's time to place the code in other works besides sacred texts. The orthodox religious fathers claim those texts as belonging to them to support their dogma and creed. Nothing could ever be further from the truth. They belong to a planet and its inhabitants.

We are looking for story tellers and poets to write the stories with the code placed within. We plan to spread it far and wide so that its always protected. It's time for a revolution of heart to spread the word of the living God.

I look forward to meeting you and your assistant. I've been told that he has a love and passion for story and rhyme. I thank you for your time, sir.

Sincerely Yours,

Miles
Davenport

"Well, what do you think Thomas?" asked Squire. "I think his words are strong and true. I think this thing he speaks of carries the weight of the heavens. I think I'm full of questions and wonder. I think it's best for me to meet this man and converse with him. I think it's something greater than honor to be a part of. I think it's time," spoke Thomas. "I agree with you young man. I believe that this man holds a key that I would love to hear more about. When he arrives, we will take up with him and welcome his words," said Squire. The two joined the others as plans were being made for the new residents of Danbury, Thomas, Mary, and Lucille Sonnet.

It was time for Carol' funeral. Squire and Ian decided to visit her grave after the woodlanders had finished with their ceremonies. It would give the two time to reflect on Carol's life in privacy.

A weeping heart will carry its cross into all forms of life until it weeps no more. Redemption sought from the heart of another can offer some relief. But it cannot heal the past nor offer another color to disguise its appearance. To the bearer it belongs and from the bearer it shall be healed. To return to a place where all things realized, and all things known sits patiently in wait for the bearers arrival.

Some of the woodlanders assembled where Carol's body rested overnight under the watch of others. It was time for her to receive a final resting place. Six men strong and true carried the oak planked coffin through the forest to a place that opened up to a glen. This is a place where the woodland people hold as spiritual. The man in the green hat led the procession. Remnants of other graves could be seen strewed about. There high on the hill was a freshly dug grave. Two men stood on either side of it. One held a pick, the other a shovel. One was crying for Carol.

This woman they came to bury touched the hearts and souls of these people whom society had casted out. She was a healer that never judged nor spoke a single word of malice. It mattered not that she was battered by one who professed love. She never failed to turn the other cheek. There were men in the camp who offered to exact the same on her abuser, but she would have none of it.

The oak plank coffin was carried to the grave as the procession followed behind. The coffin was carefully lowered in the grave by rope. The Bible and her student's book was held tight by good twine.

The one who held the green hat looked to those who came. Their eyes near to tears with heads hung low in sorrow. "Oh, Weaver of great stone mountain and valley below, who gives life and taketh away the same. We thank you for your blessings which came through this beautiful child of your creation. We as a people who flourished in her words and her songs return her to you all mighty one. We are but children in heart and know not the ways of our Father. We accept your giving's each day and know we grow in your light as we walk the path. She was as dear to us as you. Your gate we do embrace. We will sow the seeds she beard to us and prosper in the fruit it renders. Thank you oh great Weaver of earth and heaven," spoke the one who held the green hat.

"Those who came to offer gifts and blessings may come forward to honor her," spoke the one who waved the green hat over the grave. The sound of gentle weeping filled the air. One by one they came and released their gifts to the coffin below. Some returned the gifts she had given them. Others gave something that had been dear to them so that Carol would never forget them. A little girl was the last to step to the grave. She held in her hand a doll that Carol had given her.

One stormy night when the thunder shook the ground and the lightning lit the nights sky, the little girl was terribly afraid. Carol came to her with the doll. She told the little girl that the doll had come to her one night when she was a little girl. She too was afraid of a storm. The doll told her that as long as she held her no harm would ever come to her. She never feared the thunder or lightning again.

She hugged the doll one last time and released it to the grave. The doll landed face up with its button eyes looking back at the little girl. She turned to her mother and said, "The doll can protect her again, so she won't be afraid of the dark."

Soon the grave diggers and the man with the green hat were all that remained at the site. The gravediggers were aware of his admiration for Carol. The man with the green hat let out a scream that could be heard by those who were returning home. The tears came, followed by more screams. His head dropped to his chest, and he became silent. He held the green hat in both hands and with heavy eyes that looked upon her one last time. He released the hat as it fluttered like a birds wing on its journey to her embrace.

"We'll take care of her Henry. We'll see to it that she's covered with the same care she gave us," said one. "He's right sir. We be honored to have this time with her," said the other. Henry shook their hands and turned to walk away, but not in the direction taken by the others. He was going elsewhere.

He needed time alone so he could let her go. He knew if he didn't, he would never live beyond today. His heart and soul would occupy the grave with her.

The men finished their work and turned to head home. This spiritual home which held the bodies of so many passed was silent once again.

Out from the trees Mildred appeared. She was carrying a wreath made of vine and dried berries. She stepped to the grave in reverence and placed the wreath at the head of the grave. She stood, clasped her hands together and looked upwards. "She was one of us. Take her home so she may rest where she belongs," cried out Mildred. She walked back into the trees and was gone.

CHAPTER 63

If ever it be for one to look upon the eyes of the Creator, surely one would see themself.

The times were changing in the small town of Danbury. The Reverend and his wife were packing their belongings for a trip to London. His wife had a brother that owned a haberdashery shop in London. He offered them a position with adequate lodging. The attendance of the congregation had fallen off since the news about Rebecca became public. The Church of England approved his request for removal and promised to send another in his stead.

John Clayborne was expanding the inn to accommodate the increase in business. He was adding on a larger dining area with a new addition to increase the number of rooms. His sons were courting now and had other things on their minds besides work. He planned on hiring some of the woodlanders to do odd jobs and help Susan in the kitchen.

Edward was able to secure a loan to buy out the owner of the carpentry shop along with the living quarters. He was giving up the farm life for a more secure future. He and Diane would be moving to town and rent out the farm for extra income. Diane would be close to Lucy which made her happy.

The woodlanders moved deeper in the forest. They feared retribution from some for Carol's murder. One of their camps were vandalized while the occupants were at Carol's burial.

No one had seen Henry Jamison for at least a week or so. Some say he went looking for Jacob to render justice for Carol. Others said he was seen wandering the countryside near Essex.

Squire and Thomas were busy printing Bibles. They needed to employ more help to finish on time. They discussed using Ian since he was literate and enjoyed books. They also spoke how they would handle the Pope's soldiers should they reappear.

Word had been sent that Miles Davenport was two days journey away. Squire so longed to speak with him to get clarity of his letter.

Edward had been commissioned to build a false floor in Squire's wagon to conceal the Bibles while in transport to London. In turn Squire would take some of his finest furniture to London to sell on his behalf.

This town of Danbury had its growing pains. The influence of the Anglican Reformation was spreading across land. Money was flowing into the movement from the mainland and other places. Fortunes were being made and change was everywhere. No more would the rulers of Rome govern the English speaking people.

The country was divided in those days. Arguments were common and seldom civil. Some were ready to fight or die for the Pope while others favored the king and queen.

Still hearts sought the passion of love and sharing. Minds were set on survival and prosperity. Whether it be a woodlander on the hunt for daily food or the proprietor seeking investment to expand commerce. The two were drinking from the same cup.

Love of child, the love for spouse, love of church or kingdom were but a strong conviction of moral values that build character and reputation. The outer world seeks to bring all under one rule, that leans towards the conformity of all. It prefers sheep over shepherds, ignorance over knowledge, lust rather than passion.

Though all walk in life surrounded by mortal coil all are in touch with the original self, the individual within. That part which concerns itself with the prosperity of soul and spirit. It inspires to discovery of all things new.

When all the effort and all the sacrifice of the world leaves one feeling broken or lost. When all the dreams and desires failed to deliver one to the mountain top, then and only then is one ready to place one foot in heaven. A place once called home.

These souls of Danbury are but one soul family. All share a common path and destiny. Lest we forget, we are heavenly souls having a human experience.